Reading People

Also by Jo-Ellan Dimitrius

Put Your Best Foot Forward: Make a Great Impression by Taking Control of How Others See You

WITH MARK MAZZARELLA

Reading People

How to Understand People and
Predict Their Behavior—
Anytime, Anyplace

Jo-Ellan Dimitrius
and
Wendy Patrick Mazzarella

BALLANTINE BOOKS

NEW YORK

*To my husband, Randy Peukert, whose patience and
compassion are exceeded only by his devotion*
—Jo-Ellan

To my husband, Mark Mazzarella
—Wendy

2008 Ballantine Books Trade Paperback Edition

Copyright © 1998, 1999 by Jo-Ellan Dimitrius and Mark Mazzarella
Copyright © 2008 by Jo-Ellan Dimitrius and Wendy Patrick Mazzarella

Published in the United States by Ballantine Books,
an imprint of The Random House Publishing Group,
a division of Random House, Inc., New York.

BALLANTINE and colophon are registered trademarks of Random House, Inc.

Originally published in slightly different form by Random House,
an imprint of The Random House Publishing Group,
a division of Random House, Inc., in 1998.

ISBN 978-0-345-50413-5

Printed in the United States of America

www.ballantinebooks.com

2 4 6 8 9 7 5 3 1

Book design by Mary A. Wirth

PREFACE
TO THE NEW EDITION

Ten tumultuous years have passed since we first wrote *Reading People*. In that time we have survived the physical and emotional devastation of the terrorist attacks on the World Trade Center and the Pentagon, which left us both scared and angry. We have witnessed the failure of large corporations such as Enron and WorldCom, resulting from the fraud and mismanagement of corporate leadership whose honesty and fidelity we'd never questioned. We've seen the proliferation of voiceless and faceless scam artists and sexual predators lurking on the Internet, preying upon us and our children. And through it all we have tried, with varying degrees of success, to find ways not only to protect ourselves from the reality of old and new threats, but to do so without denying ourselves the many joys and fulfilling possibilities presented by life in our evolving world.

Today, there's still no skill, no amount of knowledge, no technique, and no high-tech key to opening the door to a full and fearless existence better than the ability to read people and anticipate their behavior. The lessons we taught in the first edition of *Reading People* are as applicable now as they were a decade ago, but the challenges presented to readers who seek to apply them are greater. With each new year technology brings us closer to a progressively broader spectrum of people from different cultures and with different agendas. At the same time, we have considerably less information to help determine how best to interact with them than we did in "simpler" times.

Our primary goal in revising *Reading People* is to teach our readers how to apply the original techniques for reading in a considerably different environment. Hence, you will find expanded discussions throughout this new edition of *Reading People* about the technological challenges to studying behavior, about reading people in the "Age of Terror," and about the significance of cultural differences, which are becoming more the norm than the exception.

Author Sydney Harris once wrote: "The beauty of 'spacing' children many years apart lies in the fact that parents have time to learn the mistakes that were made with the older ones." The same might be said about authors and their books. Since 1998 we have received many gratifying comments from readers who told us that *Reading People* helped improve their personal and professional lives. But we also heard criticism from some who pointed out that many of the tips contained within the book are just common sense.

Being human, our first reaction was, "If what we have to say is just common sense, why do people make so many horrible mistakes when they read people?" But once we got past our initial defensiveness, we realized that we had failed to convey our message effectively to those who articulated this criticism. And, like the parents to which Sydney Harris refers, we should learn from our mistakes. After all, those critics were absolutely correct: most of our tips, in isolation, are not earth-shattering revelations about human character. We never expected our readers to experience an "a-ha" moment when they read that a raised voice could reflect anger or excitement; or that sweating may be an indicator of nervousness, hot weather, or that a person has just exercised. True, these things are common sense. But that is not what *Reading People* is all about.

The key to reading people effectively is not so much evaluating what individual clues may mean—although the meaning of many words and actions are not obvious. Rather, what leads to great people-reading skills is, first, the ability to objectively observe and identify the clues; and second, the ability to see patterns within the multitude of clues that point consistently to one reliable conclusion.

The clues are like the tools a carpenter uses to build something beautiful. While even a novice knows what basic woodworking tools are available, like saws and drills, most of us know nothing about plunge routers or plate joiners. And even when we've assembled the best tools for the job, it is how we use these tools that makes the difference in the finished product. With that analogy in mind, we have retooled our approach to gathering behavioral clues, using what we call the Seven Colors throughout the book to reinforce and illustrate the techniques for identifying patterns and forming reliable conclusions.

Seven Colors

With so many clues swirling around us as we interact with others, it is easy to overlook even the important ones. To borrow from an old cliché, "You can't tell the clues without a score card." People reading, or at least the process of gathering clues, is much easier for most of us if we have a "score card," or checklist, to use to gather information. This may be actual notes on a piece of paper initially, and become a mental checklist that we apply automatically later on.

In our second book, *Put Your Best Foot Forward,* we described the Seven Colors as the key categories through which we all paint pictures of ourselves. Those Seven Colors are:

1. Personal appearance
2. Body language
3. Voice
4. Communication style
5. Content of communication
6. Action
7. Environment

By looking at each of these Seven Colors when reading someone, you will be able to pick up an amazing amount of information, enhancing your ability to see patterns in someone's behavior.

I was recently asked to speak to a group of plastic and reconstructive surgeons who were alarmed about the increase in violence against them by unhappy patients. The physicians wanted to know how they could better read their patients when they first came in for a consultation. They wanted to determine if new patients had realistic expectations of their particular surgical requests. In reflecting on the problem, it appeared that an initial consultation with a patient could provide the surgeon with ample information to predict whether or not the patient would likely be dissatisfied with the procedure's result—the doctor needs only look for clues within each of the Seven Colors. A surgeon would want to be aware of the patient's clothing, (outside of those lovely white paper smocks); posture (slumped over, erect, crossed arms); eye contact while asking questions and while listening to the response; vocal tone (indicating confidence, weakness, or nervousness); directness in communicating with the surgeon (does someone come with the patient, like a boyfriend or husband?); the content of her communication ("Well, I've been to five other surgeons who have told me that they can't do this surgery"); the patient's actions prior to, during, and after the consultation (lots of phone calls to the doctor, negative comments to the receptionist); and if she comes with someone, what this aspect of her "human environment" tells the doctor (is her companion sloppy or fastidious?). By evaluating these Seven Colors, a doctor is better able to understand his patient's tendencies, and thereby to address her needs.

Reading People in the Internet Age

With advancements in computer, software, and Web site technologies, curious and dangerous individuals can now attempt to read people via the Internet. One of the most frightening aspects of our evolving technosociety is that our entire lives can be exposed by the push of a button. What used to be the sacred territory of law enforcement personnel and private investigators is now open to anyone with a computer and an Internet connection. The Internet is an environment in which many people now interact, some almost exclusively. New industries have grown out of the practice of social-networking through online communication. Sites like MySpace, Facebook, Friendster, and Xanga have introduced an entirely new challenge to reading people—how to read people without seeing or hearing them. Because of this trend, which no doubt will continue at an ever-increasing pace, we explored its implications and developed techniques for addressing them throughout this edition.

Reading People in the Age of Terror

We will also address the sadly present need to read people in an age plagued by terrorism, a concern we hear with increasing frequency. The attacks on the World Trade Center, the London subway bombings in 2005, and various spoiled terrorist plots highlight the importance of accurately reading people, especially strangers. Knowing how to identify some of the red flags that might foretell of a variety of criminal activities—not just terrorism—can make both law-enforcement personnel and laypeople increasingly effective in our modern world of heightened security and constantly changing national threat levels.

Learning How to Give People What They Need

Accurately reading people will not only allow you to reliably formulate your own decisions, it will equip you to provide others with what they need the most. As expressed by Dale Carnegie, the most fundamental need people look for others to fulfill is the need to feel important. Learning how to accurately read people will help you do just that. By paying close attention to individuals' traits, actions, and patterns, you will be able to effectively decipher what they are all about, which in turn will allow you to be better able to deliver that most basic human need, tailored to your specific audience.

Don't Expect Sudden Enlightenment

If you are looking for quick answers to how to read people, you won't find them here, or anywhere, although there is no shortage of charlatans who will tout their ability to provide them. Reading people well takes time. It requires attention and focus to gather clues and patience to discern patterns from those clues. You need to pay attention to everything, as often as you can and for as long as possible to develop accurate reading-people skills.

While many of you may think you're doing this already, take a minute to complete the following quiz and see if that really is true.

Think about the people with offices next to you at work, or the offices of a couple of your friends or acquaintances.

1. Can you tell me what books they have on their shelves?
2. Have you noticed any artwork or photographs on display?
3. Can you list any licenses or diplomas they have on their walls?
4. What do they keep on their desk?
5. Do they use a specific kind of pen?
6. What kind of snacks do they keep in their office?

If you can answer all of these questions with a high degree of confidence, you are a natural people reader, demonstrated by your attention to those details that help define who people are. But if you are like the vast majority of people, who have no clue how to answer these questions and can only make educated guesses, you could learn better observation skills. In the pages that follow, we will teach you how to do that. It will be up to you to develop your new skills through practice, practice, practice. Don't be discouraged: once you start, you'll find you don't want to stop, as suddenly you will begin to see more than you ever thought possible.

But you can't quit there. As you will read time and time again throughout this book, gathering all the available clues—as necessary as it is to successful people reading—can lead to information overload, or worse, wrong conclusions. It is also important to learn how to spot patterns from within your list of clues that consistently point in the same direction. That, more than anything else, is the skill, which once acquired, will give you confidence that you are able to read others accurately. Be patient, be attentive, and be disciplined in your approach, and you will acquire that skill. It may be easier for some than others, but it is well within the grasp of us all. You have only to reach out for it. And you are already well on your way.

ACKNOWLEDGMENTS

Ten years ago the first edition of *Reading People* was conceived of and co-authored by Jo-Ellan Dimitrius and Mark Mazzarella. This updated and revised edition incorporates the concepts formulated in the original book and applies them to the changes and challenges presented in the new millennium. It is therefore appropriate that first and foremost, Jo-Ellan and Wendy acknowledge and thank Mark for his work with Jo-Ellan on the original *Reading People,* without which this edition would not have been possible.

Jo-Ellan would like to thank her children, Nicole, Francis, and Stirling, who continue to provide her with the vocabulary, ideas, and technological information that apply to the XY generation. Additionally, she would like to thank Hercules and Apollo (her dachshunds) for their comic relief during this project. Paws up, boys!

Wendy would like to give special thanks to her husband, Mark, whose unwavering confidence in her ability to breathe fresh and insightful ideas into *Reading People,* and to express them in informative and interesting ways, was the genesis of her participation in this collaborative effort. His support and encouragement throughout the process was essential for its completion. She also would like to thank her sister, Jennifer Patrick, and mother, Elizabeth Patrick, for their boundless encouragement and support in this endeavor, as in all others.

Our thanks also go out to all the great people at Random House who recognized the importance of bringing the concepts expressed in *Reading People* to bear on life in the twenty-first century, and who supported and assisted us in creating this updated and revised edition of the book. Many thanks are owed to Jane von Mehren, who first contacted us about this project. Her vision sparked our combined creative talents. We owe special thanks to Porscha Burke, our editor, from whose encouragement, creativity, and editorial talents we benefited immensely.

Lastly, while there are too many to mention individually, we thank the many family members, friends, and colleagues who contributed to this process, and whose sage advice and support are recognized and greatly appreciated by us. Thank you for everything.

CONTENTS

INTRODUCTION:
A PASSION FOR PEOPLE

When I was a child, I'd peer down from my perch at the top of the stairs above my parents' living room during their frequent dinner parties. I'd watch as my mother scurried around, carefully ensuring that no glass was empty. I remember the chubby, bald man whose booming laughter resonated throughout the house, and his rail-thin wife, who shook her head and rolled her eyes as he launched into an only slightly modified version of a story he'd told dozens of times before. I would laugh to myself as my father's friend John reached out casually for another hors d'oeuvre to add to the scores he'd already inhaled, while my dad playfully poked him in the stomach, and said, chuckling, "Make sure you save some room for dinner, little boy." I loved those Saturday evenings, when the house was filled with the laughter and conversation of a dozen people—all so different, and yet so alike. Even when I was a child, my passion was people.

Twenty-five years later, armed with nothing more than my lifetime of experiences, paper, and a pen, I sat nervously in court watching several dozen prospective jurors file into the courtroom for the first time. From among them, I would have to select the twelve who would decide whether my client would live or die. Every other decision I'd ever made about people suddenly seemed insignificant. Should I have trusted the salesman who sold me my first used car? Was I right to confide in my best friend that I had a crush on her big brother? Had I chosen a good babysitter for my young daughter? I had been reading people for more than thirty years, but this time a man's life was at stake.

For fifteen years since then, I have made my living reading people. I have sized up more than ten thousand prospective jurors, and evaluated thousands of witnesses, lawyers, and even judges. I sat for weeks next to "the Night Stalker," Richard Ramirez, peering every day into the coldest eyes I have ever seen. I shared Peggy Buckey's anguish at her unwarranted prosecution for child molestation in the McMartin Preschool case. I watched in horror as rioting spread through Los Angeles after the defense verdict in the Rodney King Simi Valley trial. In the Reginald Denny case, I tried to comprehend why four young men would mercilessly beat a complete stranger, and struggled to select jurors who would understand those motives and respond leniently. I strained to comprehend the internal torment that led John DuPont to shoot and kill Olympic wrestler David Schultz. And I endured the world's scrutiny, and often its harsh criticism, because I helped select the jury that acquitted O. J. Simpson.

It has been a wild, sometimes exhilarating ride, but not as glamorous as some might think. I have worked agonizingly long hours, and while I have been applauded by some for my involvement in unpopular cases, I have also been criticized by others for the very same involvement. My efforts to explain my deep commitment to the American system of justice and the principle that no one should be denied his liberty, let alone his life, by anything less than a truly impartial jury, have often fallen on deaf ears. My life has been threatened. I was even blamed by some for the L.A. riots in 1992 because I helped pick the jury that acquitted the four police officers charged with beating Rodney King.

Through it all, I have watched and listened. I have done my best to apply my education, my powers of observation, my common sense, and my intuition to understanding those who have passed through the courtrooms where I have worked. Mostly, I have learned. And if there's one thing I have learned, sometimes the hard way, it is how to read people.

From the day I was chosen by "the Dream Team" to become the jury consultant in O. J. Simpson's criminal trial, I have been approached from seemingly every angle to write a book. Not a book about what I do best—reading people—but about the dirt on the Los Angeles District Attorney's Office, or how the O. J. Simpson case compared with my other high-profile cases, or (and this was far and away the most popular topic) the inside scoop on the Dream Team. But writing an exposé never interested me. It was not until a very wise friend, the writer Spencer Johnson, suggested, "Write about something you know best, something that will make a difference in people's lives," that we were inspired to write *Reading People.*

No matter whom you interact with, no matter where or when you interact with them, the quality of your life will depend to a large extent on the quality of your decisions about people. Salesmen will sell more, and customers will make better purchasing decisions. Employers will make better hiring choices; prospective employees will improve their chances of landing the best jobs. You will choose your friends, lovers, and partners better, and understand your family members more. As a friend you will be more sensitive and as a competitor you will be more alert. Some of those who read people for a living, as I do, rely almost exclusively on scientific research, surveys, studies, polls, and statistical analysis. Others claim to have a God-given talent. My own experience has taught me that reading people is neither a science nor an innate gift. It is a matter of knowing what to look and listen for, having the curiosity and patience to gather the necessary information, and understanding how to recognize the patterns in a person's appearance, body language, voice, and conduct.

During college and graduate school, I spent almost a decade studying psychology, sociology, physiology, and criminology, along with a smattering of statistics, communications, and linguistics. As valuable as my formal education has been, it is not what made *The American Lawyer* dub me "the Seer" a few years back. Rather, it is my near-obsessive curiosity about people—how they look, sound, and act—that has made me an effective people reader. The empathy I feel for others drives me to understand them better.

My most important skill is my ability to see the pattern of someone's personality and beliefs emerge from among often conflicting traits and characteristics. It is a skill I learned from the time I was a little girl, sitting at the top of those stairs during my parents' dinner parties, and refined through a lifetime of experiences and more than four hundred trials. Best of all, it's a skill that can be learned and applied with equal success by anyone—anytime, anyplace.

Why am I so sure?

Because over the past fifteen years I have tested this method on more than ten thousand "research subjects." After predicting the behavior of thousands of jurors, witnesses, lawyers, and judges, I have been able to see whether my predictions came true. After the cases were decided, I spoke with the participants to explore what they thought and why. I did not always peg them correctly, especially in the earlier years. But by testing my perceptions over and over, I have verified which clues are generally reliable and which are not. I have also learned it is important not to focus on any single trait or characteristic: taken alone, almost any trait may be misleading. And I have found that the approach outlined in this book will help anyone understand people and better predict their behavior in the courtroom, the boardroom, and the bedroom.

People are people, wherever they are. The man on the witness stand trying to persuade the jury of the righteousness of his cause is no different from the salesman hawking his goods at the flea market. The prejudices shown by a prospective juror are the same as those that may surface in a job interview. A juror or witness will try to avoid answering a sensitive question in court in much the same way as he does at home or at work.

Each courtroom is a microcosm of life, filled with anger, nervousness, prejudice, fear, greed, deceit, and every other conceivable human emotion and trait. There, and everywhere else, every person reveals his emotions and beliefs in many ways.

In the first chapter, "Reading Readiness," we will explain how you can prepare yourself to read people more effectively. Chapter 3, "Discovering Patterns," will show you how to make sense of a person's often contradictory characteristics. In the succeeding chapters, you will discover how people reveal their beliefs and character through their personal appearance, body language, environment, voice, communication techniques, and actions. You'll also learn how to enhance your intuition and use it to your advantage. The final chapters will show you how to make a good impression on those who are reading you, and how to make wise and reliable snap decisions.

Throughout this book you'll be seeing what can be learned from how a person looks, talks, and acts. But the goal is not just to provide you with a "glossary" of people's characteristics and behaviors. Instead, *Reading People* aims to teach you how to evaluate people's complex characteristics and how to see the overall pattern those characteristics form—the pattern that truly can reveal and predict behavior. This method has been the secret to my success at reading people. Once you've mastered these skills, they will serve you just as well, at work and at play, today and for the rest of your life.

Reading People

ONE

Reading Readiness

Preparing for the Challenge of Reading People

"I can't believe I didn't see the signs. They were right there
in front of me! How could I have been so blind?"

We've all said something very much like this, probably more times
than we care to admit. After we've misjudged our boss's intentions, a
friend's loyalty, or a babysitter's common sense, we carefully replay the
past—and usually see the mistakes we made with 20/20 hindsight.
Why, then, after living and reliving our mistakes, don't we learn more
from them? If reading people were like driving a car or hitting a tennis ball, we'd be able to recognize our weak points and improve our
performance with every try. That rarely happens with relationships.
Instead, we interact with our friends, colleagues, and spouses in the
same old ways, doggedly hoping for the best.

In theory, thanks to the people-reading skills I acquired over the
years, it should have been easy for me to make better decisions in my
personal life—whom to let into it and what to expect from them once
I did. Yet for many years I failed to apply my courtroom abilities to
my off-duty life. Perhaps I had to reach a saturation point of pain and
disappointment in some of my personal relationships before I was
willing to analyze my mistakes and put my professional experience to
work for me.

When I finally resolved to bring that focus and clarity to my personal life, it made sense to start by comparing the courthouse with the
world outside. I was determined to figure out what I was doing in the
courtroom that enabled me to read people in that setting with such
consistent accuracy. I thought I should be able to distill that information into a set of people-reading basics that would work anywhere.

When I told my colleagues about the great difference between my people-reading successes on and off the job, I found I wasn't alone. Many of the best attorneys I knew confessed that, while they enjoyed great success reading people in court, the rest of the time they didn't do much better than anyone else. Why?

The conclusions I eventually reached led me to the keys of "reading readiness"—the foundation of understanding people and predicting their behavior. The first thing I discovered was that *attitude is critical*. In a courtroom, I was ready to focus fully on the people I encountered, to listen to them closely, to observe the way they looked and acted, and to carefully think about what I was hearing and seeing. I had a very different attitude in my private life. I rarely did any of those things. The fact is, you have to be *ready* to read people, or all the clues in the world won't do you any good.

In this chapter, you'll learn how to bring a courtroom state of mind—clear-eyed, observant, careful, and objective—into the emotional, subjective drama that is everyday life. Master the following skills, and you'll be ready to read people.

1. Spend more time with people. That's the best way to learn to understand them.
2. Stop, look, and listen. There's no substitute for patience and attentiveness.
3. Learn to reveal something of yourself. To get others to open up, you must first open up to them.
4. Know what you're looking for. Unless you know what you want in another person, there's a good chance you'll be disappointed.
5. Train yourself to be objective. Objectivity is essential to reading people, but it's the hardest of these seven skills for most of us to master.
6. Start from scratch, without biases and prejudices.
7. Make a decision, then act on it.

Discovering the Lost Art of Reading People

Unless you've been stranded on a desert island for the past fifty years, you've noticed that the world has changed. Understanding people has always been one of life's biggest challenges, but the social changes and technological explosion of recent decades have made it even more difficult. Today, many of us don't enjoy close bonds or daily contact even with the most important people in our lives. We're out of touch and out of practice.

Unless you practice the skills you'll learn in this book, you won't retain them. But that's difficult today because we live in a global society. We're in contact with people across town, across the country, or even on the other side of the world. But our contact usually isn't personal. The same technological advances that allow us such extraordinary access to others have exacted a toll—they have made face-to-face conversation relatively rare. Why meet with a client in person if you can phone him? Why have an actual conversation with Mom if you can leave a message on her answering machine? Why phone a friend if you can send an e-mail or an instant message? As long as the message gets through, what's the difference? Most of us have even phoned someone, *hoping* to leave a message, only to be *disappointed* when she's actually there to answer the call. Some of us even bow out altogether, relying on our assistants, kids, spouses, or friends to do our communicating for us. Or we settle into cyberspace, meeting, doing business, sometimes even becoming engaged—all on the basis of the sterile, electronically generated word, without the benefit of seeing someone or even talking to him.

All forms of communication are not equal. If I want to ask a favor of my colleague Alan, I have several choices. I can walk down the hall and speak with him in person; in that case, I'll be able to gauge his response accurately. Maybe he'll gladly say yes. Then again, maybe he'll say yes while wincing. Or perhaps he'll say no, but will clearly show his reservations. There's an almost infinite number of reactions I might see if I'm there in the room with him. Now, if I phone Alan instead, I'll be able to sense some of his feelings from his voice—but I may miss the more subtle undertones and I won't get any visual cues. If we e-mail each other, effectively squelching almost all human contact, I'll get just the facts. And what if I simply send someone else to ask?

Making matters worse, most of us purposely avoid meaningful conversation with all but our closest friends and family. When we do get together, we may be more comfortable saying what is expected or "politically correct" than what we really believe. Self-revelation comes hard to most people; those who confess their innermost secrets on afternoon talk shows are the exception, not the rule.

The reasons we don't like to expose ourselves could fill a book, but undoubtedly the edgy, distrustful tenor of urban life is among them. From childhood on, those of us who live in or near big cities are urged to be wary of strangers; the concept is reinforced nightly on the local news. We urbanites often return from a visit to a small town marveling at how we were treated. Instead of the averted gazes we've grown accustomed to, we're met with a friendly "Hello, how are you?" from people who really seem to mean it! That level of spontaneous, trusting communication is hard to come by in the cities where most Americans live.

Most of us did not grow up in a community where our high school classmates became our dentists, our barbers, and our children's schoolteachers. Sure, we have friends and families, but the majority of people we see each day are strangers and therefore suspect. Because we fear them, we often avoid contact, and as a result we don't use our social skills as often as we could. Our people-reading muscles have atrophied from lack of exercise.

Making Contact

If you want to become a better people-reader, you must make a conscious effort to engage other people. Even the most entrenched Internet junkie can learn the true meaning of "chat" if the desire is there, but you have to get off the couch and make it happen. Work those atrophied muscles, even if it makes you feel inconvenienced, awkward, or vulnerable.

To practice and develop your people skills, start by becoming aware of how and when you make personal contact. For the next week, each time you have the opportunity to communicate with someone, enhance the quality of that communication by moving up at least one rung on the contact ladder:

1. Face-to-face meeting
2. Telephone call

3. Letter/fax/e-mail/answering machine
4. Delegation

Instead of asking someone else to set up an appointment for you, contact the person yourself by letter, fax, or e-mail. Instead of text messaging on your BlackBerry or e-mailing your cross-country friend, call, even if the conversation has to be brief. Instead of phoning your neighbor to discuss the school fund-raiser, knock on her door and talk to her in person. Step by step, you'll become more comfortable with the increased contact.

Try to improve the quality of your communication, too, by making a conscious effort to reveal something of yourself. It doesn't have to be an intimate secret—in fact, many people will be turned off if you inappropriately reveal confidences. But you can share a like or dislike, a favorite restaurant, book, or movie. And ask something about the other person—where she bought a piece of jewelry, or whether he saw the ball game last night. Warm them up, and the conversation will start rolling.

After a few weeks, you'll become more adept at these social skills. Test yourself on the person checking your groceries, the receptionist in your doctor's office, the mail carrier, the next customer who walks into the shop. Connecting doesn't have to mean a ten-minute discussion. It can mean simply looking someone in the eye, smiling, and commenting on the weather. These brief sparks of contact aren't superficial, they're sociable, and they are where trust and communication—and people reading—begin.

Learn to See the Sheep

The more time you spend reading people, the easier it gets. Just as the anxiety and awkwardness of your first time behind the wheel of a car disappeared after a few months of everyday driving, people-reading skills that may seem unattainable today will become automatic with a little practice.

With willpower and persistence, we can sharpen any of our senses. Nothing illustrates this more clearly than an experience a client of mine had several years ago. He'd been hired by the Bighorn Institute, a facility dedicated to preserving an endangered species of bighorn sheep that live in the mountains just southwest of Palm Springs, California. Development of neighboring land was disturbing the sheep and interrupting their breeding activity; the institute wanted to do something about it.

When my client visited the institute, the director took him outside, pointed to the massive, rocky hills that rose up behind the offices, and said softly, "There are a lot of them out today." My client squinted up at the brown hills, trying to hide his amazement—not at the beauty of the bighorn sheep, but at his inability to see even one of them. Obviously accustomed to this reaction, the director tactfully called his attention to a sheep just below a triangular rock, and another on the crest of a hill to the left, and then another—until he'd pointed out almost a dozen.

The director's eyesight was no better than my client's. But he had learned to see the sheep. He knew how their shape broke the subtle patterns of the hills. He could detect the slight difference between their color and that of the rock. He had learned where the sheep were most likely to gather at a particular time of day. He had experience. He had contact. He had practice. What was virtually automatic to him was foreign to my client—until he, too, learned to see the sheep.

Stop, Look, and Listen

In the courtroom, I constantly watch jurors, witnesses, lawyers, spectators, and even the judge, looking for any clues about how they're responding to the case and the people presenting it. I listen carefully to the words that are spoken, and to how they are spoken. I pay attention to the way people breathe, sigh, tap their feet or fingers, or even shift their weight in a chair. As the jurors walk by, I notice any unusual smells—heavily applied perfume, body odor, the scent of medication. When I shake someone's hand, I take note of the feel of his handshake. I use *all* of my senses, *all* of the time.

Patience, Patience

Observing people properly takes time. Most people simply don't take enough time to gather information and reflect upon it. Instead, they frequently make critical decisions about people in a hurry, as if life were a game show in which quick answers scored more points. It's usually the other way around in life: quick answers are often wrong—and lose points.

Quick answers aren't necessary most of the time, anyway. You'll find that you often have more time to make up your mind about people than you think you do. Abraham Lincoln was once asked how long a man's legs should be; he responded, "Long enough to reach the ground." Likewise, the question "How much time does it take to read people?" can be answered: "As much time as you have." There is seldom a premium on the speed with which we read people; most deadlines for decision making are self-imposed. *If you take all the time you really have available, you'll usually have as much as you need.* If you're offered a job, the offer probably won't vanish if you ask for a few days to think about it. You seldom need to make a decision about a doctor, lawyer, accountant, day-care provider, mechanic, or purchase on the spur of the moment. So don't! Ask yourself what information would help you make the best choice, and then take the time to gather it. If you're still not sure, sleep on it.

In almost every jurisdiction in the country, the judge cautions jurors at the beginning of the trial that they must not decide the case until all the evidence has been presented. This concept has been ingrained in the law for hundreds of years, and for good reason. Just as you can't solve a riddle without all the clues, you can't make wise decisions about people if you act prematurely. To be successful, you must be patient.

Pay Attention, or Pay the Consequences

Every interview with the neighbor of a heinous criminal seems to start with "He seemed like such a nice guy." Further questioning usually reveals that the neighbor never really noticed the man, with the neighbor ultimately admitting, "He kept to himself." In fact, there were probably many clues that Mr. X was not such a nice guy after all. It's just that no one ever paid much attention.

Decisions are no better than the information on which they're based. Incorrect or incomplete information can lead to an incorrect conclusion—garbage in, garbage out. So before you can effectively read people, you need to gather reliable information about them. You can do this by using your eyes, your ears, and at times even your senses of touch and smell. When people fail to be attentive and focused, the consequences can be regrettable.

It's not hard to recall occasions when we've been inattentive to important clues. We may hire a day-care provider without spotting the faulty latch on her backyard fence, noticing how she ignored the children under her care as she spoke to us, or paying attention to her poor grammar. Yet each of these factors could have a critical impact on our child's well-being and development. We may not notice the flushed face and ever-so-slightly slurred speech of an employee who returns from a long lunch, but these may be clues he's been drinking—maybe drinking too much. This type of critical information is usually available to you—if you just take your time and pay attention.

Communication Is a Two-Way Street

During jury selection, prospective jurors sit before the assembled clients and attorneys, where they are subjected to an onslaught of personal questions—which they swear to answer truthfully. They aren't allowed to ask anyone on the legal team any questions, and we have no obligation to reveal anything about ourselves. In short, the procedure is specifically designed to let one set of people, the lawyers, read another set, the jurors.

Outside the courtroom, few people will sit politely and answer a barrage of questions without wanting to ask you a few of their own. If you're reading them, they want some opportunity to read you. If you want candid responses to your questions, you usually have to give something in return. Unlike jurors, the people you engage in everyday conversation aren't required to open up to you, and they haven't sworn to be forthcoming or honest. To coax unguarded and honest responses out of them, you need to encourage them to trust you.

The best way to establish this trust is to reveal something of yourself. Let people read you to some extent, and they will feel more comfortable. As their comfort level increases, they will open up to you. It's simple—*if you want a clear view of another person, you must offer a glimpse of yourself.*

Good trial lawyers use self-disclosure effectively to develop rapport with jurors during the jury selection process and throughout the trial. They know that even though openness isn't required of them, they can take the jury selection process to a much more meaningful level if they disclose something of themselves during the questioning. If this consistently works in an intimidating setting like the courtroom, imagine how effective it can be at a casual lunch.

Know What You're Looking For

Laurence J. Peter observed in *The Peter Principle:* "If you don't know where you're going, you will probably end up somewhere else." It's a good rule in general, but doubly important when it comes to reading people.

Long before prospective jurors enter the courtroom, the legal team and I prepare a "juror profile" that lists the personal attributes of jurors who will view our case most favorably. Sometimes we conduct mock trials or surveys of community attitudes to help us gauge the type of person who is most likely to be open-minded toward our client. I grade all candidates on their empathy, analytic ability, leadership, gregariousness, and life experiences, and on my gut reaction to them. Then I consider what other characteristics might be important in that particular case. If it's a death penalty trial, I also evaluate personal responsibility, punitiveness, and authoritarianism. In a contract dispute, I may be more concerned with prospective jurors' attention to detail or experience with legal agreements. In short, I know exactly what I'm looking for in the jurors for that particular case. If I didn't, how could I choose the right ones?

Outside the courtroom, we aren't usually so methodical. In part this is because it seems a little cold-blooded to create a list of desirable attributes. When it comes to romance, we like to think the fates will throw us together with the perfect mate. We rarely take the time to consciously evaluate even a casual friend's characteristics. By the time the bad news sinks in—"Hmmm. She doesn't keep her word"; "He's always late"; "She still hasn't taken her sick cat to the vet"— we've often become emotionally committed and find it hard to change the relationship. We devote even less forethought to people who appear less frequently in our lives—doctors, contractors, plumbers, and the like. Instead, we rely on a friend's recommendation—or, worse, an advertisement.

If we're not aware of our own needs and haven't decided what we want in a friend, a boss, or a paid professional, it's hardly fair to blame that person for disappointing us later. I recently watched a talk show in which a young man was complaining that his girlfriend of two years dressed like a streetwalker and blatantly flirted with strangers. When asked, he admitted that she had dressed and acted exactly the same way when they first met. He loved it back then, when he was focused on the immediate prospect of a few fun nights on the town; but once he decided he wanted a committed relationship, his girlfriend's wild side was unacceptable. He had failed to evaluate her in light of his long-term needs.

Before you decide whether a person meets your needs, create a mental list—or, better, a written one—of everything that is truly essential for a successful relationship of the type you're contemplating. And then don't hesitate to regularly compare your real-life candidate with the ideal one.

Whether you're looking for a husband, a business partner, or a gardener, reflect on the experience and qualities you'd like this person to have. If you're a divorced woman with two young children, it might make sense to date men who also have kids: they'll understand the demands of a family. If you're looking for a business partner, ask yourself exactly what skills your enterprise will need that you don't possess—and look for someone who has them. If you need a gardener, decide whether you want a master of topiary art or someone to reliably mow the lawn and rake leaves once a week.

Whatever you do, approach the task with absolute honesty. You won't be doing anyone a favor by pretending to have different needs and priorities than you really have. Once you know what to look for, you'll be much more likely to know whether you've found it.

Objectivity: The Essential Ingredient

During jury selection, I have only one goal: to assemble a group of people who will listen with an open mind to my client's side of the story. It's easy for me to be completely objective about this, since I have no vested interest in any particular juror serving or being excused from the jury. They aren't friends, family, or even acquaintances. Odds are I'll never see them again.

When I first tried to apply my people-reading methods to my personal life, I quickly found that the objectivity I took for granted in the courtroom was my greatest weakness. In real life, I cared very much what others thought of me. I agonized over how I'd feel if I said, "Yes," "No," "You're not right," or "You're not good enough." In order to translate my courthouse skills to the outside world, I'd have to transfer my objectivity as well. *You can't read people accurately unless you view them objectively.*

Unfortunately, as a general rule, the more important a decision is in your life, the more difficult it is to stay objective. It's easy to be objective about whether a casual acquaintance might be a good blind date for your brother. If she's a coworker, there's more at stake; if she's your boss, there's even more; if she's your best friend, all bets are off.

We all have a tendency to make decisions based on what will be painful or pleasant for us at the moment. All too often, we pick the easiest, least confrontational solution because our emotions blind us to the big picture or the long-term reality. If a woman's boyfriend constantly flirts with other women, she'll probably notice it. But if she's in love and doesn't want to admit to herself that her boyfriend has wandering eyes—and that the rest of him is probably not far behind—she may choose to think his behavior is innocent. Odds are, if he were somebody else's boyfriend, she wouldn't be so charitable. A businessman who is having trouble with a new employee may prefer to write off her mistakes to new-job jitters rather than admit he needs to replace her. And the daughter of an elderly woman suffering from Alzheimer's disease may explain away her mother's bizarre behavior rather than face the painful truth.

Whenever the truth is threatening, we tend to reach for the blinders. Just a few years ago, a friend confided to me that her teenage daughter must be lovesick, although as far as she knew the girl hadn't been seeing anyone in particular.

"How can you tell she's in love?" I wanted to know.

"Well, her grades have really started to slip. She seems to have lost her interest in everything, sleeps late all the time, stays out till all hours without calling. She just seems to be very distracted."

To me this behavior screamed "drugs," not "young love." My heart went out to my friend as I gently suggested this possibility, which she briefly considered, then rejected. It took her another six months to confront her daughter, who by that time was prepared to acknowledge her drug problem and accept help.

It is human nature to close our eyes—and minds—to things that are uncomfortable or disturbing. Leon Festinger coined the term "cognitive dissonance" in 1957 to describe the phenomenon. One symptom of cognitive dissonance is a person's refusal to accept the obvious, as my friend did with her daughter. This is a form of delusional thinking. The word "delusional" usually brings to mind someone who has completely lost sight of reality and who babbles meaninglessly or lies without any perception of the truth. But most delusional activity takes place in the minds of ordinary people like you and me as we make day-to-day decisions that may have tremendous impact on our lives. The truth is hard to see, especially when we don't want to see it.

Most lapses in objectivity are due to some degree of cognitive dissonance or delusional thinking. Even though it's difficult, we can overcome our tendency to ignore facts we don't like. First, we have to understand what it is that upsets us so much that we're willing to ignore or distort reality instead of acting on it. I've found that four states of mind most often lead to the loss of objectivity:

1. Emotional commitment
2. Neediness
3. Fear
4. Defensiveness

If you avoid making decisions while under the influence of these four mind-sets, you are far more likely to stay objective.

Emotional Commitment: The Tie That Blinds

We all feel love, friendship, contempt, and even hatred for some people in our lives. These feelings all tend to compromise our objectivity.

We don't want to think ill of those we love, and we don't want to see anything good in those we hate. To further complicate matters, most of us dislike change. For our own security and convenience, we have an emotional commitment—to ourselves—to keeping things just as they are. The same emotional undercurrent that pulls us toward the status quo also warps our objectivity when we're deciding whether to change it.

Once you're emotionally committed to a particular outcome, it can be very hard to maintain your objectivity. The stronger the emotional commitment, the greater the tendency to behave irrationally. This is why counselors usually advise against sexual intimacy until mutual respect, trust, and friendship have been well established. Once the powerful and pleasurable ingredient of sex has been added to a relationship, we tend to overlook even basic flaws until the passion subsides. By then we may be well down the road toward emotional disaster.

You can't always avoid making decisions when you're emotionally vulnerable, but if you're aware of the pitfalls, you can sidestep many of them. To begin with, try to avoid situations in which you may feel pressured to arrive at a particular answer. In those circumstances, you'll lose your objectivity. The result may be that you'll make a bad decision in the first place, then be reluctant to acknowledge your mistake even when it should become obvious later on. If you interview the daughter of a friend for a job, you may overlook her fundamental deficiencies because you're not going to want to tell your friend his daughter doesn't measure up. If you hire your neighbor as your accountant, or your golfing buddy as your lawyer, you'll tend to overlook what would otherwise be unacceptable performance because of your friendship. Whenever your worlds collide, you bring the emotional commitments of one to the other. If you mix business with pleasure, the result might turn out fine, but more likely your desire to keep everyone happy and avoid confrontation will lead you to misread people.

Another common way we create emotional commitment is recognized in a typical jury instruction: on beginning their deliberations, jurors are told not to announce their feelings about the case until after they've discussed it together. Once people publicly commit themselves to a particular viewpoint, they are reluctant to change it. Pride, stubbornness, or fear of admitting we made a mistake gets in the way. If your goal is to be objective when evaluating other people, don't hamstring yourself by announcing your feelings about someone to your friends, family, or coworkers before you've had time to gather pertinent information and carefully think it over.

If you do find yourself evaluating someone to whom you have an emotional commitment, at least be aware that your objectivity is probably impaired. Be conscious of your emotions, and thoughtfully employ the people-reading techniques discussed in the chapters that follow. Take a little extra time and effort before you form any lasting conclusions. Consider whether a trusted and respected friend who is more objective may be able to add perspective. Play devil's advocate by asking yourself how you would view the person if you weren't so close to the situation. Even if you can't eliminate the influence of your emotional commitment, you can minimize it by using one or more of these techniques.

Neediness: Don't Shop When You're Hungry

Negotiators have a saying: "The person who wants the deal the most gets the worst deal." This rule applies to relationships, too: the person with the greatest need is most likely to fill it with Mr. or Ms. Wrong. Only after he's felt the sting of his mistake will he recognize his decision for what it was—a compromise.

We first learn to compromise as children, when we fall victim to the lure of immediate gratification. We'll take the bicycle with a scratch on the fender rather than wait for an undamaged replacement to arrive because we are afraid that Dad may change his mind if we don't act quickly. As teenagers, we may accept the first offer of a date to the senior prom because we worry that no one else will ask. As adults, we continue to make bad decisions about people out of neediness. The most familiar example of this is the inevitably disastrous "rebound relationship." But neediness also drives the employer who's desperate to fill a position and hires the first passable applicant, only to find himself flipping through résumés again two months later, or the parent who settles for substandard child care rather than miss another day of work.

My mother used to say, "Don't shop when you're hungry." Good advice. When you're hungry, everything looks tempting, and you end up bringing home items you don't really need, plus some that may even be bad for you. The key is to slow down long enough to write a shopping list and maybe even have a healthy snack while you write it. Just don't let your unchecked cravings rule the day, whether you're shopping for dinner or a wife.

One crisis that has erupted throughout the country as a result of the increase in two-wage-earner households is the day-care scramble. Good day care is hard to find and often hard to keep. When the child-care provider leaves without giving her employers much notice, they're thrown into a frenzy looking for a replacement. It's hard to imagine a more stressful situation: you need a very special person to care for your child, and until you find that person, you can't go to work, which jeopardizes your livelihood. Choosing a long-term child-care provider under these circumstances is a terrible idea. Don't fool yourself into believing you can be objective under these conditions.

Whenever you find yourself reacting differently than you would if you had unlimited time, you're acting out of neediness and won't be reading people clearly. Stop and consider alternative courses of action before you go forward. It's often best to find a temporary solution to begin with, and decide on a permanent one later. The parents urgently seeking child care could put their immediate efforts into convincing a friend or family member to pitch in for a week or two, buying them time to look for permanent help. If they can afford it, they can hire a professional nanny for a while. Temporary solutions may be more expensive or inconvenient in the short run, but they'll give you the time you need to make a wise choice about your long-term selection.

Fear: The Great Motivator

Many psychologists believe our primary motivator is fear—fear rooted in our instinctive desire to avoid loss, pain, and death. With such a powerful emotion at work, it's little wonder that objectivity usually gets pushed aside.

It is hard to overestimate the influence of fear on our ability to read people. And it is impossible to remove fear from the equation entirely. We fear ending a relationship because we're afraid we won't find anyone better. We fear turning down a job: what if it's the best offer we get? We may even avoid disciplining our children because we're afraid we'll alienate them.

There's no magic pill to eliminate our fear and clear our vision while we evaluate people. Our viewpoint will always be somewhat skewed by our desire to avoid pain. But we *can* diminish our fear—and even use it to help us better read the people in our lives. If we understand *why* we are afraid, and *how* other people can either cause or eliminate the pain we fear, we can use fear to our advantage.

To repeat a point made earlier, the more important a decision is, the harder it is to stay objective. Fear is a major reason—fear that can develop into mental paralysis when a great deal is riding on a decision. For example, suppose you find yourself in a dead-end job. After several years, you get the uneasy feeling that your days there are numbered and consider leaving. Perhaps you feel that your boss is treating you differently than she used to. You've been trying to evaluate what she thinks of you and whether she is looking for a reason to fire you. No matter how hard you try to be objective, you can't help but be influenced by your fear.

To help neutralize the fear and become more objective, you should make two lists: one of all the painful experiences you might have if you stay at the job; another of the painful experiences you might suffer if you chose to leave. The first list might include ongoing stress, humiliation or ridicule by your boss, lack of promotion or raises, and, most terrifying of all, being fired. The second list might include landing another job that is even worse, loss of seniority that could make you even more vulnerable in the new job, being unable to find a new job, and failing at your new position, so that you lose it, too.

By making these lists, you start getting a grip on your fears. At least now you know what you're afraid of. If one set of fears is clearly worse, in most instances you'll choose the less painful option. But if both routes have comparable risks, you should at least be able to put your generalized fear aside and focus on gathering specific information with which to objectively evaluate your real concerns.

The best weapon against fear is knowledge. When you list your fears, you gain knowledge of yourself and your motivations. After you've gained that insight, you can go on to gather more objective information about the people who will ultimately influence your decision. If you carefully watch your boss as she relates to you and to others, perhaps you'll find she bluntly criticizes *everyone*. Or maybe you'll find she's complimentary to others and harsh only with you. From observations like these, you will eventually be able to correctly read your boss's intentions, reliably predict her behavior, and choose the best plan of action.

This is exactly the process I have found so helpful when selecting a jury. Frequently, we must decide if we should keep Juror Number One or reject her in favor of Juror Number Two. Each may present very different combinations of potential benefits and dangers. It may be more probable that Juror Number One will be critical of the prosecution's case, and therefore more likely to find the defendant not guilty—but she takes a hard line on the death penalty, so she'll probably be tough on the defendant if there's a conviction. Juror Number Two, on the other hand, may seem more likely to accept the prosecution's case, but less likely to impose the death penalty. Both options present risks and thus give rise to fear. After a trial is over, I don't want to wonder whether my client would be free if I'd picked Juror Number One or, even worse, if he'd be alive if I'd picked Juror Number Two. The only way I can sleep at night is to know that I have made the best, most objective, most rational decision possible.

By mentally listing the specific consequences I fear most about each choice, I force myself to focus on them clearly. This helps me form questions for the prospective jurors that will help me gain insights into their attitudes about those issues that are troubling me. I then discuss my observations and the risks associated with choosing each juror with the defendant and his lawyer. Ultimately, it's the lawyers and defendants who must choose if they will risk a possible death sentence in exchange for a better chance of an acquittal—but it is my job to bring as much objectivity as possible to the process. You can use the same process to make better decisions in your own life.

Defensiveness: The Fastest Way to a Closed Mind

No one likes to be attacked or criticized. We often respond by shoring up our defenses like a fort under siege. We see red and quit listening. We lose objectivity, and along with it our good judgment.

I've seen it a hundred times in court. A lawyer is cross-examining a witness and hits a nerve. The witness tenses, sets his jaw, and leans forward; he becomes confrontational, sarcastic, or argumentative. Intent on defending himself, he completely loses sight of the way he looks to everyone in the courtroom, including the jury. He doesn't see the jurors shake their heads or hear the comments they mutter under their breath. He no longer knows or cares whether he is answering the lawyer's question, and everyone sees it.

I remember a vivid example of this from a trial a few years ago involving a dispute over the ownership of a large piece of real estate. The defendant, a successful real estate developer, came to hate the lawyer who represented the investor who was suing him. The investor's lawyer quickly learned how to push the defendant's buttons, and the defendant became argumentative and confrontational. He wouldn't concede even the most minor, obvious points to this man whom he loathed. To the simple question "Isn't it true you told my client you had approval from the city to build a golf course on the property?" he snapped back, "I didn't *tell* him anything, I only wrote him letters." When the investor's lawyer continued, "Well, when you *wrote* him, didn't you say that in your letters?" the defendant responded sarcastically, "You tell me, you have copies of all my letters." After just a few moments of this, the jury was ready to throttle the man. And when the trial was over, they did—with their verdict.

As hard as it is to keep your eyes and ears open under ordinary circumstances, it's even more difficult when you're under attack—but that is exactly when you need to be most clearheaded and objective. If your boss or best customer is criticizing your performance, you should listen and learn if you want to keep your job or your key account. The last thing you should do is to misread your critic because you're focusing solely on what you're going to say to defend yourself. If your husband tries to explain to you why he's unhappy in your marriage, watch and listen carefully; don't withdraw or respond with a defensive tirade—at least, not if your marriage is important to you.

Remember, there will almost always be a time and a place for you to respond, and your response will be much more effective if you thoroughly understand what you're responding to. The only way to gain that understanding is to stifle your defensiveness and open your ears and your mind. As we tell witnesses before they are cross-examined by the opposing lawyer: "Just listen carefully to the questions and do your best to answer them. Don't argue. You'll have a chance to explain your side of the story later." Good advice, inside the courtroom and out.

Start from Scratch

The next step toward reading readiness is to clear your mind of the stereotypes and other forms of mental laziness that so often substitute for careful reflection. *You can't pour a hot bath if you start with a tub that's half full of cold water.* And if you want to evaluate people accurately, you must start from scratch, without preconceived notions of where you should end up. Think of yourself as a pipe clogged with years of deposits from an assortment of biases and prejudices. You need to scrape off those deposits and let information flow freely.

Most of us are somewhat aware of our own prejudices. Although we don't like to admit it, we often judge people by their race, sex, age, national origin, economic status, or appearance. As this book stresses throughout, hundreds of characteristics can have a significant influence on how someone thinks and behaves. But no trait exists in isolation, and no single trait takes precedence over others in every situation. It's a mistake to base your evaluation of anyone on a bias you may have about people with a particular single characteristic. This sort of stereotyping can derail your efforts to predict behavior even before you get started.

I've found that forcing yourself to recognize your biases is the first step to overcoming them. As soon as you're aware that you're making a snap judgment about a person on the basis of some bias, you can stop yourself. You can identify your prejudice and remind yourself that you can't evaluate a person when you have so little to go on. You need to evaluate a great deal of information about people before you can see patterns that will enable you to understand them. Force yourself to look for more details.

I often do this myself in jury selection. After interviewing thousands of people, I've noticed that people who share certain characteristics often think and act alike. Consequently, I have become biased. I tend to expect that the wealthy will be tougher on crime than the poor; that men with long beards will be less conservative than those who are clean-shaven; and that young people will respect authority less than older people do. Whenever I'm evaluating someone who falls into one or more identifiable groups—which means just about everybody—I make a conscious effort to put aside preconceptions as I gather and evaluate information about the person. Otherwise I can't say I'm reading ready.

Less obvious than stereotyping is shortcut thinking—taking the easiest route to a conclusion. This tendency is so common that advertisers take advantage of it all the time to sell us things. The ad that touts a car as "the best-selling vehicle on the market" appeals to us because we naturally conclude that if "everyone else" is buying the car, it must indeed be the best. Jumping to this conclusion is easier than poring through a stack of *Consumer Reports* and making an informed decision for ourselves. In fact, the car may be the worst vehicle on the market, selling so well only because it is the most heavily advertised. This kind of shortcut thinking can also interfere with reading people. We tend to assume that a person who uses big words is knowledgeable and reliable, or that a person who wears sunglasses indoors must be a shady character. But if we don't go further and test our snap judgments, we could be wrong.

The point was illustrated during jury selection in a murder case in which a middle-aged African-American man, conservatively dressed and articulate, wore sunglasses to court three days in a row. The legal team couldn't help but wonder why. What was going on? Was he bleary-eyed from night after night of partying? Was he making a fashion statement, or a political one? Could he be hiding bruises from a fistfight? Surely the sunglasses reflected on his character in some way—don't they always? There were as many theories as there were lawyers in the courtroom. Finally, the prosecutor asked the question that was on all of our minds. The prospective juror took off his glasses and revealed an injury that made one of his eyes hypersensitive to light.

If a decision is not terribly important, you may choose to take the easy route when judging somebody, just to save time. But whenever your conclusion is critical to your personal or professional success, shortcut thinking simply isn't good enough. In these circumstances, you must ask yourself whether you have started with a clean slate and validated your conclusions independently. You can't afford to jump recklessly from A to Z without stopping anywhere in between.

Technology Invites Miscommunication

The technology that we have grown to take for granted may help us better navigate today's world in most respects, but it has also created a barrier to reading people, the implications of which most of us have not considered to any great extent, if at all. The results of a recent national Harris survey found that the potential for miscommunication between adults varies predictably depending upon their opportunities to "read" one another while communicating. The potential for misunderstandings while using different means of communicating were found to be:

80%	when using e-mail
78%	when text messaging
71%	by letter or other written form
53%	by telephone
37%	when face to face

Given such findings, it is obvious that one way to reduce miscommunication is to raise the bar and push yourself to communicate one or two levels above what you normally do. The same is true with regard to increasing your ability to read other people. It's easier to do when, instead of sending off that e-mail, you pick up the phone to call your colleague, or better yet, if you walk down the hall and speak face to face.

In addition to social networking, other Web sites have been created that give additional ammunition for your ability to read people. Dating Web sites like Zogo.com, Match.com, and Matchmoi.com are replacing antiquated dating services and personal ads. In fact, I recently heard that people now participate in mobile phone dating and cell phone flirting!

Trust but Verify

The Google Web site has opened a Pandora's box in terms of making information accessible—especially information about individuals. In a recent trial in Colorado, I had the opportunity to "Google" our prospective jurors and find out if any public information about them was listed. In fact, one of the jurors had a lengthy blog detailing his views on religion. This particular trial had issues in which religion was an important factor. As such, the information I retrieved from the Internet verified my initial impressions of this individual that in fact he would likely favor the defendant's case because, like him, the defendant was a very religious Christian. But that may not always be the case. There's an old saying, "Trust, but verify." That is the ultimate validation of your ability to read people.

I recently spoke with a realtor who told me he once represented a buyer who made an offer to the seller of a home. The seller had informed the realtor that he didn't want to close the deal until after mid-January because he was involved in a number of charities that always have events during the December holiday period. After the realtor passed on this information to his buyer, the buyer didn't trust the realtor so he Googled the seller and found out that the seller was, in fact, very involved in these organizations. This is definitely a case of "trust but verify." Clearly, the buyer didn't have the utmost faith in his ability to read his realtor, so he took the next step.

Through my husband Randy, a helicopter pilot, I have learned a great deal about how to "trust but verify" in relation to the aviation field. Sites like FlightAware.com give information about a commercial or private aircraft's flight plan, owner, and its departure and arrival times. Obviously, this site isn't one that an average person will use on a regular basis. However, sites like this can be utilized by an employer wanting to check an employee's travel story, or by a girl who doesn't necessarily believe what she's been told by her boyfriend with regard to his travel plans.

The advent of social networking on the Internet has spawned the phenomenon of social-network spying. In fact, new terms like "face-stalking" and "MyStalking" have been coined to describe people who stalk their crushes, exes, or others on the Web. Not only do people have the ability to check up on whose picture is on their former girl-friend's Web page, but employers can check MySpace and Facebook for pages managed by a prospective employee. It's fascinating to see what people put on their pages, and even more fascinating to discern not only how they'd like to be seen, but what unintentional cues they may be signaling to visitors. We'll get to this in chapter 12.

Putting It All Together

Anyone can prepare for the challenge of reading others. Chapter 3 will emphasize the importance of discovering the patterns within the hundreds of clues you will uncover with patience, attentiveness, and practice. The chapters that follow will describe what many of those individual clues might—and I emphasize the word "might"—suggest about a person's beliefs, attitudes, and probable behavior. But always bear in mind that every individual is a complex and unique mosaic. Nothing you read will apply to every person or every situation.

Undoubtedly, you will disagree with some of my observations. You will have known men with scruffy beards who were very conservative; women with loud, strident voices who were soft and gentle; and men with nervous twitches who were confident and secure. So have I. There are always exceptions, which is precisely why we've stressed the impor-tance of developing patterns for decoding behavior. The conservative man with a long beard will reveal his conservatism in many ways. The soft, compassionate woman with the strident voice will show her sen-sitivity if you stay alert. And the confident man with the nervous twitch will demonstrate his confidence if you watch him long enough.

If this book could deliver but one message, it would be [this:] to read people effectively you must gather enough information about them to estab-lish a consistent pattern. Without that pattern, your conclusions will be about as reliable as a typical ten-day weather forecast. The pattern, not the individual pieces, is what reveals the person.

Make a Decision, Then Act on It

We've all complained about someone: our dentist, doctor, day-care provider, tax preparer. We've figured them out. They're sloppy, lazy, uncaring, incompetent, or dishonest—yet we keep going back to them like lambs to the slaughter. Why bother reaching the right conclusion in the first place if we're not going to act on it? Why don't we just go ahead and do the right thing?

There can be several reasons. Sometimes we hesitate out of misplaced charity or a lack of confidence in our own judgment. We may still have some doubt about our impression and feel that if we just dig a little deeper, we'll find the missing clue that will explain the person's behavior. If you're not convinced that your evidence is solid, it makes sense to go back and gather more. But remember, there's no guarantee you'll ever understand anyone completely no matter how much information you gather. And at some point you have to make a decision, or you'll be trapped in "analysis paralysis."

Some people fail to act because they simply can't bear the emotional pain or uncertainty of a difficult decision. *If you have this problem, remember that maintaining the status quo is a decision.* If a relationship isn't working, the decision not to change it is a decision to stay in it.

When you're stuck in a situation and unable to act on the information you've gathered, try a little trick. Pretend you have several choices, one of which is just exactly the way things are. For instance, if you are questioning whether your current romantic relationship is right for you, ask yourself: If I were single and I met someone exactly like the person with whom I'm currently involved, would I want to settle into a relationship with the new person, or would I keep searching? Objectively evaluate all the available information. If you find yourself recoiling from the prospect of jumping into a new relationship just like the one you're in, it may be time for a change.

I tried this very exercise a few years ago when I was unhappy with my secretary. I asked myself whether I'd hire her if I needed a secretary and she applied. I had to answer with a resounding "no." As simple as it might seem, it took this exercise to help me make the right decision.

Sometimes we delay decisions because we fool ourselves into believing that the person who has disappointed us will change. This doesn't happen just between lovers, spouses, and friends. For example, attorneys should know better, but I've seen many a lawyer accept a juror who is openly hostile to his case because he believed the juror would be swayed by his eloquence. But I've seldom seen that transformation take place. After watching thousands of people make decisions, I've learned *it's a lot easier to change the way you think about a person than to change the way that person thinks!*

Finally, there will undoubtedly be times when you've gathered and objectively evaluated all the available information, yet still find that the best choice isn't clear. In those cases you just have to make the best decision you can. You may have made a bad choice, and you may be sorry later, but you can take some comfort in the knowledge that few decisions are irreversible. If you make the wrong call about someone, you usually won't need to live with that choice forever.

One final word about reading readiness: as you go on to acquire the more specific skills described in the rest of this book, *keep practicing* the basic skills outlined in this chapter. They are the key to getting the most out of this book because they will put you into the proper state of mind to understand people better. They will help you stay receptive and alert—the very qualities you need if you're to make rapid progress.

KEY POINTS

Make contact: Communicate personally or by phone if possible; and don't forget—if you want a clear view of another person, you must offer a glimpse of yourself.

Know what you're looking for: "If you don't know where you're going, you will probably end up somewhere else." By clearly defining what you truly need, want, and expect from others, you can focus more clearly on their ability to deliver.

Stop, look, and listen: Be both attentive and patient. Don't rush to judgment. Remember, if you take all the time you *really* have available, you'll usually have as much as you *really* need.

Don't fall victim to "shortcut" thinking: Keep an open mind; not one filled to the brim with either your or other people's biases, prejudices, or stereotypes. Remember, you can't pour a hot bath if you start with a tub that's half full of cold water.

Don't shop when you're hungry: Avoid decisions when you're emotionally blinded, needy, afraid, or defensive.

If you can't be objective, at least be thorough: Make sure you've gathered as much information as possible. Play the devil's advocate and ask what you would think if it was someone else's decision; consult a trusted friend, and make lists of the possible positive and negative consequences of your more important choices.

Make a decision, then act on it: Don't let your own indecision, or the actions of others, control your fate.

TWO

Learning to Ask the Right Questions—and Listen to the Answers

I'm sitting in a restaurant, and I see a couple walk in. They ask to be seated in a corner booth, where I watch them as I finish my meal. It's clear they're just getting to know each other, probably on their first date.

They have come to a quiet restaurant, and their attention is focused on each other. I can see mild nods and gestures of understanding and interest, and what seems to be a lively exchange of information. Each listens intently as the other talks, rarely interrupting. While I can't overhear their conversation, their body language reflects enthusiasm, empathy, and curiosity. They sincerely want to learn, to understand, and to be understood.

Fast-forward a year. I'm in the same restaurant and the same couple walks in. This time they don't bother to ask for the quiet corner booth. Instead, they accept a table near the kitchen. As they hunker down with their menus, they barely bother to speak. After the waiter takes their order they sit in silence for a while; each gazes absently about the restaurant. They are so close to me that when they finally begin speaking I can hear every word. As the woman talks about her day at the office, her boyfriend sighs, stares across the room, then changes the subject to his plans for the weekend. She greets that topic with a sarcastic remark about the amount of time he spends on his mountain bike. He responds with a jealous and accusatory comment about her having lunch with an old boyfriend earlier in the week.

They're still pursuing that topic with gusto when I leave the restaurant, glad to have escaped.

What happened? They quit talking. They quit listening. Once they began to feel they knew each other, the lines of communication corroded. They no longer asked meaningful questions and listened with an open mind to the answers; they accused, denied, and bickered.

Each of us has the ability to ask meaningful questions and really listen to the answers—when we want to. The problem is, we get busy, or lazy, or too familiar, and we quit trying. Think back to the last time you met someone you were interested in getting to know, either as a friend, an employee, or a lover. Remember how you asked questions and truly listened to the answers during your first few conversations? Do you still listen as intently now that you know the person better? Chances are, you don't. And while we can't expect to maintain the intense interest we feel when we first get to know someone, many people backslide to an astonishing degree.

You'll never truly understand people unless you know how to ask good questions and listen to the answers. Without understanding them, you won't be able to predict their behavior or know how to meet their needs or whether they'll meet yours. This chapter will explain how to ask questions that matter and offer some advice about creating the best possible environment for a productive conversation. It'll also show you how to phrase follow-up questions if you don't get the information you need the first time out. Perhaps most important, you'll learn the secrets of becoming a good listener. Unless you learn to hear, *really hear*, a person's replies, all your questioning may be a complete waste of time.

The Dos and Don'ts of Good Listening

Learning to listen is more difficult than learning to ask good questions. I'm reminded of this constantly in court as I watch inexperienced lawyers question witnesses. Intent on sticking to a carefully constructed line of questioning, many of them will overlook an evasive answer or neglect to pursue important clues that a witness drops. If I taught law, I'd insist that my students learn how to listen long before they started drafting questions. Listening is critical, but because it is seemingly passive, it's frequently overlooked. It may sound like we're putting the cart before the horse, but before we cover the ins and outs of asking good questions, here's a crash course on the listening skills I've developed from years of close observation.

As you read through the following pages, consider how well you listened to another person the last time you were at a party, in the lunchroom, at an employee performance review, or having dinner with friends. If you're like most people, you'll see lots of room for improvement in several of the areas discussed. Don't worry—the wonderful thing about the process of reading people, including learning to listen to them, is that no matter how badly you've botched it in the past, you'll always have a fresh opportunity tomorrow.

First and Foremost, Don't Interrupt

Adults often listen to young children much more carefully than to other adults. We expect children to have trouble expressing themselves, so we give them the time they need; we hear them out. What's more, we really try to understand how they're feeling, not just what they're thinking. When we interrupt, it's usually to help the youngster express himself, not to change the subject or control the direction of the conversation. We tend to show the same courtesy and interest to the elderly and to those who suffer from a disability or language barrier. Why not listen to everyone that way?

The first rule of good listening is, don't interrupt. It's impossible to listen well when you're talking or planning what to say next. Even when someone is venting, keep quiet and let him get it off his chest—you might learn a lot. You can always go back later to correct, challenge, or dispute him—or, who knows, maybe even agree with him. Besides, he's more likely to listen to your point of view after he's let off some steam.

If someone's rambling, stop and listen for a while, unless you have a fire to put out. I know it can be tempting to cut her off, but what somebody rambles on about can tell you what's important to her, or at least what's on her mind at the moment, and may give you insight into her thought process or the associations she makes between one event and another.

When we interrupt someone, we derail him, even if only briefly. By the time he gets back on track and moving forward again, the spontaneity and rhythm of the conversation may be lost for good. At least half of my gray hairs come from watching this process in court. A lawyer has just gotten a prospective juror relaxed and chatting freely. I'm feverishly typing notes into my laptop and can see that the juror is just about to really open up when, out of the blue, the lawyer cuts in to ask a long, convoluted question on a completely different topic. It's like the end of a dream sequence in a bad movie: I'm snapped back to reality. The juror stops in mid-sentence, her mouth hanging open, while the lawyer finishes his question. The mood is broken. I start looking for things to throw.

Such interruptions occur regularly in our everyday conversations. There are many ways to break the flow besides a poorly timed question. The most deadly is what I call "the goldfish gulp." Just as fish come to the surface of a dirty pond as if to inhale large gulps of air, so the would-be interrupter stares at you, mouth opening to take a deep breath, as he prepares to plunge headlong into the middle of your sentence. Completely distracted, you stop talking. Why not? There's no sense talking when the other person has clearly stopped listening.

Then there are those who interrupt with sudden movements or gestures, by looking elsewhere, or even by getting up and moving away. And there are those who start taking notes feverishly. Even if their intentions are good, note-takers always make me want to stop talking until they stop writing and are ready to listen again.

Any distraction is a potential interruption, and interruptions are fatal to meaningful conversation. Learn to pay attention, and wait your turn. Think of yourself as a good referee, whose job is to keep the game moving but not to control it.

Be Empathetic: Don't Condemn, Argue, or Patronize

Don't you hate it when you confess that you don't know who the mayor of Chicago is and your companion bleats out, "You're kidding! I thought everyone knew that." If you want to make someone stop confiding in you, just be judgmental, argumentative, or patronizing. If she doesn't quit talking to you altogether, whatever she does say will be distorted by her desire to avoid your biting response. "Don't be so hard on yourself; we all make mistakes" will do a lot more for good conversation than "I can't believe you did something so stupid." "I'm sorry to hear you were laid off. Are you okay?" is much more likely to lead to meaningful dialogue than "I told you you'd get fired if you didn't quit calling in sick so much."

People who feel compelled to point out every misstatement or mispronounced word are usually insecure themselves. Belittling another may give them a temporary thrill or feeling of superiority, but it sabotages the lines of communication. *To encourage candid conversation, resist the urge to correct, criticize, or gloat.* When you really can't, in good conscience, support someone's behavior, you'll have to honestly (and tactfully) express your feelings, but those cases are relatively rare. The rest of the time, follow Mom's advice: "If you can't say something nice, don't say anything at all." This will make you the type of listener other people feel they can trust and talk to.

Stay Close, but Don't Be a Space Invader

People feel most comfortable talking to someone who is within a few feet of them. Experienced trial lawyers recognize this and, if the judge will allow, try to position themselves as close as possible to the jurors to whom they are speaking. However, they carefully avoid invading the jurors' personal space.

In most cultures personal space generally extends to about the distance of your outstretched arms. As you become closer to someone, the personal space you both want will become more flexible. Under normal circumstances, however, any time you are within arm's length of a stranger you risk making her uncomfortable. If you don't believe me, next time you get into an elevator with a stranger, stand right next to her and watch her reaction. Touching is also a risky proposition. Unless you know a person well, touching her, even in a supportive way, might make her uncomfortable and distract her from what she's saying.

Using the arm's-length distance as a guide, move in or out as seems appropriate depending on your degree of intimacy with someone. To some extent, you'll be able to judge her comfort by her body language. As you get too close she'll withdraw or grow tense. She may cross her arms or turn at an angle away from you. If you withdraw too far out of her contact zone, she may start looking around the room as if she's preparing to leave, or simply stop talking.

Be Involved, Not Intense

When we speak, particularly about something important to us, we want relatively constant affirmation that the person to whom we're speaking is paying attention. A subtle nod or an occasional "I understand" or "Right" is all it takes. We're so accustomed to hearing these subtle acknowledgments that they don't interrupt or distract us. Rather, they encourage the speaker to continue. Total quiet can be very disconcerting.

I used to work with a consultant who believed the best way to get people to talk was to say nothing, taking advantage of the fact that people hate awkward silences and automatically try to fill them. This may work for a while, but at some point the other person will become too uncomfortable or get tired of pulling the laboring oar. He won't want to talk to you anymore, and he'll think you're rude, uncaring, socially inept, or just dull.

Too much intensity, however, can be just as distracting as too little involvement. A fixed, unblinking gaze seems uninviting or even threatening. While eye contact is a wonderful tool for developing intimacy and trust, it can be overdone. The same can be said of the intent look of concern and compassion some people adopt whether you're telling them about a traumatic childhood experience or what you had for dinner last night. Inappropriate, overplayed compassion or intensity seems phony and often turns people off.

Be Aware of Your Body Language

The angle of your body or the look on your face can signal that you're about to interrupt, delivering the death blow to a good conversation. Similarly, if someone sees you grimacing, frowning, or shaking your head in disbelief midway through a story, he's likely to stop, or at least change direction.

But you can also encourage a particular line of conversation with positive body language—nodding slightly, leaning forward attentively, maintaining eye contact, and smiling. This sort of positive reinforcement comes pretty naturally to most people. The next time you're really enjoying a conversation, take note of your body language and expressions. Chances are you will realize that your physical reactions are encouraging the other person to perk up and warm to her story.

Take care, however: even positive reinforcement can be overdone. Because we all crave approval, nonverbal encouragement is a powerful force. If you don't use it prudently, the person with whom you're speaking may get carried away and overstate her true feelings or opinions just to keep getting your approval. I've seen this happen many times during jury selection. For example, in a death penalty case, a juror who is at first ambivalent about capital punishment will, after active reinforcement by the prosecutor, end up practically begging to pull the switch herself. Then the defense lawyer stands up and starts questioning her. Now the juror gets positive "strokes" every time she expresses reservations about capital punishment. In most cases, she ends up back where she started—uncertain. I know from experience that the juror's original statements probably reflected her true beliefs, and she was just trying to please everyone. If you want reliable answers, don't manipulate someone, intentionally or unintentionally, into saying what she doesn't really believe by broadcasting "Good answer!" or "Bad answer!" with your body language.

Talk About Yourself, but Don't Get Too Familiar Too Fast

Good conversation is a two-way street. Even if you ask wonderfully penetrating and thought-provoking questions, you usually won't get far unless you also reveal something of yourself. Previous chapters have stressed how important it is to engage other people and establish a rapport with them. *Disclosing something of yourself is essential if you want to keep other people speaking candidly so you'll have something worthwhile to listen to.*

Johnnie Cochran's jury selection in the O. J. Simpson criminal trial was the best I have ever witnessed. Whatever their opinion of Mr. Cochran or the case, everyone in the courtroom had to appreciate his mastery of the art of self-disclosure. It was as if he were sitting down for a cup of coffee in the living room of each juror. He laughed. He smiled. They laughed and smiled back. He struck a perfect balance, telling the jury something about himself without revealing too much. That balance is key to the art of self-disclosure.

Pick your revelations carefully, and time them just right. If you're uncertain about how much to reveal, it's usually better to err on the side of revealing less—you can always close the gap as the relationship matures. But if you reveal too much too soon, you may scare your new friend away forever.

Consider the Context

Many people are not particularly precise with the words they choose. Lawyers love to hang on every word a witness says, combing through depositions and trial transcripts looking for inconsistencies. "Aha! On page 412 she said it was a 'warm' afternoon, but on page 723, she said it was 'hot.' " Or, "Oh, I've got him. On page 114 he testified that he went straight home from work, but on page 212, he said he stopped off at the gas station." Well, the first witness probably drew no distinction between "warm" and "hot," and the second one probably did go "straight home" from work: the gas station was on the way.

To truly understand someone's words, you have to view them in the broadest context. That includes much more than where the words fall within a sentence. It may also include when, where, why, and to whom they were spoken. Consider, too, what emotions may have been at work. There is nothing more potentially misleading than taking words that were spoken in one context and transplanting them into a different context as if they were simply interchangeable parts.

Almost every married couple will have disagreements. Sometimes angry and even hateful words are exchanged. A heated argument spawned by anger, frustration, hurt, fear, or other powerful emotions can easily result in overstatements like "I hate you" and "I can't believe I ever married you." To treat such statements as if they had been spoken calmly and after deep thought and reflection may lead you to incorrect conclusions—unless, of course, they are consistent with a pattern of similar statements.

As a good listener, you are wise to be on the alert for inconsistencies that may creep into a conversation, but never forget that in real life people are rarely 100 percent accurate. *Every slip of the tongue is not Freudian, every emotional outburst doesn't reflect a person's true innermost feelings, and every inconsistency is not a willful lie. Don't view them as such.*

Listen with All Your Senses

As chapter 1, "Reading Readiness," mentioned, telephones, text messaging, e-mail, and answering machines have reduced our opportunities to speak to others in person. And that's a significant loss since the ideal conversation takes place face to face. To be a good listener, you need to be able to pick up all the available clues, with all of your senses.

In person, you'll hear nuances in someone's voice that may not carry over the telephone line. You'll be able to see the emotion in his face and the tension or relaxation in his body. When you're speaking with a more intimate friend, you can reach out and take his hand or give him a pat on the back, which may encourage him to open up even more. You may even be able to smell clues, such as alcohol, medication, or sweat. Listening may technically refer only to sound, but true understanding requires that you use all your senses. Don't hamstring yourself by using just one.

Creating the Environment for Great Conversations

Now that you've learned the basics of good listening, you're ready to set the stage for a great conversation. All face-to-face conversations have to occur somewhere—and that somewhere shouldn't be left to chance. Certain environments have a greenhouse effect on conversations, making them thrive and blossom. Others kill off discourse as thoroughly as an icy blizzard. You wouldn't ask someone a personal question during the middle of a staff meeting, or discuss her family background over the din of a rock concert.

It's rare that we don't have any choice about a conversation's environment. Even at work, there are options—your office, her office, a meeting room, the lunchroom, or even the lawn out front. The door can be closed or open. Waiting for the appropriate time and place may require a little patience, but if what you have to discuss is important, it's worth it.

What that best environment is depends on what you want to discuss, and with whom. We've all seen 1940s detective movies in which a suspect is given the third degree in a stark cell with a bright light boring into his eyes. The theory is, the more frightened and uncomfortable the suspect is, the quicker he'll "spill." In reality, most suspects are treated more humanely, but making them uncomfortable is still part of interrogation techniques today.

On the opposite end of the spectrum might be the environment a friend of mine chooses when he takes a woman on a first date. He has a favorite Moroccan restaurant where seven-course meals are eaten slowly in private booths over two-and-a-half or three hours. How better to get to know someone?

Whether you have days to plan the setting or only moments to adjust a few details, keep the following in mind.

Your Turf or Their Turf?

People are most comfortable on their own turf. If you want someone to relax and open up to you, meet in her office, at her home, or wherever else she chooses. Or, if you're already together when the conversation starts—at a party, for example—follow the other person's lead. If she suggests you move out to the patio or to a quiet corner, agree willingly. Don't be afraid to ask, "Where would you like to talk?" or "Do you feel comfortable here, or would you rather go somewhere else?"

But if *you* want to feel more comfortable and in control of the conversation, steer the other person to your turf. Have you ever noticed that when the boss delivers good news, he usually comes to the employee's workstation or office, but when he disciplines someone or terminates her, it's usually in his own office? When delivering bad news, he wants to maintain more control and authority, and he can best do so on his own turf.

There's a trade-off: control for information. It may be harder to read people on your turf because they'll be more guarded, more defensive, and less willing to reveal themselves than they would be on their home territory. You, however, will be more in control. I have found that it is seldom worth sacrificing meaningful dialogue for more control.

Avoid an Audience

In the courtroom, issues about which jurors may be sensitive are often discussed in the judge's chambers with only the judge, the lawyers, and the prospective juror present. It's embarrassing to discuss personal issues in public, so jurors don't tend to be very candid if forced to respond to such questions in open court. In daily life, too, you'll be disappointed if you try to draw personal information from someone in front of an audience.

An audience also tends to bring out the worst in people. When confronted with personal questions while others are standing by, many will respond by bragging, becoming confrontational, getting defensive, or clamming up in embarrassment. You'll never know what they might have revealed about themselves or their beliefs if you had asked the more personal questions in a private setting.

Remove Physical Obstacles Between You and a Good Conversation

Any object between you and the person with whom you're talking may interfere with your conversation. That's why many experienced speakers step away from the podium when they lecture: they don't want anything between them and the group. It's also why many businesspeople choose not to speak with clients, customers, or employees from behind a desk, but instead come around their desk and sit next to them.

If you want to have an unconstrained conversation with someone, get rid of any obstacles between the two of you. Move out from behind your desk, unless maintaining control is more important than exchanging information. At a restaurant, ask the waiter to remove tall flower arrangements, extra glasses, or any other objects that clutter the visual space between you and your tablemate. If you're wearing sunglasses, take them off. Even air is an obstacle if there's too much of it: stay close, but not too close.

Get Rid of Distractions

While I was a graduate student, I worked as the administrator of a small private school. Frequently, I met with parents to discuss problems with their children. Emotions often ran high, and I sometimes felt more like a therapist than an administrator. The last thing I wanted during these tense meetings was to be distracted by phone calls or other interruptions, so I always saw parents in my office with the door closed and instructed my secretary to hold all calls.

When you eliminate distractions, you clear the stage for candid, uninterrupted dialogue. Turn off your cell phone or pager, the TV, the radio. Choose a quiet booth in the restaurant or a peaceful park bench, away from in-line skaters and shouting schoolchildren. If you're at a party, step away from the action as much as possible so your conversation won't be interrupted by passersby or the temptation to people-watch.

Good conversation flows like a river. It twists and turns but is never broken. Interruptions are a dam in that river. Once that dam is up, the conversation may never flow freely again. By removing distractions, you'll reduce the likelihood that your conversation will be interrupted. Both you and your companion will be more relaxed and better able to concentrate on the discussion at hand. Good communication is difficult enough. Avoid putting any additional hurdles in its path.

Position Yourself to Receive Information

In both my personal and professional life, I try not to ask a really important question unless I'm close enough to clearly see the other person's eyes. A slight twitch of the eyelid, a quick tightening of the jaw, a grimace, or even a subtle slacking of facial muscles may make a significant difference in how I evaluate his response.

Reading people is all about building patterns from every possible clue you can gather. Facial expressions can be a valuable source for this information. If you choose to have an important conversation with someone while driving in your car or walking down the street, you'll be distracted, and what reactions you do see, you'll see only in profile.

This isn't to say we haven't all had wonderful discussions while taking long car trips or jogging in the park. But ideally, you should be squarely in front of the person you're talking to, where you can see her entire face and body and she can see yours.

Timing Can Be Everything

Why do some newlyweds have so many arguments? Maybe it's because they haven't yet learned what a bad idea it is to bring up important issues at the end of a long hard day. In all relationships, personal or professional, there are good times and bad times to broach any subject. Ignore this fact at your own risk.

Anger, frustration, joy, depression—almost any state of mind—may color someone's reaction to a question. If you don't bother to gauge his mood before bringing up a delicate subject, at least take into consideration how it may be influencing the response. Ask someone a perfectly civil question when he's just found out his son crashed his brand-new car, and you're likely to get a surprisingly short-tempered response. At the other extreme, you might get an unrealistically rosy answer if he's just gotten a big Christmas bonus.

Is it a good idea to ask your friend's opinion of your new boyfriend when she's three sheets to the wind? Perhaps you'll get a more candid answer. On the other hand, maybe you'll hear an alcohol-inflamed tirade against your boyfriend that has only a passing similarity to your friend's real feelings. There are those who believe you'll get more reliable information from people who are drunk or angry because they've lost their inhibitions and will blurt out "the truth." That may be so sometimes, but often people deeply regret their angry or drunken words, not because they revealed some hidden secret but because they didn't really mean what they said.

It's common for someone who is drunk, angry, or otherwise highly emotional to lose his perspective temporarily. He may ignore the big picture—or pattern—in someone's behavior and focus on an isolated event that dominates his thoughts at the moment. Whatever he says in these circumstances may have no resemblance to what he would say upon sober reflection.

To have a successful discussion, pick your time carefully. Make sure it's good for the other party, too. Avoid discussing a sensitive issue with someone who's been drinking or is already agitated and angry. Don't try to force someone to sit down and talk with you when he says he's too busy; he'll be distracted, unfocused, and ultimately unresponsive to your needs.

Go Slow and Easy

The normal progression of communication between two people moves from the general to the specific, the casual to the meaningful, and the impersonal to the personal. The process needn't take weeks or months. I've seen good attorneys develop a bond with prospective jurors or witnesses in minutes. There is nothing like a broad smile and a self-effacing, self-disclosing manner to make jurors relax; they quickly start trusting the lawyer, who can then elicit candid answers to difficult questions about their biases and personal beliefs. But before he begins probing, the great lawyer establishes rapport. He warms the juror up.

If you move too quickly from general, unthreatening questions to penetrating inquiries about someone's faith and marriage (for instance), the conversation may skid to a halt. Many people will simply clam up; others will be offended and think you're rude and insensitive. Some might conclude that you're socially inept. What replies you do get may not be very reliable. People may simply say what they think you want to hear so you'll back off and leave them alone.

I saw an excellent example of this at a recent seminar that featured a mock trial and jury selection. The case involved a schoolteacher who'd been fired for teaching the Christian doctrine of creation in violation of a school board policy—a reversal of the famous Scopes "Monkey Trial" featured in the play and movie *Inherit the Wind*. Naturally, during jury selection the questions quickly turned to the jurors' religious beliefs. The jurors pleasantly answered the lawyers' questions: "Yes, I'm a Christian, but I don't go to church much"; "I never did get into that"; "I'm a devout Catholic." They did not appear to be put off by the questions, and everything went smoothly—until we got to one elderly lady. "Do you consider yourself a religious person?" the lawyer asked her abruptly. She bristled and through clenched teeth replied, "I think that's a matter for me and my creator." *Whoa*, I thought. Never forget that what one person believes is perfectly appropriate, another may find deeply offensive. Most of the jurors were comfortable with the pace at which personal information was elicited. But everyone's threshold for self-disclosure is different.

Should I Let Him Think About It?

You have a question you want to ask. The answer is critical to you, and it must be reliable. You don't want it tainted or manipulated in any way. Do you give the person you're asking as much time as he needs to answer, or do you ask for an answer on the spot? It depends.

We face this dilemma all the time in litigation. On the one hand, before trial we can present written questions to opposing parties, who then have weeks to prepare written answers. In theory, this gives them plenty of time to provide the most truthful and complete answers possible. In practice, they generally use the time to carefully massage their answers. Our other option is to wait until the person is seated before us in court before we spring the pivotal question on him. We certainly get a more spontaneous answer this way, but often it's not very complete or well thought out.

Most lawyers believe that you're much more likely to get a truthful answer from somebody if he must respond immediately, particularly if the question raises a sensitive issue. This applies outside the courtroom as well. While there are exceptions (you can't always demand that somebody decide right this minute whether to accept a job, buy a car, or elope to Paris), *in general if you want reliable answers to delicate questions, don't allow somebody too long to ponder his possible replies.* When you crave spontaneity, but also need reflection, ask for a quick response; once you get it, suggest: "Think about it more overnight and we'll talk again tomorrow."

The Dos and Don'ts of Good Questions

The questions you ask, like the time and setting, should take into account all the circumstances, including what sort of information you need. There are times when you must have precise answers, in which case your questions must be equally focused. And in rare cases, you may even need to get tough with your questions. Usually, however, you'll learn more from broader questions that trigger a free flow of information. In any situation, you'll get better results if you plan your inquiries before you actually sit down with the other person.

Preparing Your Questions

A good lawyer wouldn't dream of winging her examination of a witness. But the *best* lawyers don't remain wedded to a particular line of questions, either. They pay close attention to other leads that crop up during the testimony. *Whether you're on a first date, interviewing for a job, or looking for a day-care provider, plot out the questions in advance that will get you the information you really need.* By doing so, you'll achieve several goals. First, you'll save time during the actual conversation. Second, you'll ask more precise and illuminating questions than you would if you winged it. Finally, if you prepare your questions beforehand, then during the conversation you can focus on the other person's answers and body language instead of thinking about your next question. This will make the conversation not only more informative but more spontaneous as well. You'll be able to go with the flow, knowing you can always return to your prepared questions after you address whatever topics might pop up unexpectedly.

Preparation doesn't mean making up a set of flash cards to flip through during the course of a conversation, although sometimes it's not a bad idea to write down questions in advance. Physicians sometimes suggest patients do this before an office visit so they don't lose track of their concerns. I always write down any questions I have before an important meeting. Even if you don't take the list with you, writing down your most pertinent questions before any important encounter will etch them more firmly in your mind.

What Should You Ask?

Tell me the nature and history of the relationship and what each party wants from the other, and I would be able to fashion some useful questions for them. The truth is, there are as many good questions as there are moments of human interaction. The cardinal rule is to be clear on what is important to *you*. If you're a divorced man with young children looking for a long-term romantic relationship, your potential mate's attitude toward children is obviously something you'll want to explore. If you're a dentist interviewing for an assistant, you'll want to know about the person's schooling and experience.

Three general traits tend to shed most light upon all others: compassion, socioeconomic background, and satisfaction with life. (This will be discussed in more detail in chapter 3, "Discovering Patterns.") In any context, knowing about them will give you a substantial head start on understanding someone and being able to predict his or her behavior. So if you can't think of anything else to ask, focus on these.

Many of the questions we ask prospective jurors before trial are designed to enlighten us about these three key areas. We ask questions like

Where were you born?

Where were you raised?

Where do you live now?

What did your parents do for a living?

What do you do for a living?

How many brothers and sisters do you have?

What do you do in your free time?

What books and magazines do you read?

What TV shows do you watch?

Do you belong to any organizations or clubs?

What are your goals for the next five years?

What did you want to be when you were in high school?

Since people love to talk about themselves, these questions can be just as useful outside the courtroom. Just remember to proceed slowly and tactfully and watch for clues that might indicate you're getting too personal too soon.

I find it especially helpful to know about people's family lives when they were growing up. Did their parents help them with their homework? Did they play Little League, sing in the church choir, take dance lessons? If so, did their parents come and watch? These questions can be asked of almost anyone, and the answers will indicate what kind of socioeconomic background someone has.

Questions that will help you gauge someone's satisfaction with life are also always worth asking. One of my favorites is "What did you want to be when you were in high school?" If the person didn't do what she wanted to, ask why. Even a few questions along this line will quickly provide you with some insight about whether she has achieved her objectives in life and how she feels about missing those goals if that's the case. Again, sensitivity is everything. Don't forge ahead like a reporter with a hot lead if you can tell the other person wants to avoid the subject.

You can learn whether someone is compassionate in any number of ways. Is he close to his family, especially his parents? Does she do any volunteer or charity work? How does he feel about the homeless, about paying taxes to support public schools, about the minimum wage? You can always formulate a few questions that can be tossed casually into a conversation to get a sense of someone's degree of compassion. Also watch for revealing behavior and body language: How does he treat cashiers, waitresses, and others in service positions? What's her reaction if someone bumps her accidentally, or absentmindedly cuts her off on the freeway? People's attitudes and behavior will enable you to determine their place on the hardness scale within an hour or two of meeting them.

By preparing some general questions concerning these three important areas, you'll be able to learn more about people more quickly than you have in the past. In all but the most casual encounters, you'll probably want more specific information as well. To get it, you can use three types of questions: open-ended, leading, and argumentative.

Different Questions for Different Circumstances

Say what you will about lawyers, the great ones definitely know how to ask good questions. While a scathing cross-examination may be what comes to mind when you think of a lawyer interrogating a witness, that type of blitzkrieg happens only rarely. Good lawyers devise their line of questioning to coax out truthful answers. Sometimes one approach works best, sometimes another.

All witnesses and jurors are sworn to tell the truth and most do, at least most of the time. But some are, let's say, reluctant. Others are so eager to please they just need to be pointed in the right direction and turned loose. For these reasons, good lawyers have developed a keen sense of which types of questions work best in various circumstances.

When you think of the different types of questions that you can ask, visualize a funnel. The wide-open end represents open-ended questions that call for a "wide-open" narrative explanation and give someone latitude to answer however he wants. The argumentative or "pointed" questions are at the narrow end of the funnel. These are very focused, often confrontational, and may call for just a one-word or two-word response. In between lie leading questions, which focus the person's response but leave some room for explanation, though not as much as open-ended questions do.

Each type of question is more appropriate in some circumstances than others. Knowing when to use which type can be critical to getting reliable information from others.

The Open-ended Question

The open-ended question is an invitation to chat. The key aspect of this type of question is that it doesn't suggest what you might like the answer to be. That is its great advantage: since the other person can't tell what answer might please you, he's much more likely to say what's really on his mind. *For gaining objective, untainted information, open-ended questions are usually your best bet.* In addition, because open-ended questions give the person so much room to wander, the answers will almost always include extra information that may be very revealing.

There are some drawbacks to open-ended questions. One is that because they're so broad, the answer may wander entirely off the track so that you'll never get the information you really need. Another is that open-ended questions take time to answer and so are best used when time isn't a priority. A third disadvantage is that an open-ended question leaves the other person more room to avoid answering altogether.

Even if you need very specific information, however, a good strategy is to start with a few open-ended questions and become more focused as you go. This gives you the opportunity to develop a rapport with the other person while at the same time getting some valuable background data. It just takes a little patience, which is essential anyway if you want to get honest, reliable information.

In most instances, open-ended questions are the best way to find out what you need to know. For example, let's assume a woman has decided she wants to have children, and have them relatively soon. She's been dating a man for several months and thinks he could be Mr. Right. At some point, she'll want to find out whether her new love shares her priorities. If the relationship is developing nicely, she might be inclined to confide in him, "Becoming a parent and raising kids is extremely important to me. How about you?" If the purpose of this question is to find out how he really feels, she's botched it.

First, her question clearly broadcasts the "correct" answer. This taints the response, making it unreliable. Second, suppose the man was to reply, "I feel the same way"? This tells the woman nothing about when the man wants to have children, how many he wants to have, how he believes his life will be changed by having children, or much else of substance. They could have completely different ideas about all of these important issues. However, the woman will probably be delighted to get such an agreeable response, and will go home blissfully believing that she has found her future husband, who wants to build exactly the same life she does. Not necessarily.

Now let's assume that, instead, the woman simply asks: "How do you see your life five years from now?" This is a truly open-ended question. If the man responds, "I want to be married, have a couple of kids, a house with a picket fence, a dog, and a motor home for family vacations," the woman might justifiably conclude that he shares her dreams. However, if his reply does not specifically include children, perhaps parenthood is not a priority for him in the near future. If he doesn't mention children at all in his response, she can follow up with a more focused but still somewhat open-ended question, such as "Where do kids fit in to your future plans?" By phrasing her questions in a general, nonsuggestive way, she'll receive more reliable information from which she can read his intentions better.

The same holds true for job interviews. If you want to hire a secretary who will be satisfied in that position for a long time, ask, "What do you see yourself doing five years from now?"—not "I'm really looking for someone who will be happy being my secretary for the next five years. Would you want to stay in the same position that long?" Similarly, instead of asking, "Are you willing to work overtime?" a better question would be "What is your preference about working overtime?" Even if you plan to ask your new employee to work overtime regularly and feel compelled to warn her of that fact, hold off. First find out what her real preference is. Maybe she'll volunteer that she needs extra money and would love the opportunity. Maybe she'll say she has commitments most evenings and weekends. Whatever her response, you can ask her about her willingness to meet the job's actual requirements after you've found out what her preference would be.

During jury selection, I'm able to see the tremendous improvement in the quality of information lawyers obtain if they're good at phrasing open-ended questions. In capital punishment cases—particularly high-profile ones—we frequently encounter people who are eager to be on the jury. When they are asked by the prosecutor simply, "Do you believe in the death penalty?" they almost always respond, "Yes." However, this doesn't tell us why they believe in the death penalty, how strongly they feel about it, or whether they think there ought to be exceptions to its application. Even those who generally support the death penalty have some reservations. The key is to find out what they are.

In the Night Stalker case, one of the prospective jurors, an African-American man, was asked how he felt about the death penalty. He said he thought it was appropriate in many instances, but that it had been "disproportionately applied." The prosecutor thought he would be a good juror for the prosecution. As the consultant for the defense, I disagreed. The well-phrased open-ended question allowed the man the freedom to express his feelings. It was extremely significant that in his relatively brief reply he pointed out that the death penalty was disproportionately applied. Obviously, the prospective juror was troubled by the fact that African-American defendants in capital cases are sentenced to death more frequently than defendants of other races. From this answer, I believed he would be a hard sell for the prosecution. People don't like to enforce rules they think are unfair.

We decided to leave this man on the jury. Just before the trial began, another juror reported that he had announced to the other jurors that he could never vote for the death penalty. At that point, the judge excused him. I'd been right, but only because the prosecutor's open-ended question allowed the man the freedom to give me the information I needed to read him correctly.

The Leading Question

Whereas open-ended questions don't focus the answer to any great degree, leading questions do. Sometimes it is helpful to restrict the scope of an answer. Because leading questions direct a person's response, they can avoid a lot of wasted time and energy. If you want to know when your employee arrived at work, don't ask, "So, what did you do today?" Instead, ask a leading question: "When did you get to work?"

Leading questions are also essential if you want to get a straight answer from someone who is trying to sidestep you. You can ask some people open-ended questions until the cows come home and never get a straight answer. At some point, the open-ended question has served its purpose: it has demonstrated the person doesn't want to talk about the issue. If you want to find out why, you'll need to ask a leading question.

On some occasions, leading questions can be helpful precisely because they do influence the response. A life insurance salesman effectively used this technique with me shortly after the birth of my first child. "Can you think of anything more important than having your daughter financially secure if something were to happen to you?" he asked. The question wasn't meant to gain information, but to make me focus on the importance of providing for my child in the event of my death.

Another very handy use of the leading question is to let the other person know that you're aware of certain facts. For example, many businesspeople make it a habit to learn everything they can about a prospective new customer before they meet in person. They then prepare a few leading questions, such as "Does this project have anything to do with your acquisition of the ABC Company last year?" A few well-planned leading questions along this line impress the customer, encourage his confidence, and prompt him to share more information.

In your personal life, leading questions often smooth the way to closer relationships. I have a friend who is gay but doesn't reveal her sexual orientation publicly. It was obvious to me from the first time I met her that she was gay, but it was equally obvious that she didn't want me or anyone else to know. As I got to know her better, I wanted our friendship to be more open. So I picked an appropriate time and asked her if she had a "partner"—a term that's often understood as meaning a same-sex spouse or lover. This gave her the choice of either letting the matter pass or dropping her guard, realizing I had guessed her sexual orientation. As it turned out, she *did* have a partner, and she was eager to talk about her. This leading question enabled us to move more quickly to a relaxed, honest friendship.

Sometimes Things Get Ugly: The Argumentative Question

Argumentative questions are just that: argumentative. While they're often handy in the courtroom, they're seldom productive elsewhere. But sometimes it's necessary to get in someone's face if you want to learn crucial information or uncover a lie.

Those who watched the O. J. Simpson trial may recall F. Lee Bailey's confrontational examination of Detective Mark Fuhrman about his use of "the 'N' word." You might have expected Detective Fuhrman to crack under such a barrage. On the contrary, he faced Mr. Bailey's onslaught with little sign of emotion, denying he had used the word at all in the past ten years. When the Laura Hart McKinny tapes were revealed, Detective Fuhrman's staunch denial in the face of such aggressive questioning made his lie even more damaging to the prosecution.

In daily life, the most common use of argumentative questioning is to force someone into a reluctant admission: "Fine. Here's what you want to know—now leave me alone." It's not unusual for people who have revealed information under such interrogation to later claim they said it only to get you off their back. Such reversals should be viewed skeptically. Except in the movies, even under the most aggressive assault, people rarely confess to crimes they didn't commit or admit nonexistent "facts."

The drawback of badgering someone is that although it may get you the facts you need at the moment, it usually exacts a stiff price. In life outside the courtroom, we actually have to maintain relationships with most of the people we question. Argumentative questioning can permanently alter those relationships. So bullying or threatening someone into sharing information with you should be a last resort.

If at First You Don't Succeed—Follow Up!

No matter how carefully you choose your questions and listen to the answers, there will be times when you don't get what you're after. Perhaps the person honestly doesn't know the answer or has trouble sticking to the topic. Maybe she's responding evasively. Or maybe you didn't ask the question clearly or loudly enough and she didn't hear it correctly. In any case, don't give up if the information is important to you.

The first rule of good follow-up questions is to ask them as soon as you realize you need to—ideally, while the original conversation is still taking place. To do this, you have to be a good listener.

Steer the conversation back on course if you realize it's veering away from the topic you want to discuss. There are many ways to do this without being rude or offensive. Before you step in, however, let the person finish speaking. Remember, don't ruin the spontaneity by interrupting. Once there is a natural pause in the conversation, make your move.

One of the most effective approaches is to take full responsibility for the lack of communication. After all, it may well be that your question was unclear. Why not give the other person the benefit of the doubt? You might confess you don't remember whether she gave you the information you needed: "You may have already mentioned this, but I don't remember—what did you do at your last job?" Or acknowledge that you may not have grasped her explanation: "I don't really understand how that happened. Could you explain it again?" Unless the person is being evasive, she'll be glad to comply.

A little self-disclosure before you ask the question again may warm someone up, relaxing him enough to reveal what you need to know. Consider the boy who's reluctant to tell his father about his fear of trying out for the school football team. When his dad asks about it, the youngster may do everything possible to skirt the issue because he doesn't want to admit he's afraid he won't make the cut. If the father perceives this and confides that when he was his son's age, he was afraid to try out for the team, chances are his boy will respond by acknowledging the same fears. Now they're out on the table and can be discussed. But when you use this technique, be alert to the possibility that you're tainting the response. Maybe the boy's real reason for not wanting to try out is he doesn't like sports and doesn't want to admit that to his father. His father's suggestive self-disclosure has given him an acceptable out, which he has pursued gladly. Because of this risk, I don't suggest using this approach unless others have failed.

If the person won't respond to any of these approaches, try another strategy. Go all the way back to some safe ground—something that the person feels comfortable talking about. Reconnect there, and work forward again to the area where the apparent sensitivities were. If that still doesn't work, let the matter go for a while. Wait for a better time or circumstance, or until your relationship with the person matures to a point where he feels comfortable talking with you about even sensitive issues.

Sometimes there is no subtle way to pursue the information being withheld. If the salesman won't give you a straight answer, you have to be very direct: "Can you tell me whether or not this car has ever been in an accident?" Or ask the prospective employee, flat out: "Were you fired from your last job?" The more difficult it is to pry information out of someone, the more significant the information may be. In fact, at some point the entire exercise becomes meaningless— the person's secretive and possibly dishonest behavior itself should steer you away from him.

Getting Information from Outsiders

After reading this chapter about drawing other people out, you ought to be able to get most of the information you need, most of the time. But there are occasions when you need more than you can tactfully ask for, or more than the person has any intention of giving you. In those situations, you'll find you can learn an extraordinary amount from third parties.

It's not this book's purpose to train private eyes, but those so inclined can learn immense amounts about others from public and private records. It's amazing what personal information is housed in sources like the Internet, Dun & Bradstreet, credit reporting services, court files, school records, professional licensing bureaus, and motor vehicle departments. During a recent American Bar Association program on legal issues raised by the electronic revolution, one of the speakers demonstrated how he could pull his outstanding home mortgage balance out of cyberspace. It's scary, but with a little effort and ingenuity many of our best-kept secrets are accessible for all the world to see.

Closer to home, we can learn much about someone from his friends, family, coworkers, and even acquaintances, such as the clerk who waits on him at the local market. You can usually tell how others feel about someone simply by watching their interaction. Do others treat him with respect, deference, fear, intimidation, love, concern, humor, friendship? How does he treat them? And you don't have to rely on observation alone: ask!

It makes sense to check personal references, just as an employer would check education or job references, yet we seldom do. Partly, this is because of social taboos. You can't casually call up your boyfriend's ex-fiancée and ask her opinion of him. However, there is nothing awkward about remarking to his mother, "It must be nice to have Joe come visit." There's a broad range of potentially revealing responses from "It sure is—he never calls or stops by anymore" to "I never get tired of him stopping by or calling, even though he does it all the time." The first response paints a picture of a neglectful son. The second suggests he is considerate and devoted.

You'll be impressed by what you can learn if you take a little time to pose productive questions to others who already know the person you are just getting to know. And you don't have to pry. Ask your boss's wife at a party, "Do you play golf with your husband?" The question may elicit a number of responses, all of which can tell you a lot about your boss's character and priorities. A quick "You've got to be kidding—he takes that game way too seriously" tells you how competitive he is. "I would love to, and I keep hinting, but he never asks me" reveals a selfish and insensitive side. "We've played every Sunday morning at seven o'clock for the past six years, rain or shine" demonstrates both his commitment to his wife and his obsessive adherence to schedules and routines. This in turn indicates that he expects to see loyalty, organization, and promptness in his employees. Any of this information would help you to better understand what is important to your boss and to predict his behavior accordingly.

Once you're looking for them, you'll discover many opportunities to learn about people from third parties. Each can provide you with a different perspective, and the more perspectives you have, the more reliable your picture will be.

KEY POINTS

Learn to listen: Even great questions won't help you "read" if you don't know how to listen. The cardinal rules of good listening are:

- Don't interrupt
- Be empathetic: don't condemn, argue, or patronize
- Maintain a comfortable physical distance
- Be involved, but not too intense
- Don't let your body language impact the free flow of information
- Self-disclose, but not too much, too soon
- Don't take what someone says out of context
- "Listen" with all your senses

Create an environment for great conversations: Consider where and when your conversations should take place, and who else, if anyone, should be present. If the conversation is important, don't leave the setting to chance.

Be patient: Let others move at the speed with which they are comfortable.

Prepare questions: Productive conversation is stimulated by good questions. Whether preparing for a job interview or a first date, think of a few questions to keep the conversation moving and information flowing your way. Questions that call for information about the three most predictive traits—compassion, socioeconomic background, and satisfaction with life—are always a good place to start.

Learn to ask the three different types of questions:

- Open-ended questions are an invitation to chat, and usually lead to longer, more informative answers.
- Leading questions focus the response on a particular issue and help keep the dialogue on track, but may produce less spontaneous or complete answers.
- Argumentative questions are usually your last resort, but may be necessary to ferret out the truth when you have to be confrontational.

If at first you don't succeed—follow up: If you don't get an answer to the question you asked, either repeat it or rephrase it, but ask it again as soon as possible.

THREE

Discovering Patterns

Learning to See the Forest,
Not Just the Trees

In 1939, Sir Winston Churchill called Russia "a riddle wrapped in a mystery inside an enigma." He could have been describing any of us. Even saints have a darker side, and the devils we encounter may reveal elements of honesty and charm. No one is entirely consistent, and most of us are a hodgepodge of often conflicting thoughts, values, and behaviors. But no matter how complex a person may be, patterns of behavior emerge from their seeming inconsistencies. Once you learn to identify those patterns, you'll be able to understand others and predict their behavior.

Collecting a mountain of miscellaneous data about somebody by scrutinizing her looks, body language, environment, voice, and conduct will do little good unless you know which traits can be important indicators of character and which are relatively inconsequential. After you've identified someone's potentially important characteristics, you then have to sort through them and find out how the pieces fit together. You need to learn to see the big picture—the forest, not just the trees.

It's All About Character Development

Learning to read people effectively calls upon many of the techniques gifted storytellers use to develop a character and bring him or her to life. Think about how the creators of Walt Disney's *Beauty and the*

Beast transformed the Beast into a sympathetic hero. A huge brute with fangs and thick fur is frightening, not sympathetic. But the film-makers found ways to make the audience see that there was more to the Beast than first meets the eye. First they dressed him in princely clothing, a clear sign that this is no ordinary monster. Then they used body language to reveal additional aspects of his human character. To this they added dialogue and actions which imply that the Beast may be a sheep in wolf's clothing. A central clue to the creature's real identity comes from an outside source, the narrator, who explains that the Beast is really a prince who has been transformed as a punishment for his uncaring actions years earlier.

By the movie's climax, the pattern is complete. The audience sees not a Beast but the kindhearted hero who lives within. The gradual revelation of the Beast's true character, layer by layer, is what makes the movie a masterpiece. The audience doesn't have to work to develop the pattern that reveals the Beast's nature. The writers and animators make it unfold before our eyes. But in life, we have to search for the pattern of traits that divulges each person's character.

Discovering a predictable pattern is more than just gathering information by following steps A, B, and C. Once you have all the available information, you must sift through it and weigh it until finally you can step back and look at the whole person. It's not unlike the process a physician goes through when trying to diagnose an ailment. If you come into the office with a painful wrist, he might ask to see how much you can move it. He'll probably feel it and manipulate it himself; ask what recent activities might have hurt it; and then take an X-ray. Each of these diagnostic techniques provides a different piece of information. When all are considered as a whole, he is able to make the best possible diagnosis.

In the same way, you should look at as many different clues as possible when you evaluate someone. Which criteria are most influential depends on the circumstances and on what you need from the relationship. If I'm hiring someone to tile my patio, my needs are simple and clear-cut: he should be good at his craft, honest, and reliable. I don't have to spend hours contemplating all the criteria taught in this book. But if I'm deciding whether to enter into an intimate relationship with someone, I should put a lot more energy into determining what my needs are and carefully consider all the information available about the man.

The following section describes the process I generally follow when I'm trying to get to know and understand someone. The process is the same whether I'm in or out of the courtroom: people are people, whether in the jury pool, the office pool, or the car pool. Although the material is presented in the order that works best for me, it usually won't matter which area you reflect on first, as long as you keep all of them in mind when you're sizing someone up. With a little practice, you'll develop your own approach; eventually much of this process will become second nature to you, as it has to me.

To discover meaningful and reliable patterns:

1. Start with the person's most striking traits, and as you gather more information see if his other traits are consistent or inconsistent.
2. Consider each characteristic in light of the circumstances, not in isolation.
3. Look for extremes; the importance of a trait or characteristic may be a matter of degree.
4. Identify deviations from the pattern.
5. Ask yourself if what you're seeing reflects a temporary state of mind or a permanent quality.
6. Distinguish between elective and nonelective traits. Some things you control; other things control you.
7. Give special attention to certain highly predictive traits.

You Have to Start Somewhere—
Begin with the Most Striking Traits

The amount of information I'm able to gather about prospective jurors is trivial compared with what's available in everyday life. We often see people in many different settings: casual, formal, business-related, social. And we often get to know them over the course of months or years. In fact, we have access to so much information it's easy to feel overwhelmed, unless we have a game plan designed to keep us focused.

Anyone who has assembled a jigsaw puzzle has learned that without some logical approach, one can fumble endlessly with the hundreds of pieces on the table before finding a single match. To get started, most people begin by putting together the edge pieces—not because they show what the finished puzzle will look like but because they are relatively easy to identify and assemble. Once the edge of the puzzle has been completed, we have a framework to help us determine how the other pieces fit into place.

Within the first few minutes, or even seconds, of meeting someone, I've usually gathered a tremendous amount of readily observable information about age, sex, race, physical characteristics, vocal mannerisms, and body language. With a few questions, I can quickly learn about my new acquaintance's education and marital status, the number, sex, and age of his children, what he does for a living, and his family history, hobbies, club or organizational memberships, and favorite television shows. This represents just the first layer of information available to those who are trying to read people.

A second, more subjective level of information is based on physically observable traits that require interpretation: the meaning of body language and mannerisms, the significance of vocal qualities, and the importance of specific actions, to name but a few. Here, you need some understanding of the possible meanings of each of the person's observable traits.

And there is a third level of information, which reflects conclusions about the person's character based on analysis of the information revealed at the first two levels. Is a person considerate or rude? Stingy or generous? Violent or passive? Hardworking or lazy?

After years of trying, I still can't read and interpret all this information at once, and I have never met anyone who could. Yet all of this information goes into the recipe for reading people. To bring order to the chaos, *when I meet someone new I usually take note of the two or three characteristics that stand out most clearly:* his size, clothing, voice, mannerisms, speech quality, or actions. Or I may even have a sense of his emotional and mental state. From these most striking characteristics, I form a first impression. But I never forget that first impressions are just that—*first* impressions.

People often try hard to make a good first impression. The challenge is to continue to examine your first impression of someone with an open mind as you have more time, information, and opportunity. Otherwise, you may overlook essential clues that lead in a completely different direction.

I constantly test additional information against my first impression, always watching for patterns to develop. Each piece of the puzzle—a person's appearance, her tone of voice, hygiene, and so on—may validate my first impression, disprove it, or have little impact on it. If most of the new information points in a different direction than my first impression did, I revise that impression. Then I consider whether my revised impression holds up as even more clues are revealed—and revise it again, if need be.

Stay particularly alert to new information that does not match your first impression. As mentioned in the last chapter, once people have formed an opinion about someone, they resist changing their minds. If you yield to this temptation, you'll often end up with the wrong impression of people. Every relationship deepens and evolves. It sometimes takes months or even years to get past a first impression and more accurately see the complex patterns of a person's behavior.

Everything Must Be Seen in Context— Not in the Abstract

As William Shakespeare aptly noted, "All the world's a stage, and all the men and women merely players. . . . One man in his time plays many parts." *To accurately identify patterns in people's traits and behaviors, you need to consider the stage upon which they appear.* If you told me simply that a young man wears a large hoop earring, you couldn't expect me to tell you what that signifies. It might make a great parlor game, but in real life I would never hazard a guess based on so little information. If the man is from a culture in which most young men wear large hoop earrings, it might mean he's a *conformist.* If, on the other hand, he's the son of a Philadelphia lawyer, he may be *rebellious.* If he plays in a rock band, maybe he's *trendy.* If it's Halloween, maybe he's on his way to a party, dressed as a pirate.

Think again about the jigsaw puzzle. A single blue puzzle piece could be part of the sky, a pool of water, a building, the side of a truck, or a man's shirt. Relying on a single trait to predict the beliefs, character, or probable actions of a complex human being is like picking up that one piece and proclaiming it to be the left side of a blue 1982 Ford pickup. Good luck!

To illustrate the point, I'll describe some characteristics of a man I knew almost ten years ago. When I first met him, he was sitting at a table. He was thin and somewhat hunched over; he looked like a bird with a broken wing, afraid and isolated. He had a nervous smile and an awkward way of doing just about everything. Soon after, when he got to know me better, he began drawing pictures for me, usually of small animals. Rabbits were his favorite. He was quite a good artist.

You probably imagine a small, timid man who wouldn't hurt a fly— but I'll add a few more pieces to the puzzle: The table this man was hunched over was the defense counsel's table in the courtroom where he was on trial. He was handcuffed at his wrists and ankles. He was afraid, isolated, and nervous because he was facing the death penalty for killing thirteen mostly elderly women. And why did he draw me pictures of small animals? I don't know. I suppose it was because he liked to draw and it kept his mind off the trial. He was Richard Ramirez, "the Night Stalker," who remains on death row today.

Always bear in mind, there are many interpretations of almost every aspect of a person's appearance, body language, environment, vocal intonations, words, and actions. Unless you consider them in light of all the available information, your effort to interpret them will be little more than a shot in the dark.

Look for Extremes

I recently overheard an amazing conversation between two women at the coffee shop I frequent on Saturday mornings.

"My daughter came home last night with a tattoo," said the first woman. She almost sobbed.

"You're kidding!" her friend said quietly, leaning closer.

"No, I'm not. I can't believe it. I'm not sure what I'm supposed to say. At this point, I guess there's not much I can do."

"I'm so sorry. But I'm sure it'll be okay," her friend said as she grabbed the first woman's hand to console her.

They went on like this for at least ten minutes. It was impossible not to eavesdrop—they were sitting at the next table. I was having a hard time not turning around and blurting out: "Okay, I give up. Where the heck is this thing? How big is it? And, for Pete's sake, what does it look like?" Were they assuming, because the young woman got a tattoo, that she was doing drugs or hanging out with a motorcycle gang?

Tattoos are revealing, but a small butterfly on the ankle is very different from a large rose on the breast. The woman in the coffee shop may have been agonizing over nothing. In fact, *the significance of nearly every trait depends on how big, small, intense, or subtle it is.* In other words, it's a matter of degree.

An excellent illustration is the shoe-shining obsession of a lawyer I knew. I'm used to the pricey, clean-cut, conservative clothes attorneys wear—they want to make a particular kind of first impression—but this fellow went to extremes when it came to his shoes. The merest scuff, and he'd be off in search of a shoe-shine stand. Was he a neat freak, or incredibly vain? Did he suffer from obsessive-compulsive disorder? Perhaps he came from a family in which he was taught from a young age to keep his clothing perfectly neat. Or maybe he had a military background: servicemen are trained to keep their shoes spotless, and many never lose the habit.

Without knowing more about him, it would have been impossible to attribute a particular meaning to his remarkable quirk. But whatever the truth was, I knew it would provide an important clue to his character. And it did. As I got to know him, I learned he'd grown up so poor that his parents could afford to buy him new shoes only once a year, at the beginning of school. He was self-conscious about his poverty and learned to take extraordinarily good care of his shoes so they wouldn't reveal his family's financial plight. It was a habit he retained into adulthood, and it enabled me to understand him much better. It explained his extremely frugal nature as well as his insecurity and obsessive drive for success.

The significance of any trait, however extreme, usually will not become clear until you learn enough about someone to see a pattern develop. As you look for the pattern, give special attention to any other traits consistent with the most extreme ones. They're usually like a beacon in the night, leading you in the right direction.

Focus on Deviations from the Norm

Anything unusual is usually important in understanding people. That certainly applies to deviations from what you may have come to recognize as someone's normal pattern. There are two types of deviations to watch for. The first is a trait that clashes with a person's other characteristics—call it a "rogue trait." The second is conduct inconsistent with a person's normal habit or routine. Call this a "rogue action."

Your initial reaction might be to dismiss rogue traits, because, by definition, they're "out of character." But most often that's a mistake. The rogue trait is usually worth examining closely. In rare cases, it reveals the true nature of a person who has managed to disguise every other clue to her personality. More frequently, the exceptional trait simply provides you with valuable insight into the complexity of her character.

If you saw my brother-in-law, Amal, and his conservative attorney, you would know exactly what I mean. Amal is from Morocco and makes leather clothing and jewelry, much of which he sells to rock musicians. The hoop earring he wears fits in well with his trendy clothes, long hair, and casual manners. But what if his lawyer sported the very same earring along with his Brooks Brothers suit, wing tips, and erect posture? You would certainly want to look for more clues to explain this unusual feature.

Even a small deviation in someone's pattern can expose his priorities. A very small but distinctive rogue trait provided me with great insight into the character of the chairman of the board of FTI Consulting, the company I work with. As the head of a successful, publicly traded company, Dan dresses well and very conservatively. He is poised, confident, and always professional. There's clearly a pattern. What sticks out on Dan, and reveals a different side of his personality, is that he always wears "friendship bracelets" braided by his children—whether he's at a casual gathering or presiding over a board meeting. When I got to know Dan better, I realized that this choice to wear his children's bracelets wherever he goes is a sign of how important his family is to him. Not only is he a proud father, but he also wants to make his children happy by wearing their gifts, even if they clash with his wardrobe. This rogue trait turned out to be highly predictive of Dan's caring, compassionate nature.

The significance of rogue traits can be illustrated a thousand ways. The young woman in a tight dress and spiked heels reveals that this isn't her usual attire when she wobbles across the room like a toddler taking her first steps. The socialite dressed in a thousand-dollar gown who proudly wears the simple engagement ring her husband gave her when they were struggling students thirty years earlier shows her traditional values and self-confidence by her decision not to "upgrade" to a five-carat rock. And the man who appears calm and poised during an interview but whose fingernails are chewed to the nub is probably less tranquil than he appears.

Rogue actions can be even more revealing than rogue traits. Most people are creatures of habit; they love routine and stick to it unless something specific causes them to change. If your normally talkative child is suddenly quiet as a mouse at dinner, you know something's up. If your typically upbeat and friendly employee shows up one day quiet and sullen, you should wonder why. And if your boyfriend calls you like clockwork every Thursday night to make plans for the weekend, then one week doesn't phone until Saturday at noon, it's behavior worth investigating.

One isolated lapse from a routine shouldn't automatically shake your belief in the accuracy of the pattern you have seen develop. But it should get your attention. Even if you're confident that your child is happy, your employee friendly, and your boyfriend faithful, rogue actions deserve exploration. Whatever the explanation, it probably will help you understand the person better.

Are You Seeing a State of Mind or a State of Being?

An occasional outburst of anger does not make someone an angry man. You're not introverted because sometimes you don't feel like talking, or fundamentally selfish because last Thanksgiving you took the last piece of pumpkin pie, or insecure because you asked your boss if he was happy with the last project you completed.

Child-rearing experts always caution parents not to tell children they're bad when they misbehave, but rather to scold them for doing *bad things*. This concept applies to adults, as well. Good people occasionally do bad things, and bad people sometimes behave like angels. In looking for patterns, it is critical not to confuse occasional behavior or feelings with a more permanent personality trait or quality.

If you're considering rehiring someone who worked for you a few years earlier, you'd be wise to recall your past experiences with him. But you'd be ill-advised to base the decision on a single occasion when he disagreed with you, unless you saw other behavior that indicated he was argumentative by nature. Isolated episodes don't usually reveal a permanent state of mind. As you search for patterns, ask yourself whether the clue you are evaluating is just an isolated event. If it is, don't give it too much weight unless it can be characterized as truly extreme.

Some Things You Control, Some Things Control You: Elective and Nonelective Traits

The perspectives most people have on life are shaped to some degree by the way their bodies look and function. A man who is six feet tall will probably have a very different take on the world than his five-foot-tall brother. That foot makes an incalculable difference that neither man can control entirely, and it's not just about reaching the top shelf in the closet.

Physical characteristics fall into two main groups: elective and nonelective. Elective traits include things that can be controlled: for instance, clothing, tattoos, makeup, and accessories. They tend to reveal who we would like to be, or at least what we want to project to others. Nonelective traits are those that cannot be controlled—height, race, body proportion, complexion, coloring, facial features, physical handicaps, and, to a lesser degree, voice. These nonelective traits that significantly affect someone's experiences in life also tend to reveal the most about his or her character, way of thinking, and behavior. This is especially true of traits we've had since birth.

Nonelective Traits

Traits people were born with, particularly those that present physical challenges or make it more difficult to be included in normal social settings, usually have a deep-rooted and permanent effect on personality and behavior. For that reason, I rely heavily on such traits for clues to the core of a person's character.

Someone confined to a wheelchair from birth has spent a lifetime compensating for what the able-bodied take for granted. He has suffered discrimination and been pointed at, laughed at, and talked down to as if his mind functioned no better than his legs. In most cases, such experiences can't help but cause his handicap to become central to his life. The same can be said of the attitudes of many minorities, the obese, the physically challenged, those who suffer from debilitating diseases, as well as the mentally and emotionally challenged, such as an autistic man or a young woman suffering from Asperger's syndrome who can't control her speech and body language very well and constantly suffers from the reactions she gets from others.

When searching for patterns among the traits of those whose life experiences have been drastically affected by their nonelective traits, I first focus on what the effects have been, and on what the people have done to try to overcome the obstacles they face. Are they fighters, who struggle with a walker rather than yield to a wheelchair? Are they independent? Do they choose to read Braille, rather than rely on a helper? Are they confident enough to venture out in public without hiding their deformity? When they go out in public, are they self-assured, or do they avert their eyes to avoid the stares of young children and insensitive adults?

Some people meet with enthusiasm, resolve, and good nature whatever challenges the fates have thrown their way. Others retreat, defeated and bitter. Most find a path somewhere in between. The course they choose may reveal much about their personalities.

Most nonelective traits are less significant than those just discussed. If they aren't extremely unusual, facial features, height, body proportion, and the like generally don't warrant special consideration—unless someone decides to alter what would be a permanent nonelective trait but for the miracles of modern medicine. Whenever

I meet someone who has invested the time, energy, and money required to permanently alter some aspect of her physical appearance, I look particularly hard at what that says about her desires and priorities. Whatever significance a trait might normally have will apply twofold if someone wanted it badly enough to go shopping for it.

Not all nonelective traits are physical. Financial status, for example: the average person can't wake up in the morning and decide, "Today I think I'll move into a million-dollar home and drive a Porsche to work." Like someone with a physical handicap, a person with a limited income will learn to cope in some way. How people choose to spend whatever money they have can speak volumes about their beliefs and values. If someone on a fixed income dresses in expensive clothing, it might suggest she's impractical and insecure and longs to gain social acceptance. If there's little money left over for the kids' clothes, she's also selfish and self-centered. If a wealthy woman purchases the very same clothing when she can afford to spend more, it *might* reflect the exact opposite: confidence, frugality, security, and no particular concern about how others view her. However, I would also look for other clues; maybe she dresses down because she *does* care about how others perceive her and wants to be seen as down-to-earth. Only after completing the pattern-building process would I feel comfortable deciding which is the case.

Elective Traits

Because people can change elective traits from day to day or minute to minute, I view them very differently. A person's clothing, jewelry and accessories, and even mannerisms can be altered almost at will. They change as we change settings and circumstances. Most of us don't dress for work the way we do when we're lounging around the house or going to a party. We speak differently when talking with old high school friends than we do with our boss or a customer.

When you're identifying patterns, it is particularly important to keep in mind that elective traits often fluctuate. If you rely on them in isolation, you may not see the truest picture of someone's personality. If you saw me in my sweats at the market on a Saturday afternoon, you would draw very different conclusions about me than you would if you saw me in business dress, entering the courthouse. Either set of conclusions would miss the mark to some degree. Don't assign too much significance to someone's elective traits, unless you've seen him enough times and in enough different circumstances to form a well-rounded picture.

Remember, also, that we alter our nonelective characteristics as we mature. The woman who gets a nose ring as a fashion statement or a form of rebellion when she's nineteen may have forgotten it completely by the time she's thirty-five. The nose ring was more a reflection of youthful experimentation than of her core character. Of course, if she's fifty-five and still sporting a ring in her nose, I would consider it an extreme trait and pay it much closer attention.

All Traits Are Not Created Equal

He's short, dark-haired, slightly overweight, well-dressed, smiles a lot, has a college degree, is married with two young children, teaches high school history, belongs to the Rotary Club, loves gardening and old movies, speaks with a slight Southern accent, and comes from a large, close family. And he has a thousand other characteristics. I have five minutes to decide whether he can give my client a fair trial. So many clues, so little time!

I often face this type of pressure in the courtroom. A wrong decision could literally be fatal to my client. I usually have more time in life outside the courthouse. But I also accumulate even more information in which to look for patterns. With so much to look at, the only way to ever reach a meaningful conclusion about someone's personality or beliefs is to focus on those traits and characteristics that will most likely predict how a person thinks and behaves.

Over fifteen years, during which I've evaluated thousands of individuals at hundreds of trials, I've learned that while every case and every person is different, some characteristics are consistently more telling than others. Bear in mind that these are generalizations and can sometimes be entirely off the mark. Usually, though, you'll find them to be accurate guides.

Before a legal team selects a jury in a big case, we often conduct research designed to identify "predictive traits," characteristics likely to have the greatest influence on a juror's beliefs about the issues in the case. We conduct community attitude surveys over the telephone and live mock trials with people who fit the profile of the typical juror who might be called to serve in the upcoming trial. We ask these people everything we can think of that will provide clues about how they might feel about our case. We record their age, sex, and race, and we question them to gather information about their employment history, hobbies, education, marital status, what they read, what TV shows and movies they watch, what political, social, or fraternal organizations they belong to, and so on. We also ask them about their life experiences: where they were born and grew up, what their parents did for a living, how many kids were in the family, whether they have been involved in a lawsuit, and much more. Then we gather even more information about their attitudes. How do they feel about the death penalty? Do they think people sue too much or are awarded too much money? Should oral contracts be treated differently from written ones? If someone lies once, is he likely to lie all the time?

Next, we tell our mock jurors the key facts about the case and ask for their initial reaction to the principal issues. From their replies, we determine which traits most frequently appear in people who view the case in a particular way. In one case we may find that young, single, college-educated women with high incomes tend to favor the defendant, while older married men in blue-collar jobs favor the prosecution. In another, with different facts, it may be just the opposite.

After studying the information obtained from the mock jurors, we prepare questionnaires for the real prospective jurors. These questionnaires help us determine which traits each prospective real juror has. We can't ask them in advance how they would decide the case, but if we know how others with similar traits would have decided it, we can make an educated guess.

Next, when the lawyers are questioning the jurors face to face, we focus on the traits we've found to be the best indicators of how someone would decide the case. We also focus our questions on individual jurors' unique characteristics; this is usually the most critical aspect of the process. The fact that most older married men in blue-collar jobs favor the prosecution doesn't mean the one in the jury box will. We may find during the oral questioning that he was once wrongly charged with a crime and is likely to be very suspicious of the police and the prosecution.

I have worked through this process hundreds of times in every conceivable type of case—not only criminal cases but also civil lawsuits involving personal injuries, breach of contract, employment disputes, fights over movie rights, family quarrels, and more. Almost no issue has escaped scrutiny, from attitudes toward the police and other authority figures, to views about when individuals should take responsibility for their own actions, to biases against large companies, to employers' responsibilities to their employees and vice versa.

The traits and beliefs I evaluate at work are no different from those you will see in every company, household, street, and neighborhood. And the lessons I've learned have proved equally applicable wherever I am. First among those lessons is one we've already emphasized and will continue to stress throughout this book: no trait or characteristic means the same thing in every person or in every circumstance. However, I've identified three key characteristics that provide consistently reliable insight into almost everyone, almost all the time:

1. Compassion
2. Socioeconomic background
3. Satisfaction with life

As I try to identify patterns in someone's characteristics, I always focus intently on these traits because they are blind to gender, age, race, sexual orientation, and other characteristics by which we often stereotype those who belong to an identifiable group. Concentrating on these three traits forces me to look through any stereotype and to the person's underlying qualities and experiences. We'll illustrate how the process can be used to cut through gender, age, and racial stereotypes, but the same analysis can be applied to any bias.

I have found women much less likely to vote for the death penalty in murder cases than men. But it would be a critical mistake for me to tell my client to select a woman over a man to sit as a juror in such a case on the basis of her sex alone. Sex isn't the real issue—it's the juror's level of compassion for others. Women, as a group, tend to be more compassionate than men because women are more frequently raised to be caregivers. A man who grew up in a compassionate, loving home and acquired those traits would be a much better choice as a juror in a capital punishment case than a bitter, hardened woman. The relevant question isn't "What is the juror's sex?" but "Is he *or* she compassionate?" or "How was he *or* she raised?"

Similarly, should you consider only women candidates when hiring a nurse for your elderly grandparent? Of course not. Even if you were able to prove that two out of three women are more caring and attentive than the average man, a decision based on gender alone would still be wrong a third of the time. That's certainly not good enough for me in the courtroom, and it shouldn't be good enough for any of us outside of it.

Elderly people often tend to be more conservative than the young. But it's not because they're old; it's because *most* elderly people were raised during more conservative times and usually in more conservative households than *most* young people. Elderly people who vividly recall struggling through the Great Depression have beliefs and values that were affected by that aspect of their socioeconomic background. But if I wanted to select a conservative jury, I wouldn't just pick the twelve oldest prospects. One of them might have been raised by a free-spirited vaudevillian and be the most liberal of the lot. To identify those who will think and act conservatively, I need to know their backgrounds, not just their ages.

Of all stereotypes, those based on race are undoubtedly the most prevalent. And once again, it's foolish to act on such a bias rather than gather information upon which to base an informed decision. A person's experience, not the color of his skin, dictates his view of the world. Until we become a truly color-blind society, racial background will undoubtedly impact our experiences. Even so, the son of an African-American Beverly Hills doctor will usually share more beliefs with his white neighbor than he does with an African-American man raised in the projects.

Of course, there are exceptions, but they are typically based at least in part upon shared experience, not just shared skin color. For example, almost to a man, the hundreds of young African-American men I've seen asked about their attitudes toward the police have expressed hostility. But the origin of their attitude can almost always be traced back to an experience in which either they or someone close to them had an insulting or frightening encounter with a police officer. If our hypothetical son of an African-American Beverly Hills doctor had been pulled over and harassed for no better reason than that he was black and driving a BMW in Beverly Hills, odds are he would also have a hostile view of the police. But it is important to understand why he would share that view. The incident occurred because of his race, but his attitude toward the police was formed by the incident: it's a result of the incident, not of his skin color. So when I am helping to select the jury in a police brutality case, the relevant issue is not whether a prospective juror is white or African-American, but whether he has had good or bad experiences with police officers. Anyone, regardless of race, who has been unnecessarily roughed up by a cop would likely have a negative attitude.

It's almost always easy to tell someone's gender, age, and race, but don't draw any conclusions based upon these isolated facts. Instead, as you explore the many chambers of someone's personality, keep an eye out for anything that answers these questions: Is he compassionate? How was he raised? Does he believe he's had a fair shake in life? Throughout, whether discussing appearance, body language, environment, voice, or actions, this book will emphasize these essential questions. The answers will provide a solid foundation for understanding almost anyone.

Compassion

After even a brief encounter, most of us walk away from a person thinking to ourselves "He seems like a really nice guy," "What a jerk," or something in between. We'll usually have some initial impression, based on the kindness of his face, the warmth in his eyes, his smile lines, his openness or friendly words, or his sincere handshake. Scientists have developed a "hardness scale" for categorizing minerals. I have my own personal hardness scale for people. On one end is the cold, unemotional, uncaring person; on the other is the warm and compassionate soul. When I'm evaluating someone, one of the first things I do is try to place them somewhere on this scale. Where someone lies on it often tells me more about how they are likely to think and behave than any other single fact.

I'm not alone in my belief that an individual's level of compassion is a very good predictor of how he will think and act. Time and again, when I've asked attorneys what type of juror they're looking for, they'll say: "We need nice people, the type who will understand that no one's perfect and we all make mistakes. People who won't judge our client too harshly." Or they'll tell me, "We want real taskmasters. Judgmental people who won't believe the other side's witnesses and will make them pay dearly for any mistakes."

The closer people are to the compassionate end of my personal hardness scale, the more they tend to be generous, fair, sincere, affectionate, gentle, family-oriented, forgiving, and understanding of human frailty. They are inclined to give other people the benefit of the doubt and are more inquisitive and patient than people who lack compassion. They may have a harder time coming to a decision than those who are less compassionate, but only because of their desire to do the right thing. They don't want to hurt anyone, so they are unlikely to be dishonest. They tend to believe that what goes around comes around.

People who fall on the uncaring end of the scale tend to be more critical, intolerant, unforgiving, harsh, punitive, and self-centered. They are also frequently more analytical, more likely to scan the facts and make a quick decision. By the same token, they tend to be more judgmental, impetuous, and inclined to act before all the information is in. Their motto frequently seems to be "What's in it for me?"

If I peg someone as either very compassionate or unusually cold and harsh, I already know more about them and how they are likely to behave than their age, educational background, employment, physical appearance, and sex combined could ever tell me. Because of that, when the following chapters describe traits that reflect whether someone is compassionate, take special note. You will be well on your way to an excellent understanding of a person whenever you've added this piece to the picture puzzle you're assembling.

Socioeconomic Background

A person born with a silver spoon in her mouth will almost always view life very differently from someone born and raised in poverty, regardless of what other characteristics they may share. But socioeconomic background is not measured only by family income. It consists of a combination of social and economic factors. The love and support we receive as children, our exposure to learning and other worldly experiences, the environment in which we are raised, and a thousand other factors come into play. Our attitude toward life is greatly influenced by whether our emotional and physical needs have been fulfilled. Often, financially secure parents are able to meet more of their children's needs than parents who are struggling to make ends meet, but there are frequent exceptions.

I know a man who was raised on a farm in Idaho with thirteen brothers and sisters. It was all his parents could do to put shoes on their feet and food on the table, but the family was very supportive and their actions were grounded in strong religious convictions. All my friend's emotional and physical needs were met. As a result, he does not view the world from the perspective of someone who has lived a life of denial, even though his family had only a little more money than a family on public assistance. Money isn't the only measure of need fulfillment.

Generally, a person's socioeconomic background will have a significant impact on his outlook and behavior. People who have had to scratch and claw for everything they have, whether financial or emotional, may develop a siege mentality and retain it all their life, no matter how much money or success they eventually achieve. They may become hardened and lack confidence; they may be insecure, unkind, inconsiderate, stingy, intolerant, defensive, and unwilling to reveal much of themselves. Because they had to fight so hard to survive, they tend to be more watchful and to believe the ends justify the means. On the positive side, those who have pulled themselves up by the bootstraps also tend to be focused, hardworking, and dedicated to achieving their objectives.

People who have always had their needs fulfilled, on the other hand, tend to be more confident, secure, kind, generous, tolerant, forgiving, and open. But if everything has been handed to them, they also may lack drive and intensity and be rather materialistic and egocentric.

If we experience prejudice as children, we may become suspicious and defensive. If we live with constant criticism, we are more likely to become judgmental and intolerant. If we are treated with kindness and compassion, we will probably become caring. If we had to struggle to make ends meet, we may become less giving. And it doesn't matter whether we're tall or short, black or white, male or female, young or old. That is why socioeconomic background is always a key predictive trait.

Satisfaction with Life

It may seem logical that a person's degree of compassion and her socioeconomic background would be among the three key predictive traits. The importance of the third key characteristic—satisfaction with life—might not seem so obvious. But it almost always has a wide-ranging effect on how people think and how they treat others.

Personal or professional success can't be measured on an absolute scale. One person always dreamed of becoming a doctor, but never made it through medical school; she became a nurse instead. Another has struggled to overcome huge obstacles and has achieved her lifelong goal of becoming a nurse. The second will see life through the eyes of a successful person, while her colleague feels like a loser.

Financial success, too, must be measured in light of the individual's expectations. Someone who dreams of wealth and has set his sights on earning a million dollars a year will be horribly disappointed with a $50,000-a-year salary. Another, who never dreamed of making half that much, might view that same $50,000 job as an achievement beyond his wildest imagination. He will think, "Life is great," and act accordingly.

Over the years, after paying particularly close attention to this characteristic, I have found that people who have achieved their goals tend to believe in personal accountability and responsibility. They tend to be more compassionate, supportive, at peace with themselves and others, and optimistic. They also tend to be more forgiving, hardworking, and industrious.

Those who have not achieved their goals often have a victim mentality. They can be quick to place blame on others and may be bitter, angry, negative, pessimistic, and vengeful. Usually, they are less industrious and more critical and cynical than achievers.

Like the other key predictive traits—compassion and socioeconomic background—the degree of someone's satisfaction with life tells me more than I could learn from any number of other traits. And it's usually not difficult to find out how satisfied someone is. A few simple questions, such as "What did you want to be when you were in high school?" or "How do you like your job?" or "If you could change your life, what would you do?" will usually prompt responses that make it clear whether someone has achieved personal success. That information will be another key piece in the puzzle you are assembling.

Why Do We Need to Read in Seven Colors?

Sure, most people already know that someone sitting with crossed arms may be feeling defensive or angry, someone who doesn't look them in the eye while speaking may be lying, and someone who is speaking in a soft voice may be shy. Unfortunately, many people end their analyses there, resulting in knee-jerk conclusions. Accurately reading people only *begins* with those first observations. While first impressions have emotional impact and can consequently be hard to change, in order to really understand what someone else is about, you must acquire lots of additional information against which to test your first impression.

If you told me the person with crossed arms was sitting in the San Diego courthouse, for example, given my familiarity with the building, I would explain that the reason for the crossed arms was as likely because she was freezing as it was that she was defensive or angry. Most of us cross our arms and legs in that building in an effort to keep our body temperature up against the perpetual onslaught of blasting air-conditioning. Environment, and not inner feelings, in this example, might be the most likely explanation for this particular body language. But, that is not to say that the person wasn't, in fact, revealing defensiveness or anger. Cold people can be defensive and angry, too! But tell me that the person is also shaking his head, gritting his jaw, turning his body to the side, and at some point, it will become clear that he is, in fact, upset or angry, whether or not he is cold. But to arrive at that conclusion with a high degree of confidence, many clues must be gathered and evaluated, not simply one—that his arms were crossed.

Similarly, someone who refuses to make eye contact may be distrusted in American society because she is seen as shady and dishonest. But if you learned she is from a culture where lack of eye contact is considered a sign of respect or submission, you might reach the opposite conclusion and view her in a very different light, realizing her downcast eyes are a sign of respect and humility. Or, if you notice many signs of severe shyness, you could arrive at the conclusion that the lack of eye contact had nothing to do with her honesty and everything to do with her discomfort at the moment.

We all recognize in theory how important it is to stop, look, and listen. But in the rush of modern society, even the most highly observant people cut corners in this regard, and consequently miss critical pieces of information. Remember that decisions are no better than the information on which they are based. The G.I.G.O. principle applies here as much as anywhere else—"garbage in, garbage out."

In the fast-paced world in which we live, it is tempting to notice someone's flashy car or wild hairdo and conclude right away, "Aha, I've pegged him!" Almost everyone has the ability to read the cues that form first impressions, and most of us tend to stop there, or at least pay significantly less attention once we've made up our mind about someone. But why? Would we rush to the salesman's office to sign a contract to buy a new sports car just because it "looked" fast? Not the prudent buyer. He would want to know more details about its engine, transmission, suspension, and more. He would read a test report or two from automotive enthusiasts' magazines. And he would want to "take it out for a spin," the longer the better.

Likewise, it is important to examine as many of the seven important aspects of a person's personality as possible in order to gather enough information to form a complete and accurate impression without falling prey to the lure of stereotyping or shortcut thinking. By practicing the techniques described in the chapters that follow, you will be able to hone your people-reading skills to an extent that will bring your social interaction to an entirely new level—a level that will enable you to better understand other people, predict their behavior, and alter yours accordingly.

Consider this example: a new mother, Darla, is interviewing Cassie, a potential nanny for her young child. Right away, she notices that Cassie's appearance is neat and polished, and her body language reflects a poised and friendly manner. As they speak further, Darla notices that Cassie communicates directly and her voice is both inviting and authoritative, as she asks questions about relevant information that will give her a complete grasp of her job description. But when she asks Darla about who is likely to show up during the day, her voice changes and becomes tentative and shaky, and she breaks eye contact. These observations give Darla pause. Is Cassie thinking of sneaking her boyfriend over? In order to gather more information, Darla should also take note of the woman's environment, if possible. Is Cassie's purse neat and well organized, or are various papers and objects bursting through the zipper? Is it buzzing with a constantly ringing cell phone (her boyfriend)? Darla should go outside and look at Cassie's car. If it is littered with trash and clothing and appears not to have been washed in months, Darla will have learned something about Cassie's habits that was not otherwise revealed. And if the car was left unlocked, Darla may justifiably worry that this reflects the level of security she can expect Cassie to exercise with her child, or perhaps the soundness of her judgment in general.

Although we don't have the space to identify every possible trait, quality, or characteristic that might exist in the Seven Colors, the next chapters illustrate the process for interpreting many of each color's cues. You will then be able to test your observations against information perceived through the other colors, identify patterns, and eventually arrive at reliable conclusions about those with whom you interact. Once again, remember, the key is not just knowing the range of possible meanings that can be given to individual traits and characteristics. It's having the attentiveness, patience, and objectivity to gather as many clues as possible, and identify the patterns that develop as you do.

KEY POINTS

Look for patterns: Single traits or characteristics seldom hold the key to someone's character or emotions. True understanding comes from identifying recurring themes.

You have to start somewhere: Begin by forming a first impression based on a person's most striking traits. Then keep testing, and if appropriate modifying, that impression as you acquire more information.

Remember, anything unusual is important: Watch for extremes and any deviations from a person's norm.

Don't confuse a temporary state of mind for a permanent state of being: Whatever someone's typical character may be, everyone has good and bad days. Reserve judgment until you spot a trend.

Ask yourself, "Is this trait the result of free choice or fate?": Elective or voluntary traits (like choice of clothing) reveal who we would like to be, or how we would like to be viewed *at the moment*. They can change like the wind. Nonelective or involuntary traits (like permanent physical characteristics) cut deeper into our psychological makeup, and have a more pervasive and permanent effect on our beliefs and emotions.

All traits are not created equal: Someone's level of compassion, socioeconomic background, and satisfaction with life almost always reveal more about him or her than any other traits. Give special attention to information that sheds light on these three key predictive traits.

FOUR

First Impressions, Part One

Personal Appearance

I recently observed a clean-cut, impeccably dressed man entering a Los Angeles courtroom. His navy suit was perfectly tailored, his shoes were polished, and his nails were clean. An impressive figure, he collected stares of admiration from both the men and the women in the audience. Noticing his monogrammed briefcase, expensive cuff links, and TAG Heuer wristwatch, the bailiff assumed he was one of the high-powered attorneys on the civil litigation calendar and asked him which case he was on and who he was representing, in order to be helpful to this obviously powerful man. When the man began to speak, however, the image began to crack. His voice was weak, his words halting, and his vocabulary limited. He spoke softly so as not to be overheard, as he explained to the bailiff that he was not an attorney and was not here on any of the civil cases. He was actually looking for *his* attorney: this polished, conservatively well-dressed man was on the criminal calendar as the defendant in a sexual assault case.

This goes to show that anyone can dress the part. So what other cues could we have noticed to complete the picture in this example? If we had noticed how this man arrived at court, we might have seen him get off a bus instead of roll up in a Lexus, or he may have been dropped off by several other men driving a beat-up jeep with a broken taillight, dressed as if they had just rolled out of bed. We may have noticed him constantly adjusting his suit as he was walking, signs of discomfort at the irregular style of dress. Or, as is often true in cases involving sex crimes, the man may have been very successful and entirely accustomed to wearing a tailored suit, and otherwise dressing to the nines—but in this environment, he felt afraid, intimidated, and embarrassed.

It is important to notice everything you can about someone's personal appearance because it not only conveys the image a person intends to project, but it also unintentionally conveys information they wouldn't necessarily want you to know, as in the example of the professionally dressed businessman with fingernails chewed to the nubs. And because personal appearance usually provides the material for first impressions—and, because first impressions are hard to change—we need to pay attention to everything from clothing to hairstyle to accessories. But remember: no matter how many clues we may derive from someone's personal appearance, six other colors can surprisingly change the way that picture ultimately develops.

It's tempting to note a wild hairdo or weak handshake and assume you've pegged someone's personality. That's rarely possible. If reading people were simply a matter of matching a few traits to standardized meanings, you could carry this book around like a foreign-language dictionary and "interpret" anybody you meet, within minutes. Appearance and body language can reveal a lot, but they are seldom reliable predictors of human behavior unless they're viewed together with the other traits discussed in this book. But they're a good place to start.

It would be impossible to list every physical trait and body movement people can display. Even absorbing the most common ones, many of which we've included in Appendices A and B, is a daunting task. It's best tackled after you've read the rest of this book, when you can review the appendices at your leisure, armed with a fuller understanding of the people-reading process. The information there will be even more valuable then. Almost all aspects of physical appearance and body language can mean many different things. At this early stage, the important thing is to recognize that most features of a person's appearance and body language can have a wide range of meanings, and to learn what to watch for as you gather more clues about his personality or emotions from other sources.

The Thin Line Between Appearance and Body Language

There isn't always a clear distinction between appearance and body language. You might look at a woman and notice the shape of her eyes, their color, the type of makeup she's wearing, her crow's-feet, and whether or not her eyes have a kindly expression or maintain contact with yours. Makeup can clearly be put in the "appearance" column, but what about shifty eyes or kind ones? Eye contact certainly belongs in the "body language" category. But the expression of the eyes might be classified as either appearance or body language.

Although the categories of appearance and body language may overlap, they often reveal very different aspects of a person's character. We can consciously choose our attire, and to a great degree we can determine the way our bodies look. Most of our body language, however, is beyond our control.

All elective physical traits, such as the way someone combs his hair, reflect conscious choices, so they tend to reveal how he wants to be seen by the outside world. Even nonelective physical traits can often be altered. A short man may wear stack-heeled boots and a hat; a particularly tall woman may stoop a bit; a woman who must use a cane may choose either a stylish walking stick with a carved head or a hospital-issue version.

Someone's jewelry and accessories can supply clues about her religion, alma mater, hobbies, degree of economic success, taste, and much more. Clothing may point to a certain value system or lifestyle choice—for instance, does this person prefer the practical or the extravagant? And personal grooming habits can reflect on many aspects of someone's personality. But even when read together, attire, accessories, and grooming sometimes reflect only the beliefs, values, and image the person *consciously wants to project* on a particular occasion.

Body language, on the other hand, provides more basic information. Few people are aware of all their physical reactions to the world around them, and fewer still can always control those actions even if they want to. Manners and poise may be consciously learned, but facial expressions, eye blinking, leg crossing, and nervous tapping are difficult to consistently repress. I've seen enough people on the witness stand to know that it's nearly impossible to control body language, even if one's fate depends on it.

Body language, then, tends to reveal inner character and emotions—fear, honesty, nervousness, joy, indecisiveness, frustration, and much more—that aren't obvious from grooming or attire. Although appearance and body language usually provide different types of information, the knowledge that can be obtained from each of them is equally important. Sometimes appearance and body language point in the same direction, sometimes in opposite directions. The important thing is to keep your eyes and your mind open.

Appropriateness for the Occasion

Any trait that is extreme or that deviates from the norm is worth special attention. The same is true of any trait—either appearance or action—that is inappropriate for a particular occasion.

A tank top may be fine at the company picnic, but not at the company Christmas party or in the office. A conservative suit says one thing about a person when worn to church, quite another if worn to a child's Saturday morning soccer game. And a big smile and a slap on the back may be called for at a retirement party, but would raise questions at a funeral.

Be careful to stay objective. An unusually short skirt worn to a conservative job interview would raise eyebrows. The woman's good sense, her understanding of office behavior, and the reasons why she would choose attire that might sexualize the interview all deserve your attention. But the same skirt worn out to dinner with her boyfriend would not deserve the same scrutiny unless it was so revealing that it was remarkable even for that occasion. The difference doesn't lie in whether you personally approve of short skirts, but in whether they are appropriate attire for a certain situation. If you evaluate her attire solely on the basis of your own tastes or moral standards, you won't learn much about her character, except that the two of you don't share the same attitude toward short dresses.

The same can be said about behavior. You may be very reserved personally and uncomfortable with loud, outgoing types; and there are certainly times when familiar behavior or boisterous conduct would be inappropriate by most people's standards. But if you measure others' behavior by yours alone, you won't learn much about who they are, only that they aren't just like you. So measure people's behavior by what is normally considered appropriate conduct. If, by that standard, someone's behavior is still extraordinary, you should wonder why.

Inappropriate clothing, makeup, and hairstyles, as well as inappropriate gestures or other body motions, can reflect many things. Most commonly, the person may

- be seeking attention
- lack common sense
- value comfort and convenience over all else (in the case of attire)
- be trying to show he is spontaneous, rebellious, or a nonconformist and doesn't care what other people think
- not have been taught how to dress and act appropriately
- be self-centered and insensitive to others
- be trying to imitate someone he admires
- not have the right attire for the occasion

I can make that last point from experience. Last year I traveled to the East Coast for a very important meeting with the general counsel and senior officers of a large corporate client.

Unfortunately, my luggage was lost en route, and I didn't have time to buy new clothes before the meeting. I had no choice but to show up dressed in the jeans and boots I'd worn on the plane. Believe me, I was quick to explain the circumstances.

If someone's appearance or behavior seems inappropriate on occasion, take note of it, but don't jump to conclusions. Try to identify probable reasons, by asking the person (diplomatically, of course), asking a third party, or waiting to see whether a pattern appears regarding how the person dresses and acts on other occasions.

How Important Are Looks?

Physical appearance is just one of the many pieces you'll use to fit together the puzzle of someone's character. But it's a large piece, and like most, it should come with a warning: things are not always what they seem. For instance, it might be natural to assume that an obese woman who sports a brightly colored dress and a large hat adorned with ostrich feathers has a flamboyant personality. Why else would she wear such flashy clothes?

In fact, there might be several reasons. She may simply like bright colors. Or her motivation could be more complicated. People whose appearance is outside the norm tend to make other people uneasy, so they are often ignored. This woman may have chosen her outfit out of insecurity and to attract attention and comment, thus breaking through the discomfort barrier. On the other hand, some people with an unusual appearance feel self-conscious and want to be ignored. Perhaps this woman thinks loud colors will actually distract observers from her body. To her, the outfit may feel like camouflage. Or maybe the woman doesn't even like these clothes, but wears them because they're a gift from her husband. Then again, maybe she really is just flamboyant.

Not only can physical traits have more than one possible meaning, but people can also change their appearance from day to day and situation to situation. To further complicate matters, almost any physical trait can have virtually opposite meanings, as in the example above.

Of course, there are times when you can draw a very accurate conclusion from a strong and consistent set of physical features. I remember a case in which two men were charged with throwing a third man out of an airplane. When I met the defendants, I noticed immediately that one had tattoos on virtually every visible portion of his body. I presume he had more on those portions that weren't visible. His partner wore ostrich cowboy boots, gold chains, and a gaudy gold-and-diamond pinkie ring. His shirt was open and he carried an exotic men's leather handbag. I assumed the jury would have little trouble reading this pair.

The message sent by a person's outward appearance is normally a bit more subtle. Almost every aspect of a person's appearance will point in several directions—and then you need to add body language, environment, voice, and behavior to the mix. *The key is to identify enough traits pointing in the same direction that you can safely conclude you're on the right track.*

If you're so sure about the reliability of a single trait that you think you don't need to trouble yourself to look for a pattern, you'll usually be off target. I've heard every off-the-cuff conclusion you can imagine:

"The two-inch-long fingernails tipped me off to her: gold-digger, right?"
"Any guy who wears a tiny bikini bottom to the beach has to be gay, doesn't he?"
"If he's wearing sunglasses indoors, doesn't that mean he's dishonest?"
"Anyone with dirt under his fingernails must be a slob at home. Doesn't sloppy always mean lazy?"

Wrong!

Two-inch-long fingernails could also reveal rebelliousness, non-conformity, or trendiness (depending upon the person's peer group), artistic leanings, or a need for attention. Or maybe this is someone just having some fun. A tiny bathing suit on a man could mean he is foreign (usually my first guess), is a bodybuilder or swimmer, has a huge ego, is an exhibitionist, or is wearing the suit to please his girl-friend even though it makes him feel uncomfortable. A person may wear sunglasses indoors not because he's hiding shifty eyes but be-cause he thinks they're stylish. He could be covering up a black eye or other evidence of violence. He may be sensitive to light because of physical trauma, a recent eye examination, or allergies. He could be covering up bloodshot eyes or dilated pupils that might reveal drug or alcohol abuse. He may be rebellious or simply forgetful. And as for a little dirt under the fingernails on occasion, what of it? It may just mean the fellow is human. You won't know whether it might mean more unless you look elsewhere for clues.

Even when several physical clues seem to point in the same direc-tion, you may be misled if you don't gather more information. A friend of mine tells a story about his father, who worked for RKO Theaters many years ago. The company's offices were in a plush suite atop Rockefeller Center in New York City. One morning, as my friend's father crossed the office lobby, he noticed a scraggly-looking man with dirty, uncombed hair. The man was dressed in rumpled clothes and sneakers. My friend's father wondered why the man was there and how he'd gotten past building security into RKO's private offices.

A few minutes later, as he sat at his desk sorting through the day's work, his boss buzzed him and asked him to come down to his office immediately. When he arrived, his boss turned and gestured toward the same man he had seen in the lobby. "Mr. Wexo," he said, "I'd like you to meet the new owner of our company, Howard Hughes."

Every aspect of a person's appearance can offer clues to his emotions, beliefs, and values. If you were to stop and catalog all of them, the list would be overwhelming. In Appendix A we've listed over a hundred different aspects of physical appearance. They are classified generally under these headings:

- Physical characteristics (body, face, extremities, skin, and physical irregularities/disabilities)
- Ornamentation/jewelry
- Makeup
- Accessories
- Clothing
- "Bodifications" (elective alterations of the body)
- Hygiene

And these are just the most common features.

In Appendix A there is also a discussion in some detail of what twelve of the most common physical traits or characteristics may mean under different circumstances. They are:

- complexion
- hygiene
- fastidiousness
- writing, logos, and pictures on apparel
- tattoos and other "bodifications"
- tastefulness
- regional style
- cultivated images
- flamboyance versus conservativeness
- practicality versus extravagance

- sexual suggestiveness
- dowdiness

As mentioned at the beginning of this chapter, we don't recommend that you read the appendices until you've finished the rest of the book. Perhaps more than any other traits, isolated physical characteristics cannot be interpreted accurately without also taking into account other physical traits as well as body language, environment, voice, and actions. Throughout this book, along with the discussion of clues that can be obtained from other sources will come constant references to physical traits that tend to reinforce that information. You must put everything into the mix and stir for the recipe to turn out right. To illustrate the point, consider some of the possible clues provided by someone's hair. Hair was chosen as our example for two reasons. First, the people you meet won't always wear hats, belts, or shoes. But everyone has something to look at on the top of his or her head, even if it's just skin. Second, a person can elect to change almost all of his or her hair's natural features—color, curliness, and even amount. So it's a common means of personal expression.

Even though hair is an important feature to notice, don't assume that it's more relevant than other traits just because it's highlighted here. In many respects, hair says the same about someone as any number of other traits might. For example, a person generally makes the same statement with flawlessly groomed hair as with immaculate clothing or manicured nails. A flashy or radical hairstyle or color usually means the same thing as gaudy and flamboyant clothing or jewelry. Once you realize what can be learned from someone's hair, and why, you can easily apply that knowledge to other physical features.

The Secrets Revealed by Hair

Hair is often an excellent predictor of someone's self-image and lifestyle. Your hairstyle can reveal how you feel about aging, how extravagant or practical you are, how much importance you attach to impressing others, your socioeconomic background, your overall emotional maturity, and sometimes even the part of the country where you were raised or now live.

Keep current fashions in mind when using someone's hair to predict beliefs and behavior. For example, in the 1960s and 1970s long hair on a man indicated rebellion. In the 1990s, a redneck trucker might wear his hair as long as a teenage rock star. Also, bear in mind the person's age: Waist-length hair on a fifteen-year-old girl says something quite different than it does on a woman of fifty, just as a ponytail on an eighteen-year-old man reveals much less about him than it would if he were fifty-five. And, as with all other traits, consider how hair fits into the entire package.

Men's Hair

LONG OR SHORT The conventional wisdom is that short hair indicates a conservative bent, while longer hair indicates a radical or artistic nature. This is true sometimes, but not always. Very short hair on a man may indicate that he

- plays sports
- is in the military, or was at one point in his life
- works for an organization that requires short hair, such as a police force or fire department
- is trendy, artistic, or rebellious (if his hair is dyed an unusual color or cut particularly short)
- is conservative
- is undergoing or recovering from medical treatment
- thinks he looks better with short hair
- keeps his hair short for practical reasons

The last category is the one most people overlook. Many men have closely cropped hair simply because it's convenient. Also, hair length is no longer a reliable indication of a man's political views; be careful not to jump to conclusions about someone's politics. Short hair may indicate nothing more than a practical temperament.

COIFFED HAIR When a man wears highly styled hair—precisely cut, blow-dried, and sprayed—it's usually part of a "power" image that includes expensive clothes, shoes, and accessories. The package, designed to reflect financial success, usually indicates vanity, a big ego, and a concern with impressing others. Relatively few men have the time, money, or inclination to have their hair regularly styled at a salon. In our culture, it's unusual for a man to pay this much attention to personal grooming. All other things—the suit, the shoes—being equal, the man with the coiffed hair is almost guaranteed to be more concerned with status, power, and image than the man whose hair is neatly cut but not styled or sprayed. Much the same can be said of any similar extraordinary grooming habit, such as manicured fingernails.

HAIR LOSS Telling information can often be gained from the ways men deal with hair loss:

- *Extreme comb-overs or obvious hairpieces* always suggest vanity, but to me a more important fact is that they usually reveal poor judgment and unawareness of others' perception. When I see a man with his few remaining hairs carefully combed from his left ear, over the top of his head, and down to his right ear, the first thought that comes to mind is "Does he really think we don't notice?"
- *Hair plugs and other hair-replacement surgery* also can indicate vanity or a lack of self-acceptance. Men have hair transplants in an effort to look younger and more attractive. If that's worth the time, energy, and money to them, it's a safe bet they're feeling insecure and uncomfortable because of the loss of their hair and the youthfulness it represents. These remedies may also point to a healthy income, although some people save every penny to pay for the surgery. That would indicate an obsession with appearance.
- *Baseball caps, hats, and ponytails* on a balding man can also indicate resistance to growing older (or growing up). But bear in mind that many balding men have to wear a hat outdoors to avoid sunburn on their scalp or for warmth in cold weather. If the hat stays on indoors, that's another story. The wearer may be self-conscious and insecure because of his hair loss.

DYED HAIR It has become more commonplace for men to dye their hair when it starts turning gray. If they do a good job, you may not notice and therefore won't be able to use this as a means to evaluate them. Dyeing indicates a certain amount of vanity, although not as much as coiffed hair does. Most revealing is a poor dye job or one inappropriate for the man's age. Jet-black hair looks very strange on a balding seventy-five-year-old man. I question his judgment and his ability to correctly assess how others view him. It takes a certain level of self-centeredness, along with a detachment from reality, to adopt such an obviously unnatural style.

Men's Facial Hair

BEARDS AND MUSTACHES Some people believe that any facial hair indicates a secretive nature. This is rarely true—hiding a weak chin with a beard doesn't indicate secretiveness. More often, it's just a cosmetic choice.

Beards and mustaches can indicate that the man wearing them

- believes he looks better that way
- is young and trying to look older
- is trying to hide his age by growing a beard to cover the wrinkles
- is trying to conceal a facial flaw
- has a rebellious or artistic nature
- works in a job where there is no restriction on facial hair

Carefully consider the length, style, and maintenance of beards and mustaches. Long beards and mustaches may reveal liberal political leanings. Unkempt or dirty mustaches or beards, like unkempt or dirty hair, can be a sign of laziness, lack of concern for appearance, physical or mental illness, poor judgment, and the other traits poor hygiene generally reflects.

OTHER FACIAL HAIR Big, bushy, unkempt eyebrows, like excessive nose hair or ear hair, often indicate that grooming and personal appearance are not among a man's priorities, or that he's oblivious to how odd these features appear. Many men with these features also believe that plucking or trimming such hair is not masculine.

RADICAL CUTS, COLORS, OR STYLES Whether on a man or a woman, a radical, outrageous, unique, or striking haircut, color, or style is worth noticing. No one just wakes up that way. And they didn't go to a salon or barber bent on the usual trim, only to be held at gunpoint while the stylist gave them a purple Mohawk!

A radical cut, color, or style may suggest

- nonconformity
- rebelliousness
- an adventurous nature
- an expressive, artistic nature
- an unconventional job and lifestyle
- a desire to appeal to a particular peer group
- trendiness
- disregard for personal appearance
- a need to be different and noticed
- cultural influence (age, race, social group)

Don't simply conclude that someone with a wild hairdo craves attention, though that option deserves serious consideration. Particularly among the young, an expressive hairdo may be a short-lived feature, and one which says little about the person's essence. However, a bizarre hairdo on an older person, or one worn for an extended period of time by a younger person is a very significant feature.

Women's Hair

Because so many hairstyles are acceptable on women, most stylistic deviations don't indicate much about a woman's personality. Extremes of length, volume, style, and color are the most telling aspects of a woman's hair.

LONG OR SHORT   In our culture, women's youth and sexiness are often associated with long hair. For that reason, women's and men's decisions to wear hair long or short have very different implications.

When a woman has very short hair, keep in mind the following:

- *Short, chic, carefully cut hair* can signify an artistic nature. Like any high-maintenance hair, it may also reveal financial well-being. But keep in mind that many women with average paychecks spend a small fortune on their hair. Spending a significant percentage of one's income on hair—or any other aspect of personal appearance—suggests vanity, a need for acceptance, concern about others' perceptions, and possibly insecurity.

- *Less styled short hair* may indicate a practical nature. Long, curly hair is particularly hard to maintain. If other physical clues point to practicality, short hair is probably not otherwise significant.
- *Dramatically short hair attracts attention.* If the woman's clothing is flamboyant, this hairstyle fits right into the pattern.
- *She may be recovering from or undergoing medical treatment,* such as chemotherapy.

If a woman has very long hair, bear in mind the following:

- Since long hair is associated with youth in this society, a woman who is past forty and has waist-length hair may be resistant to growing older. Sometimes women with this trait are caught in a time warp and still think of themselves as teenagers or college students rather than as grown-ups. Such women may be fairly unrealistic in their outlook on life as well as in their perception of themselves.
- A woman may wear her hair long, even though it's not particularly attractive that way, because she believes it makes her more sexually appealing.
- Long hair sometimes indicates a bohemian spirit. To many women, long hair means freedom from conventional style. If that's the case, the woman's clothing usually reflects this attitude.
- Long, unkempt hair may indicate a lack of judgment, a rebellious nature, illness, laziness, or an unwillingness or inability to put time and energy into good grooming. A woman with long, stringy hair either doesn't realize how it looks, or doesn't care. When the hair is downright dirty, you should wonder if some of the other "poor hygiene" traits we discuss in Appendix A might apply to her as well.

BIG HAIR Big hair is usually an indication of age or regional background. Women in the South and other areas with a strong "country" influence frequently like their hair more teased and styled than do women elsewhere. This preference cuts across the socioeconomic spectrum, from the wealthiest Dallas society lady to the farmer's daughter.

Older women often favor teased, sprayed hair as well, but this is usually because such styles are easy to maintain between visits to the salon. Also, older ladies may experience hair loss; teasing is sometimes necessary to get any volume at all. Finally, they were raised in an era when poufy hair was stylish, and they may simply have retained that cultural influence.

COLOR Many women color their hair. Unless the color is extraordinary, it is not significant. But a woman who chooses to let her hair go gray may be making a strong statement. Chances are she is comfortable with herself and her age. She doesn't rely on the opinion of others, but decides for herself what looks good on her. Women who go gray may also be doing so for practical reasons, in which case their clothing will be practical too. Some women, allergic to hair dye, have little choice in the matter, so their graying hair says nothing about their personalities.

BODY AND FACIAL HAIR In the United States, the cultural norm is for a woman to shave her legs and armpits, pluck very shaggy eyebrows, and remove other facial hair. Many other cultures are not as hairphobic. A woman who doesn't shave her armpits or legs may be from another country. Unshaven body hair on a woman who was raised in this country usually signifies rebelliousness, feminist ties, or a bohemian nature. If a woman has long stubble on her legs or under her arms, indicating she hasn't shaved recently, she may be ill, depressed, or lazy, or she may lack interest in her appearance and how others perceive her.

I've found that extremely noticeable facial hair, such as a light mustache or very unkempt eyebrows, is usually a conscious choice, not an oversight. The woman who chooses not to change that aspect of her facial features is often saying: "Here I am, like it or not. This is me." This may indicate a very strong will and a defiant attitude toward societal expectations. It may also signal that she is not appearance conscious, either because she is comfortable with herself and not seeking others' approval or because she grew up in a family or culture in which facial hair wasn't a big issue. She also may opt to leave things as they are rather than endure the pain, inconvenience, or expense of waxing or plucking her hair.

Interpreting Other Physical Characteristics

As you can see, various aspects of people's hair can have many meanings, sometimes conflicting ones. The same is true of all physical traits. Usually, you can decode their significance only after you gather and interpret other clues. To make the point, I'll tell you more about the heavyset woman we mentioned at the beginning of this chapter.

I met Clara years ago through a charity with which we were both involved. She was not only fond of wearing very expensive, brightly colored dresses and plumed hats, she also preferred four-inch-high spiked heels (she was only five feet tall) and very heavy makeup. From her dress alone, I guessed that she was insecure and trying to get attention, but I couldn't be sure.

As I got to know Clara better, I learned that she was married to a wealthy doctor who worked very long hours. She spent most of her free time volunteering for a number of charities and entertaining "the ladies" at her beautiful home, which she loved to show off. She had to be the center of attention at social events. She would bounce from group to group, speaking rapidly in a slightly high-pitched and always excited tone—that is, until it came time to volunteer for a project that involved something other than entertaining. Just the mention of forming a committee to write a proposal to the city, or meeting to discuss building plans with the architect who was working on the center's new building, and she was off to the powder room.

Taken together, Clara's appearance, body language, environment, voice, and actions left no doubt in my mind about what made her tick. She was seriously overweight. Her husband worked all the time. She didn't have enough confidence in her own abilities to become involved in a project that would have required her to venture into uncharted waters. Given all this, her brightly colored clothes and gaudy hats made sense. As I'd suspected, she was insecure and her dress was one way she could make people notice her. But I couldn't be sure of that "diagnosis" without many more clues than those provided by her physical appearance alone, striking though it was.

Piercings

I was in line at the DMV last year in order to correct an important error that occurred in processing my vehicle registration; if not corrected it could have landed me a ticket at any time. I was already tense as I remembered my last DMV mix-up and the amount of time it took to be fixed, and I desperately hoped to be able to speak with someone competent and more helpful. As I neared the front of the line, my heart dropped as I caught my first glimpse of the woman behind the counter. A trendy-looking twenty-something with a large ring through her nose. Oh, no, I lamented, not today!

In reality, this young woman may have been perfectly capable of solving my problem, but her choice of piercings did not project the capability I was seeking, and I did not have the time nor the vantage point to observe the other six of her Seven Colors. I would have perceived her as more capable if, instead of a nose ring, the woman's piercings consisted of small pearl earrings which, unlike a nose ring, generally point toward professionalism and competence.

Body piercings can be analyzed in a fashion similar to tattoos. While women are virtually expected to have pierced ears in modern society, and such is acceptable in all professions and walks of life, piercings in other locations or numerous ear piercings have not gained such widespread acceptance. And as with tattoos, quantity counts. There is a huge difference between someone who shows up with a tiny rhinestone stud in her nose and someone who comes to work looking like Dennis Rodman.

What Does Society Expect to Be Pierced?

The first question you might ask is, "What society?" Other cultures may not bat an eye at extravagant piercings on men and women. One of the most commonly accepted piercings worldwide, however, is women's ears. Most women get their ears pierced at a very young age, and this bodification is not only accepted but expected in virtually every profession. Pierced ears on men, however, has not gained universal acceptance. In conservative professions such as law and banking, for example, a man who showed up sporting an earring may raise eyebrows, although that's less true today than it was twenty-five years ago. If the earring was the type that dangled, he might be instructed by his boss to take it out.

Another more recent phenomenon with ear-piercing is the piercing known as "gauge." A gauge piercing is similar to the earlobe-piercing practiced by certain Ethiopian and Ecuadorian tribes. It is a piercing where a large disc or gauge is placed in the earlobe to stretch it out. As with the tribal tradition, it would appear that people who get these piercings view this as a canvas of expression. It's also interesting to note that the smaller the gauge the larger the lobe. So a ten-gauge would create a hole smaller than a five-gauge.

I can't help but wonder if people with this type of piercing are aware of the fact that as you age your ears grow. Have they taken into consideration that at sixty or seventy years of age, they will have a hole in their earlobe that is big enough to put a fist through?

In a more liberal environment, however, a man wearing two hoop earrings who may stand out at a Wall Street firm might look right at home in the workplace in the fashion or entertainment industry. Herein lies the challenge of reading people based on their accessories. In order to decide what his choice of jewelry says about him, you need more information about a particular man. If he is a record producer, he is probably reflecting the style of his industry. If he comes from a wealthy, conservative family and is unemployed, however, he may be a bit rebellious. In other words, the same item, such as an earring, can have opposing meanings—conformity or rebellion—depending upon other factors.

Surprisingly, nose and eyebrow piercings are showing up in a wide variety of people and professions. If the piercings are small enough, they are tolerated by lots of different employers. Like a lower-back tattoo, they can signify identification with one's peer group and a nonrebellious attempt to fit in. Tongue piercings, however, are a different story. Not only are tongue piercings almost painful to view (as we imagine what it must have felt like to have that stud put in), but they can significantly interfere with the person's speech, thereby creating issues with employability and competence. A young woman with a tongue piercing that interferes with her speaking ability is not likely to succeed in a profession that requires interaction with the public. Even taking orders at McDonald's and Subway require the ability to communicate clearly with customers. While many people are willing to take the piercing out on the job, this may nullify the reason the person got the piercing in the first place: to show it off. Another issue regarding nose and tongue piercings is the reality of infection. Our delicate facial areas are especially sensitive, and a person's willingness to ignore that susceptibility in the name of body art is also a factor to consider regarding her priorities and judgment.

Tattoos and Other "Bodifications"

When we actually alter our bodies, I call the changes "bodifications." Like clothing and jewelry, many bodifications are temporary, just like the states of mind they may reflect. For that reason, I give traits such as severely plucked eyebrows and false nails the same analysis as other ornamentation. But sit up and take notice when someone makes an affirmative decision to *permanently* alter her body with tattoos, implants, or dramatic body piercing.

Tattoos, for example, are revealing on many levels. The subject matter alone may be telling. A small flower or butterfly may indicate that its wearer is artistic and is trying to add beauty or interest to her life. Someone in the military may get a tattoo that symbolizes his branch or unit. Regardless of their subject, large, obvious tattoos may demonstrate

- a need to be different
- rebelliousness
- nonconformity
- an artistic or bohemian nature
- membership in a peer group, such as the military or a gang
- working-class socioeconomic background (you'll seldom see a wealthy person with tattoos)

If someone has chosen to get a noticeable tattoo, it usually indicates that she's individualistic and nonconformist. You can expect original thinking and spontaneity. You may also encounter a bit of an "I don't give a damn what other people think" attitude. The bigger, brighter, bolder, and more outrageous the tattoo or tattoos, the more revealing of these personality traits they become.

You are discussing potential changes to your life insurance policy with an executive at the insurance company. This important decision has been weighing on your conscience and you want to make absolutely sure you are choosing the right terms and conditions. The woman assisting you seems to be very knowledgeable, and looks quite credible, in her navy blue suit, pearls, and hair up in a bun. You are about to sign the documents memorializing your new changes, when she drops the pen she was handing you. As she leans over to retrieve it, her suit rides up in the back and you notice to your surprise, a huge tattoo of a serpent and flames along her lower back. This visual takes you aback, as you never would have guessed this conservative, professional woman would do such a thing to her body. But in context with everything else about both her appearance and her demeanor, should her choice of body art kill the deal?

Unlike the woman in the coffee shop in chapter 3 who thought her daughter's life was over because she came home with a tattoo, most people in modern times would not react this strongly. Tattoos have become so commonplace, we are used to seeing them on all kinds of people from all walks of life. But although they are much more common and acceptable than they were twenty-five years ago, we can still glean a wealth of information from someone's tattoos by noticing, what they are, how old they are, and where they have them.

Size Matters

Size and placement of tattoos makes a world of difference in determining how to read this type of bodification. There is a major distinction between someone who sports a small rose on her ankle and a huge dragon covering her entire back. Similarly, we can read different characteristics into someone who has something tattooed across his forehead as opposed to someone who has a tattoo in a place that is almost always covered up with clothing.

And make sure to consider the rest of the package. Take, for example, a woman I saw in the courthouse not long ago. She was middle-aged with gray hair in a bun, and wore a floral dress and pearls.

Thinking she might be a prospective juror, I considered her outfit as very appropriately designed to show respect for the judicial system. As she passed me, however, I noticed through her nylons that she had a small marijuana leaf tattoo on her ankle. That threw me for a minute, and forced me to consider the range of possible explanations. Was the tattoo something left over from a rebellious youth, or was she the kind of criminal defendant described previously who may merely be dressing the part for court? If she had been wearing a juror badge and I learned she had just gotten the tattoo the week before, I might suspect her to be a "stealth juror," trying to look the part in order to be selected as a juror on a case for less-than-civil-service-minded reasons—a book deal, for example. On the other hand, my opinion of her might change completely if I learned she was dying of cancer and carrying a medicinal marijuana card.

Following the Crowd or Making a Statement

If you are losing sleep over the tattoo your teenager snuck out and got against your wishes and what it means for her future, before you discontinue her college fund and write her out of your will, find out how many of her friends have similar tattoos. If the answer is several, all of whom appear to function quite normally, you may not need to give up on your child. This tattoo does not mean that she is throwing away her life or demonstrating how rebellious she can be. She is merely following the crowd and has acquired the tattoo merely as a rite of passage.

On the other end of the spectrum are those who demonstrate their individualism by acquiring unique personal tattoos: many people tattoo the names of their spouse, family members, or deceased relatives. While such tattoos may certainly still affect employment opportunities, they are read very differently than a gang moniker would be. These people have adorned themselves out of a desire to visibly display their love and devotion for another person. Similarly, religious tattoos are becoming more common. In coauthor Wendy's seminary classes, several of her classmates have verses of Scripture tattooed in large print across their backs and biceps. These students explain that in addition to serving as outward displays of their dedication to Jesus

Christ, their tattoos are also valuable conversation starters they use as witnessing opportunities.

Other elective bodifications, such as implants, are also very important clues about someone. Each of the many ways we can change or enhance our bodies will point toward what a person values, both in herself and in others. Someone who elects to have breast implants usually wants to enhance her sexuality. She is vain and concerned about what others, particularly men, think of her. A man who has liposuction to remove his love handles is also conscious of his appearance and attractiveness. He is vain and usually financially secure enough to afford to be. As with tattoos, it's important to note the degree of any surgical enhancement. A little tuck around the eyes isn't the same as a dramatic face-lift, and small breast implants don't say what huge ones do. Such extremes emphasize the traits we've already discussed. If the surgical alterations are what most people would consider outlandish, I also can't help but think the person's self-centered and emotionally needy nature is clouding her judgment and ability to accurately understand how others perceive her.

KEY POINTS

Scan from head to toe: You'll never know where you'll find that critical clue—hairstyle, watch, shoes, chewed fingernails—unless you look everywhere.

But don't judge a book—or a person—by its cover: Our physical appearance, dress, and body language always provide clues, but seldom definitive answers, about our personalities and character.

Remember, it's easy to dress the part: Characteristics that can be consciously adopted—like hairstyle, dress, and even a distinctive walk—generally have less meaning when viewed in isolation than involuntary actions—like a nervous laugh or furtive eyes.

Look for consistent combinations of clues: If you're on the right track, the signs should point in the same direction.

First Impressions, Part Two

Body Language

The prosecution has rested and the defense case is under way. The defense attorney calls his client, the impeccably dressed man described at the beginning of chapter 4, on trial for sexual assault. As the defendant raises his right hand to take the oath, his arm is shaking. His voice cracks as he states "I do," in affirmation of the oath to tell the truth. As he walks toward the witness box, his gait is uncertain and his eyes downcast. Sweat is already visible across his forehead as he states his name and spells his last name for the record. He fails to make eye contact with any of the jurors, he taps his fingers incessantly on the podium and sips water constantly. In short, his current state of being is much better "read" through all of the things that he can't control, rather than how he consciously dressed before he came to court.

Given the nature of the charges, however, consider that this man's dress and body language might not necessarily be inconsistent—a professional, well-dressed, and successful man could be expected to show signs of nervousness and embarrassment under these circumstances, whether he is guilty or not. If the charge was not sexual assault but grand theft auto, you might expect entirely different body language.

Basic Information

While personal appearance portrays lots of information about what traits a person chooses to display, body language provides more information that the person frequently can't help but display. Few of us are aware of our physical reactions to the world around us, and even fewer of us can control all of our actions even if we want to.

Body language tends to reveal inner character and emotions such as fear, honesty, nervousness, joy, frustration, and much more. These things are not obvious from our grooming or attire. Sometimes appearance and body language point in opposite directions, in which case remember that body language is much more reliable. While people can manipulate their personal appearance to "dress the part," they cannot control their involuntary responses. Note also that some body language can be cultural. Some cultures have far smaller personal space zones than others. Some shy away from a lot of eye contact. All of this needs to factor into your analysis. As with the other colors, consistency is the most reliable way to figure someone out.

One of the most powerful demonstrations of why body language will give you a much more reliable read on someone is seen through videotaping. If any of you have had the experience of being videotaped doing something and then watching the video, you know why this is so. Most of us are horrified to watch ourselves on videotape because we see things we do that we can't believe. "Turn it off!" we yell at the videographer lest we embarrass ourselves any further. Why is this? The explanation is simple; we can't control it. Unlike personal appearance, which can be manipulated, you are not in control of the unusual or distinctive body movements you are observing as you watch the videotape.

Involuntary Body Language

Involuntary body language may be the only observable sign of "negative" emotions or traits. We have all learned to disguise dishonesty, resentment, and other socially undesirable traits. But stay alert, their signs will often leak out only through someone's body language.

During the 2000 presidential debates between George W. Bush and Al Gore, much of the commentary following the second debate focused on Gore's body language. He often shook his head and rolled his eyes as Bush spoke. The adverse effects of his nonverbal behavior outweighed the content of his presentation.

Recently, CNN's Wolf Blitzer asked me to analyze the body language of the Democratic presidential candidates during the first

YouTube–sponsored debate. While there was a great deal to evaluate about the body language of all the candidates, the most interesting dynamic occurred between Senators Hilary Clinton and Barack Obama. Whenever either of these two candidates answered a question, they never looked in the other's direction. Contrary to that, whenever any of the other candidates answered questions, both Clinton and Obama looked at the speaker. This interaction demonstrated the tremendous tension between the two, making very obvious their mutual opposition and refusal to acknowledge each other.

In looking at the candidates in the next set of debates, it would be important not only to look at their body language and listen to their voice intonation during the time they are speaking but also to notice these traits when one of the other candidates is answering a question. Are they standing erect? Tapping their fingers on the podium, or gazing at their notes? Do they look bored or engaged in the process? These observations are critical because people often reveal the most telling clues about themselves when they are not on stage, and consequentially less self-conscious.

Jeffrey Skilling: A Case Study

In 2006, I had the chance to work with the United States Department of Justice in prosecuting Ken Lay and Jeff Skilling for their roles in the collapse of the Enron Corporation. It was a unique opportunity to follow Jeff Skilling's body language from the time he appeared in front of the House Committee on Energy and Commerce's hearings through the first day of the criminal trial. The change in his voice and demeanor as the details evolved spoke volumes about his involvement.

I remember watching Skilling's testimony on C-SPAN several years ago. I was captivated with the growing investigation of Enron's bankruptcy and wanted to evaluate the body language of the man whose name had become a regular part of American vernacular. During his three hours on the stand, two interesting characteristics stood out. First, he maintained a rather rigid body posture at the hearing table; he wasn't hunched over or slouching in his chair. Second, his voice fluctuated from a regular tone to a loud, accusatory tone. This certainly was not the body language of a weak-kneed pushover; these signals are classic demonstrations of self-assuredness, righteous indignation, and aloofness. Skilling's brazenly overconfident body language communicated his obvious disregard for the authority of the court.

The hearings dragged on, and although public interest in the events waned, the Department of Justice's Enron Task Force asked me to consult in the jury selection for the criminal trial, which began in January 2006. It may be helpful to set the stage for that one day of jury selection. Each prospective juror had already been evaluated in the month prior to the jury panel's arrival in Judge Sim Lake's courtroom. Each legal team (the prosecution, Lay's defense, and Skilling's defense) had analyzed the questionnaires away from the presence of the jurors during the Christmas holiday. On the day that was designated for jury selection to begin, I sat at the prosecution's counsel table, approximately six feet away from Jeff Skilling and his defense table, which was approximately the same distance away from Ken Lay's defense table. All eyes were on the jurors as they filed into the courtroom. Once the jurors settled into their seats, Judge Lake introduced the case and the charges, and I noticed how Jeff Skilling was looking at the jurors. Not just a casual look over the entire crowd, he appeared to be actually staring down the jurors. This fascinated me because these signals mirrored Skilling's body language during the time he had been testifying at the congressional hearing. His mannerisms again demonstrated overconfidence and braggadocio, exerting his superiority over the jurors and officers of the court.

Unfortunately, I never had the opportunity to talk with the jurors after the verdict was returned. I would love to know if any of them noticed Skilling's blatant staring—an approach that disregards the comfort zone all people have around themselves. While the corresponding physical comfort zone covers a space of about one arm's length from your body, I have found through my experience selecting juries and speaking to countless jurors after trials that the gaze comfort zone is limited to about two to three seconds at any one individual if it is "eyeball to eyeball."

Open or Closed

Many aspects of body language can be categorized into two types: open and closed. Someone with open body language is relaxed, sitting square to you, making good eye contact, and not placing anything—their arms, hands, purse, or other objects—between you and them. A person with closed body language may have their arms or legs crossed, be facing away from you or to the side, or hold something in front of them, between you and them. Whether someone is open or closed may be indicative of their comfort level, their culture, or their level of extroversion.

One of the most classic examples of closed body language is crossed arms. Instead of immediately assuming a prospective juror with arms folded across her chest is behaving defensively, I must take the time to decipher the context of her body language. If her crossed arms are coupled with a scowl, perhaps my knee-jerk conclusion that she's defensive may be correct. But having selected countless juries in a multitude of counties and courtrooms, one of the most frequent explanations for a juror's crossed arms I've encountered is their attempt to stay warm because courtrooms are often iceboxes. Of course, crossed arms may mean something totally different if a person is sandwiched between two large people on an airplane, in which case she may be desperately trying to maintain some personal space. Or maybe the woman just has a big stain on her shirt. The list of possibilities is endless. Knowing the classic body language cues is a great step, but following them up with information from the other colors is critical.

Inconsistencies: When Language and Body Language Collide

It often takes a trained eye to pick up the subtle nuances of nonverbal communication. This is where I weigh in as a jury consultant. What people admit or conceal in response to questions is often apparent in their body language, as they respond to questions not only verbally but also with their mannerisms, revealing true answers that may contradict their spoken words.

The personal nature of many voir dire questions gives me an excellent opportunity to observe the attitudes and personalities of the prospective jurors. Questions about sensitive topics may reveal defensiveness, uneasiness, or marked shyness in jurors who are uncomfortable disclosing private information. I pay close attention to those jurors who make faces or otherwise exhibit uneasiness, even when the specific questions are not directed at them. Some jurors will also engage in inappropriate laughter or other nervous behavior while trying to answer questions. Conversely, outgoing or self-confident jurors will exhibit little or no hesitance or discomfort as they answer any type of question, however private. They may even give humorous answers to entertain the rest of the panel. I often caution lawyers to be aware, however, that jurors who crack jokes during the questioning may be doing the same thing, if selected, back in the jury deliberation room.

A Bad Attitude or a Bad Hair Day?

We all have moments when we are "not ourselves." How do you tell the difference between a negative personality trait and someone simply having a bad day? Kinesics, the study of body language, is one of the most widely misunderstood "sciences" ever to have ridden the wave of popular culture. With the publication of Julius Fast's *Body Language* in 1970, people everywhere began to study the crossed legs, facial tics, and pants-hitching habits of their friends and acquaintances. Like kids with secret decoder rings, they hoped that a few behavioral quirks would reveal a person's deepest feelings and motivations.

It doesn't always work that way. Fast himself cautioned that mastering body language is a formidable proposition: "A study of body language is a study of the mixture of all body movements from the very deliberate to the completely unconscious, from those that apply only in one culture to those that cut across all cultural barriers." Any system so complex isn't exactly user-friendly. But despite Fast's own warnings, reading body language became all the rage. A generation later, plenty of people still think twice before crossing their arms at a meeting.

Toward the end of *Body Language,* Fast pinpoints one of the most troubling problems with kinesics. He discusses that always intriguing posture, crossed legs: "Can crossed legs . . . express character? Do we, in the way we hold our legs when we sit, give a clue to our inner nature? As with all body language signals, there is no simple yes-or-no answer. Crossed legs or parallel legs can be a clue to what the person is feeling, to the emotional state *at the moment*, but they may also mean nothing at all."

Body language often reflects just a physical condition (such as a bad back) or a temporary state of mind (like frustration), not a more permanent character trait. A person's body language may shift from moment to moment and setting to setting. So if you've only met somebody once it's risky to judge her personality by her body language. Everyone gets tense at times; that doesn't mean we're all a bunch of nervous Nellies. But if someone seems tightly wound every time you meet her, you've probably spotted a character trait—or, at the very least, a recurring theme in her life—not just a bad hair day.

Consistency, then, is one key to interpreting body language. If you don't know the person and haven't watched her closely in different situations, you won't know what her normal behavior is like, so you won't have any point of comparison. The insight you gain from body language is most useful as you begin to see more of a person's character. And to know someone's character—this point bears repeating—you must identify the patterns not just in her body language but in all the areas described in this book.

User-Friendly Body Language

Somewhere between the serious study of body language and parlor-trick analysis lies a workable method for day-to-day interpretation of people's movements. Appendix B lists scores of body movements that may help you interpret a person's emotional state or personality. But, like physical characteristics, most body movements can have many meanings or no meaning at all, depending on the circumstances.

The best way to sort the meaningful information from the unimportant details is to learn how various emotions are usually revealed in an assortment of movements that typically occur simultaneously, rather than to memorize separate body movements and their possible meanings. For example, poor eye contact can be a "symptom" of dishonesty, anger, nervousness, defensiveness, embarrassment, fear, arrogance, boredom, and other emotions. You can tell which only if you look at other clues that point in a particular direction. So it's not very helpful to simply list all the different emotions that a particular trait or behavior—poor eye contact, for instance—might reflect. Instead, this book describes the combinations of movements that typically reflect various states of mind. At the end of this chapter, nine of those basic emotional states are discussed. Thirteen more are discussed in Appendix B. The nine included here will demonstrate how seemingly similar emotions can be revealed through very different body language, and how very different emotions can be expressed with many of the same body movements.

Although you shouldn't rely too heavily on body language alone, there is no denying that it can provide valuable information. For example, if you have a hunch that someone's lying to you, you can try to force the person to tell you the truth, find evidence such as a paper trail, or perhaps confirm your suspicions with information from a third party. But unless you know the physical tip-offs to dishonesty, you may never think to question someone's truthfulness in the first place. Most people are very uncomfortable lying, so it's not too difficult to spot a lie if you know what to look for. You might not be able to prove your conclusions in a court of law—but then again, you probably won't need to. Once a person's body language has signaled to you that he might be lying, you can confirm your hunch through these other sources if the situation warrants it.

Emotional Hide-and-Seek

Many of our basic mind-sets, such as dishonesty or anger, are generally thought of in negative terms. Others, such as surprise and attentiveness, are neither always positive nor always negative; you may welcome them in one situation and avoid them in another. Some feelings, like happiness, are almost always perceived positively.

It's safe to make a generalization: negative emotions are harder to read than positive ones. With the exception of the person who's secretly gleeful at another's misfortune, is playing hard-to-get with a potential sweetheart, or is negotiating a deal, most individuals gladly express their positive feelings. It's not hard to read an emotion when there's no attempt to conceal it.

But the less desirable shades of the human psyche aren't so well received. We are uncomfortable around complainers, people who are indecisive, people who are anxious. We expect all but our closest friends and family to keep their depression, anger, and frustration to themselves, or to deal with it somewhere else. So people often hide these emotions from others. If you need proof that they're unwelcome, the next time an acquaintance asks, "How are you?" when you're having a really bad day, tell him. Then watch his reaction!

People also hide their negative emotions because they fear a confrontation. "What's wrong?" "Nothing." is no doubt one of the most often repeated exchanges in the English language. If you judge from someone's body language that he's upset or anxious, don't just ignore your conclusion. Give some thought to whether it would be best to resolve the issue then and there, wait for a better time, or watch further to see if it blows over. Even if you decide not to pursue the issue on the spot, once you recognize that there is a problem you'll be better equipped to deal with it when and if it does erupt.

There's nothing wrong with these unspoken rules of emotional hide-and-seek—they help keep life civil. But just because people don't feel comfortable showing their negative emotions doesn't mean they're not feeling them. And if you don't know how to identify them, you can't respond appropriately. But if you can learn to recognize, for example, when someone feels frustrated with you, you can try to meet the problem head-on rather than leave it to simmer and turn from frustration to dislike to hostility.

The beauty of knowing how to read body language is that, try as people might to cover up their "unacceptable" feelings, it's nearly impossible if you know what to look for. We mentioned earlier that even those whose lives depend on appearing cool, calm, and honest on the witness stand often fail at their task. The truth shows through in their body language, usually in conjunction with other traits. Unless someone is an accomplished actor, he just isn't going to be able to mask his emotional state.

If you learn which clues point to which basic emotion, you can do much more than just sniff out discontent in those around you. By studying the following pages, you'll be able to tell the customer who's paying attention to you from the one you're boring silly; the nervous employee from the indecisive one; the frustrated friend from the angry one. By the same token, you'll become more aware of your own body language and what it may be signaling to other people, even if they're only picking up the clues subconsciously. If you are aware of body language you can help fine-tune the way you present yourself to the world. Once you realize the power of body language and what it reveals about you, you might even choose to avoid particularly sensitive situations where you don't care to share your feelings. This might even be one time when you decide to make a phone call rather than have a face-to-face meeting in which you're likely to reveal too much. Any way you use it, the knowledge is a very valuable tool.

Reading Body Language

On the pages that follow, nine types of body language are discussed. Each is preceded by a visual image designed to help you remember which movements indicate which emotion or trait. The nine states of mind discussed are

- honesty and dishonesty
- attentiveness/pensiveness
- boredom
- anger/hostility
- frustration
- depression
- grief/sorrow
- indecision
- nervousness

Discussed in Appendix B are

- arrogance/humility
- confidence/leadership
- confusion
- defensiveness
- drug and alcohol use
- embarrassment
- fear
- resentment

- secretiveness/openness
- sexual or romantic interest
- surprise
- suspicion/disbelief
- worry

These lists are not all-inclusive; human beings possess an inexhaustible repertoire of emotions. But if you learn to identify these, the others won't be too difficult to interpret. As we mentioned earlier, you will find it more helpful if you review the additional detailed discussion you'll find in Appendix B after you've learned more about how environment, voice, and behavior can help you better incorporate particular body movements into overall patterns.

Honesty and Dishonesty

Imagine a young boy insisting to his mother that he wasn't the one who took the cookies out of the cookie jar. He can't bring himself to look her in the eye for more than an instant. He's shifting from foot to foot, and stuttering to beat the band.

Honest people are generally relaxed and open. Dishonest people aren't. *Any trait that shows tension, nervousness, or secretiveness indicates possible dishonesty.* In chapter 11, "Sometimes Things Aren't What They Appear to Be," we'll discuss the characteristics of four different types of liars: occasional, frequent, habitual, and professional. Two of those types, habitual and professional liars, are difficult to spot by body language alone. The habitual liar is so accustomed to lying that he may not care or fully realize he's lying, so he usually won't show it. The professional liar has rehearsed his lies so well that his behavior will give little away.

Like drug and alcohol abusers, people who lie won't usually admit it. But lying is often easy to detect when you know what to look for. The symptoms listed here are reliable tip-offs to the occasional liar and frequent liar. These physical clues generally appear only when someone knows he's lying and is at least somewhat troubled when he does. Luckily, most people are at worst occasional liars and reveal their discomfort in many ways.

Symptoms of dishonesty include:

• Shifty or wandering eyes
• Any type of fidgeting
• Rapid speech
• Change in voice
• Shifting back and forth on one's feet or in a chair
• Any signs of nervousness
• An exaggerated version of the "sincere, furrowed-brow look"
• Sweating
• Shaking
• Any activity that obscures the eyes, face, or mouth, such as putting the hand over the mouth while talking, rubbing the nose, or blinking the eyes
• Licking lips
• Running tongue over the teeth
• Leaning forward
• Inappropriate familiarity, such as backslapping, other touching, and getting too close (invading personal space)

The signs of honesty are just the opposite of those listed above. Honest people are relaxed and calm. They usually meet your gaze. A sincere smile and the warm, kind eyes that most of us know when we see them also indicate honesty.

When things get stressful, it can be difficult to tell the difference between honest nervousness or defensiveness and dishonesty. If your employee has made a horrible mistake and you've asked him in to explain it, chances are he'll look nervous and defensive no matter how truthful he is. I've watched hundreds of nervous witnesses, and I've found the surest way to detect a lie in a stressful situation is to watch for their patterns of behavior, looking for consistencies and deviations.

Several years ago, I worked on a case in which the owner of a real estate development company was being sued by his partner for fraud. One of the key witnesses was an employee who had worked closely with both men. A very nervous woman under the best of circumstances, she shook like a leaf from the moment she was sworn until the moment she left the witness stand. She showed all the classic signs of dishonesty: failing to maintain eye contact, shaking, fidgeting in her chair, and fussing with small paper cups on the witness stand. But I couldn't conclude from this that she was lying because had she been dishonest, she probably would have been more comfortable during at least some portion of her testimony—when describing her professional background, for instance. The fact that this woman's discomfort was constant revealed that she was nervous, not necessarily dishonest.

You have to pay close attention to someone's normal pattern in order to notice a deviation from it when he or she lies. Sometimes the variation is as subtle as a pause. Other times it's obvious and abrupt. I recently saw a news interview with an acquaintance who I was certain was going to lie about a few particularly sensitive issues, and lie she did. During most of her interview she was calm and direct, but when she started lying, her manner changed dramatically: she threw her head back, laughed in "disbelief," and shook her head back and forth. It's true the questions dealt with very personal issues, but I've found that *in general, no matter how touchy the question, if a person is telling the truth her manner will not change significantly or abruptly.* But you won't see those changes if you're not watching carefully.

Attentiveness/Pensiveness

Think of a lioness stalking her prey: body still, eyes fixed, she's motionless except for a slight twitch of her tail.

Attentiveness and pensiveness are both generally characterized by an absence of movement. The stillness, like that of a stalking lioness, indicates concentration either on what another person is saying (attentiveness) or on some private train of thought (pensiveness).

The classic representation of someone deep in thought is Rodin's *Thinker,* who sits with his elbow on his knee and his chin resting on his hand, gaze fixed. *Stillness, a fixed or set gaze, and the chin on the hand are all signs of pensiveness or attentiveness.* Sometimes the person will engage in a simple, repetitive movement, rather as a lioness's tail might twitch as she prepares to pounce. But there's a distinct difference between these small motions and the body language of boredom (discussed next). The thinker's motions are usually unconscious, and they remain constant for long stretches of time. For example, if the person is twirling a pencil, she won't suddenly stop twirling and start tapping her feet, then stop tapping her feet and start shifting in her chair.

Other symptoms of attentiveness or pensiveness are

- maintaining strong eye contact
- gazing steadily at an object
- general stillness
- tilting or cocking one's head
- chewing one's lip or pencil
- furrowing one's brow
- folding one's arms and staring into space
- leaning back in one's chair
- looking upward
- scratching one's head
- holding one's head in one's hands
- resting one's chin on the hands/fingers

It may be tempting to assume that someone who doesn't exhibit the signs of attentiveness must be bored, but someone can be inattentive for many reasons: she may be preoccupied, depressed, ill, drunk, sleepy, or confused, to cite but a few possibilities.

Boredom

It's the last class period on a warm day, twenty minutes before school lets out. Most of the students are gazing off into the distance. A few are whispering, some yawn, others are passing notes, and they're all wiggling like earthworms on hot pavement.

People who are bored want to be somewhere else, doing something else. The less you care about what's going on around you, the more you itch to get up and leave. When someone is bored and longs to be elsewhere, it's almost as if his body wants to move to that fantasy place or person. That tension between mind and body is uncomfortable, so *people who are bored usually try to distract themselves with physical activity.* They may literally twitch in their seats.

Symptoms of boredom include:

- Letting one's eyes wander
- Gazing into the distance
- Glancing at watch or other objects
- Sighing heavily
- Yawning
- Crossing and uncrossing legs and arms
- Tapping fingers, twiddling thumbs
- Tapping feet
- Fiddling with pens, eyeglasses, paper, etc.
- Doodling
- Pointing one's body away from the other person
- Shifting weight
- Leaning forward and backward in one's chair
- Moving one's head from side to side
- Rolling the eyes
- Stretching
- Cradling one's chin in hand while glancing around the room
- Picking at fingernails or clothing
- Attempting to do another task

Boredom is one of the more difficult states to conceal. Many of the signs just listed are really efforts to stay awake or alert—the bored person sometimes simply must yawn or stretch, or he'll nod off. It takes considerable talent to appear attentive and interested when you're actually bored. Watch for one or more of these telltale twitches if you fear you might be boring someone. And if you're bored and don't want to show it, try to stay still.

Anger/Hostility

Imagine a fuming baseball manager and a defensive umpire, chests thrust out, jaws set, faces red. The manager's arms are flailing and the umpire's arms are crossed resolutely in front of him.

Anger usually manifests itself in one of three ways: aggression, defensiveness, or withdrawal. Aggressive anger like that demonstrated by the baseball manager is usually hard to miss. But most people are not comfortable expressing anger, so it's crucial that you also watch carefully for defensiveness and withdrawal.

The following are signs of all types of anger:

- Redness in the face
- Arms, legs, or ankles crossed
- Hands on the hips
- Short or rapid breath
- Frequent repetition of certain phrases
- Pointing of fingers
- Rapid speech
- Rapid body motions
- Tenseness
- Locked jaw
- Tightly closed lips
- Frozen expression or scowl
- Stiff, rigid posture
- Shaking
- Fists clenched
- Frustrated, almost uncontrollable arm movements
- False or sarcastic laughter

Someone who is extremely angry may express his anger by invading another's personal space, literally "getting in his face"; sticking out his face, jaw, or chest like the angry manager previously mentioned; or glaring intently, as if trying to stare someone down.

A person who has become defensive may set her jaw, cross her arms, scowl, or close her lips tightly. But you probably won't see rapid body motions, redness in the face, and changes in her breathing patterns. Nor will she display the more aggressive behaviors cited in the preceding paragraph. Instead, you'll see a stiffening, as if she has hardened to protect herself. Her limbs will draw closer to her body and will be positioned between you and her. Her face will set. Often she will avert her gaze to avoid direct eye contact.

If her anger is expressed by withdrawal, you will often see more exaggerated versions of the same symptoms. She may try to avoid contact by turning her body and eyes away. She'll become quiet and might even sulk. In extreme cases, if these behaviors don't relieve her stress, she may get up and leave the room.

Be alert to all the possible signs of anger; relying on just one could mislead you. Redness in the face, for instance, can be caused by recent exercise, a medical condition, embarrassment, sunburn, bad makeup, or even a face peel. If you relied on that clue alone to decide whether someone is angry, the odds are you'd be wrong.

Frustration

Think of a teenager aggressively pitching the notion to his dad that he should have his own car. His arms are flailing. He's staring intently and frequently pointing. Unsuccessful, he tosses his hands in the air, shrugs, sighs, turns, and walks out of the room, shaking his head as he leaves.

Frustration comes in two flavors: confrontation and surrender. If someone believes she can correct whatever is frustrating her, she may show signs of confrontational frustration by attacking the problem head-on. Many of the signs of confrontational frustration resemble the signs of anger. But once a person thinks a situation has become a lost cause, she'll exhibit signs of surrender frustration—an irritated passivity—not signs of anger.

Symptoms of confrontational frustration include:

- Frequent direct eye contact
- Uttering repetitive phrases
- Closeness to the other person, frequently within his or her personal space
- Gesturing with the hands
- Pointing
- Shrugging

Surrender frustration may begin with

- sighs
- rapid exhaling
- grimacing
- hands on the hip
- hands on the head (in exasperation)
- exaggerated or melodramatic movements

Once the point of total surrender has been reached, the signs are

- rolling the eyes or closing them
- shaking one's head
- throwing one's hands in the air
- shrugging
- turning and walking away

It's important not to mistake confrontational frustration for anger, although sometimes it turns into anger, as it appeared to do in the tense exchange between Laura Hart McKinny and prosecutor Christopher Darden in the O. J. Simpson trial (as described in chapter 1). Ms. McKinny began her testimony about Detective Fuhrman in rather neutral tones. However, after being aggressively questioned by Mr. Darden, she became frustrated and demanded, "Why are we having this adversarial conversation?" Ms. McKinny clearly wasn't about to surrender to Mr. Darden's badgering, so she confronted him. When he didn't back off, she appeared to get angry, and her testimony became more critical and more damaging to the prosecution.

Likewise, be careful not to misinterpret boredom as surrender frustration. Many signs of boredom resemble those of surrender frustration, but bored people aren't necessarily frustrated.

Depression

Visualize an ice statue in the noonday sun, slowly melting into a formless puddle.

Severe or "clinical" depression is a very serious illness. People suffering from clinical depression can become virtually nonfunctional. They may suffer from severe eating disorders, completely neglect personal hygiene, be unable to concentrate on anything, even their work, and ultimately require medical intervention to recover. This discussion isn't concerned with clinical depression, but rather with the type of gloom each of us has experienced for short periods of time as we cope with the stresses and disappointments of everyday life.

That kind of depression is usually revealed not only by physical appearance and body language, but also by voice and actions. However, it's usually possible to identify depression simply by watching someone. People who are depressed move differently. There is no spring in their step, no twinkle in their eyes. They will seem tired and listless. The depression has taken the wind out of their sails.

Symptoms of everyday depression include:

- Isolation and avoidance of social contact
- Poor concentration
- Inability to focus or plan ahead
- Low and quiet speech
- Relaxed, slackened body
- Downcast eyes
- Slow and deliberate movements
- Change in appetite (some people quit eating, others overeat)
- Inattention to hygiene and dress
- Forgetfulness

Grief/Sorrow

A young boy is holding a small, lifeless bird that has fallen from its nest. His head is bowed. His eyes are filling with tears and his shoulders are slumped.

You might expect depression and grief to "look" alike, but sometimes they don't. Nor are they always related. Sometimes depression is not the result of grief, and occasionally someone who is grieving does not act depressed. If you focus on just the body language common to both, you may misunderstand someone's emotional state.

Grief can lead to somewhat contradictory types of behavior. Most frequently, those who are grieving have lost their positive energy, and their appearance and body language reflect that. Their loss tends to dominate their mind and override most other emotions. In these cases, grief and sorrow are usually accompanied by some degree of depression, so you may see signs of that as well.

It's easy to tell when someone is suffering from grief when it is accompanied by depression. In the early stages of the grieving process, however, people often experience denial, anger, and searching. Their body motions may actually appear exaggerated and animated. They may seem "hyperactive," talk quickly, or ramble from subject to subject just to keep the conversation moving and their mind off their sorrow. If you carefully watch someone you suspect is compensating in this fashion, you will usually notice brief moments when she stops. In that moment, she allows her grief to creep through the barricades she has erected. Her face will slacken, she'll stare off into the distance, and then she'll quickly recenter herself and be off again.

The typical signs of grief or sorrow include:

- Tears
- Listlessness
- Inability to complete normal daily tasks
- Isolation
- Apathy
- Downcast eyes
- Signs of depression and confusion
- Relaxed facial muscles
- Slumped or slackened body
- Motionlessness, or slow and deliberate motion

Indecision

A baseball player is stuck between first and second base. The pitcher has the ball. Which way to go? The base runner glances right, glances left; he leans one way, then the other.

People who are trying to decide between two options—to agree to the deal or reject it, to say yes or no, to leave or stay—usually will reveal that indecision in their body language. They will literally "go back and forth."

Symptoms of indecision include:

- Shifting back and forth in one's chair
- Looking back and forth between two fixed objects
- Tilting head from side to side
- Opening and shutting hands, or moving one hand, then the other
- Opening and closing one's mouth without saying anything

My friend David is a serious poker player and tells a story that describes the back-and-forth of indecision. In poker, body language that reveals a person's hand is called a "tell." David was playing seven-card stud with a woman he suspected had a full house. She had two queens and two sevens faceup on the table before her. He noticed that she quickly glanced back and forth several times between the three cards she held and the four that were faceup on the table. David knew that if she wasn't holding a seven or a queen in her hand she would realize it immediately, and would not need to double-check. But if she *was* holding a queen or a seven, before she increased her bet she might glance back and forth between them and those on the table to double-check. He had seen this many times before. Because of this "tell," David folded, even though his hand would have beat hers if she did not have a full house. He was right.

Interestingly, David tells me many high-stakes poker players wear sunglasses even in dimly lit rooms so their opponents can't see even the slightest involuntary flicker of their eyes. They even motion for their cards in silence, so their voice doesn't betray them. Their counterpart in business is someone who chooses to communicate by phone or in writing to avoid revealing emotional "tells."

Nervousness

Stare at a dog. Watch his eyes dart back and forth to avoid yours. His head will start turning left to right as he glances back at you. He'll shift his weight from foot to foot. Maybe his tail will twitch or he'll turn his body away.

Like boredom, nervousness is uncomfortable. To ease the discomfort, the nervous person requires distractions, and he creates them with body motion. Although it's fairly easy to spot *severe* nervousness, sometimes the signs are not so obvious. I recall, for instance, a witness who at first glance appeared to be absolutely calm. No shaking, no tapping, no shifting in her chair. But during her testimony, she repeatedly reached for the water pitcher, carefully poured, and thoughtfully drank. I think she went through a gallon of water. Maybe she was just thirsty, but I doubt it. I concluded that she was nervous, and that she channeled her nervousness into the water-pouring-and-drinking ritual so that it wouldn't be revealed in more obvious ways.

Someone who is nervous will need an outlet for his nervous energy. In the world of high-stakes poker, where reading and disguising emotions is a prerequisite to success, smoking is common; it provides a physical release for players' nervousness and prevents other, more obvious signs from creeping out. As smoking is banned in more and more casinos and card rooms, many players are revealing "tells" they used to be able to hide. The nervous energy that had gone into smoking is spilling out in other ways.

Common symptoms of nervousness include:

- Eyes darting back and forth
- Tensing of the body
- Contraction of the body (curling up)
- Shifting one's weight from side to side
- Rocking in one's chair
- Crossing and uncrossing the arms or legs
- Tapping hands, fingers, feet
- Adjusting or fiddling with pens, cups, eyeglasses, jewelry, clothing, fingernails, hair, hands, etc.
- Wringing the hands
- Clearing the throat
- Coughing nervously
- Smiling nervously (nervous people often smile, then resume a normal expression, over and over, very quickly)
- Biting the lip
- Looking down
- Chattering nervously
- Shaking or quaking (in extreme situations)
- Sweating (in extreme situations)
- Chewing nails or picking cuticles
- Putting one's hands in one's pockets
- Rotating side to side with the upper body
- Becoming silent

Because there are so many symptoms of nervousness, many of which can indicate other states of mind, you must not rely on isolated clues. For example, although sweating can signify nervousness, it also can mean that someone feels hot, has just exercised, is ill, or is even having a menopausal hot flash. Most nervous people show more than one symptom.

A Final Word of Caution

If life were a silent movie we would have to rely on appearance and body language as we struggled to read and understand people. And if people overplayed their emotions in real life the way actors did on the silent screen, we might be fairly successful. But life is not silent, and most of us rarely exaggerate our dress or mannerisms enough to broadcast our emotions unambiguously. The villains among us don't have long handlebar mustaches to finger gleefully as they commit their dastardly deeds, and heroes don't all wear white hats. In real life, distinctions in physical appearance and body language are often very subtle and may convey many different and often contradictory meanings. A woman may cross her arms because she's angry, defensive, or nervous. She may also just feel cold.

Physical characteristics and body language are what you'll often notice first, but file those observations away for a while. Unless you absolutely must, never evaluate another person solely on the basis of his attire or the way he walks across a room. You need much more information to make a sound judgment. These are just the first steps along the path to understanding others. Don't stop here—continue the journey.

KEY POINTS

Remember, involuntary body language may be the only sign of "negative" emotions or traits: We've all learned to disguise dishonesty, resentment, and other socially undesirable traits. Keep alert; their signs will often leak out only through someone's body language.

Actions that are inappropriate under the circumstances deserve special attention: An isolated lapse of propriety may simply mean someone was caught off guard. But if someone consistently dresses or behaves inappropriately—wears skirts too short, speaks too loudly, or behaves too casually or too formally—find out why, and you'll find a critical key to his or her character.

Watch out for anything that is peculiar or peculiarly unique: Whether mannerisms or grooming and clothing, if something stands out, it's usually significant.

SIX

Voice—It's Not What You Say, It's How You Say It

Learning to Hear More Than Just Words

When I was a child, my mother used to tell me, "It's not what you say, it's how you say it." Years later, I find myself saying the same thing to my own kids. Their behavior reminds me daily how much of our attitude is revealed not by words but by the way they are spoken.

Two dialogues really take place in every conversation; one uses words, the other tone of voice. Sometimes the two match, but often they do not. When you ask someone, "How are you?" and get the reply "Fine," you're not usually relying on the word "fine" to tell you how she feels. Instead, you let her tone tell you whether she really is fine, or whether she is depressed, anxious, excited, or feeling any of a dozen other emotions. When you listen to tone, volume, cadence, and other vocal characteristics, you tune in to the nonverbal conversation, where the true substance is often found.

Anyone with normal hearing can detect the signals people convey with their tone of voice, but few of us understand all of them. This is partly because when we're interacting with someone, there's a lot of competition for our attention. We size up their appearance and body language, listen to the content of their words, and watch their actions. We may even struggle to identify some intuitive reaction we're having to the person or situation. Vocal subtleties can get lost in all this. It's easy to notice the message someone sends with a pouty, sad, or frustrated tone of voice, but a fleeting note of anxiety, fear, or embarrassment may slip right past you if you don't pay close attention.

I've trained myself to listen for these vocal clues and recognize their nuances since such a momentary glimmer may be the only tip I get about a prospective juror's doubts or true feelings toward a client. This chapter will explore the ways people communicate intentionally and unintentionally through tone of voice, explain how you can tune in to these often elusive vocal clues, and decode the messages contained in the most common vocal traits.

Hearing Between the Lines

Outside the therapist's office, few of us are willing to announce, "You hurt my feelings," or "I'm sad and I want to talk about it," or "I'm frustrated with my work and would like to complain to you about it for an hour." Instead, we signal these feelings with vocal clues. *We play emotional hide-and-seek.* Someone who is sad may be longing for sympathy but feel she needs your "permission" to broach the subject. She'll sigh, speak softly, answer questions briefly, and couple these vocal clues with body language such as downcast eyes and limp, lifeless gestures. Eventually, you'll get the message and ask what's wrong, thus giving her the permission she seeks.

Such behavior might seem manipulative, but it's a product of our socialization. We're taught not to ask openly for sympathy, express resentment or jealousy, or show anger, hurt, or other unpleasant emotions. But sometimes we badly need to express ourselves and, not wanting to come out and say so, we use tone to convey the message. This nonverbal communication is nearly universal. You can test it yourself: tune in to a TV channel in a language other than your own. Find a soap opera, turn your back to the set, and listen to the dialogue. You may not be able to follow the plot, but you'll surely be able to pick up on the actors' emotions.

Two recent trials in which I was involved illustrate just how important it is to pay attention to the way words are spoken. The first case involved the family of a young man who was in a car accident and died because a paramedic misread the label on some medication he administered. The family argued that the bottle wasn't labeled clearly enough and sued the pharmaceutical manufacturer, which hired me to help pick the jury. The jury had to decide who was at fault and how much money, if any, should be awarded to the man's family.

During jury selection, the family's attorney asked a middle-aged, conservative white man whether he would put any cap on the amount of money he would be willing to award to compensate the family for the death of a loved one. The man responded, "There is no amount of money that could compensate someone for the death of a loved one." The plaintiff's lawyer thought he had a great juror, who would award virtually unlimited damages. The man had "said" the right thing.

But the plaintiff's lawyer missed the vocal clues that revealed the juror's true meaning. The man had spoken almost critically, even sarcastically. That tone suggested to me he resented the attorney's asking him to put a price tag on the young man's life. The juror's response was also crisp and to the point, which indicated a certain emotional distance from the case. Given all this, I understood him to mean not that unlimited damages were warranted, but rather that he felt it inappropriate to attach a dollar figure to a human life. We left him on the jury, and as it turned out, we were right. He voted with the others, who after only thirty minutes of deliberation found the pharmaceutical company wasn't responsible for the young man's death.

The second example comes from the criminal trial—the one in Simi Valley—of the four police officers accused of beating Rodney King. During jury selection, a young Hispanic woman said that one of her sons wanted to become a police officer. She also said, with apparent sincerity, that she had no personal belief the four police officers were guilty. Officers Larry Powell and Stacey Koon recommended that she be retained. Because of her son's ambitions and because she seemed open-minded, they believed she would make a sympathetic juror.

I was wary, however, of how she responded to a number of other questions. When asked whether she had spoken with anyone about the case, she said that she had discussed it with her husband. She also acknowledged that he believed the officers were guilty and should be punished. While she promised not to allow her husband's views to influence her and not to talk to him about the case during the trial, I had my doubts. As she spoke of her husband, it was clear from her very deferential tone that she had a traditional marriage, in which she took care of the house and children and he wore the pants in the family. There was no reservation or qualification in her voice when she relayed her husband's strong feelings about the officers' guilt. His opinions were spoken as if they were gospel. When she promised to try to keep an open mind despite his beliefs her voice grew softer and much more tentative and uneven. That suggested she was nervous and not confident of what she was saying. I believed she would have to overcome a significant psychological barrier to vote "not guilty," given that to do so would incur her husband's wrath and disrespect. As it turned out, she was one of three jurors who voted to convict Officer Powell.

You will be able to respond to the potentially critical messages embedded in a person's tone of voice if you understand what various vocal clues mean and teach yourself to listen for them. You can do so by following these steps:

- Focus on the voice—not the words—from time to time during the conversation.
- Ask yourself whether the voice reflects elective (voluntary) or nonelective (involuntary) characteristics.
- Look for patterns. Ask yourself whether the voice is different now from its usual tone or is in any way exaggerated. (That is, listen for deviations and extremes.)
- Compare the voice to the person's body language and words.
- Consider the environment.
- Decode the vocal clues.

Focus on the Voice

You can absorb only so much information in a given moment. It's difficult to concentrate on someone's words while simultaneously cataloging her jewelry and noticing whether she's crossing and uncrossing her legs. With so much competing for our attention, it's easy to pass over tone of voice unless it's extreme. We tend to pay more attention to words than to tone for the simple reason that words require a reply. Sometimes, if we take our attention off the content of the conversation, we'll lose track of it altogether.

Even so, in every conversation there are moments when you can briefly turn down the content and turn up the tone. It takes only a second, and with practice you'll be able to listen to words and tone simultaneously. The trick is to do this in short spurts rather than minute-long segments. There are bound to be moments when you can mentally step back and attend to nonverbal clues even in a fairly complex conversation. And almost always, if you really listen to someone's voice, you will enrich the meaning of their words.

Distinguish Between Elective and Nonelective Vocal Characteristics

The significance of characteristics both elective (intentional and voluntary) and nonelective (involuntary, resulting from genetic or socioeconomic background or an uncontrollable response to other circumstances) was discussed in chapter 3, "Discovering Patterns." What's tricky about vocal patterns is that many typically nonelective vocal characteristics, such as a high-pitched or raspy voice, can be due to some temporary medical or emotional condition (nonelective) or can even be intentional (elective). When someone is purposely altering his or her voice, he is often trying to manipulate the listener. Sometimes, you have to listen carefully to the content and consider the circumstances to determine whether a vocal trait is elective or not.

I recently had a chance to witness a master of voice manipulation during a meeting with two new clients, whom I'll call Steve and Sarah. Both were intelligent, well-educated, and articulate. Steve was a successful businessman, while Sarah had been a homemaker and mother to their now adult children for most of her life. Outwardly, Steve was aggressive and domineering. Sarah was passive and submissive, with a high, little-girlish voice and a gentle manner.

I quickly concluded that Sarah had learned to manipulate situations with her voice rather than communicate her feelings and ideas with words. When she had something negative to say about someone, she'd adopt a victim tone, complete with slightly lowered voice, hesitant speech, and a whine, to accentuate her main points. The message she sent was "This bad, mean person is hurting me by his behavior. Help me." She used a different vocal technique when she had an idea to contribute. In their household, Steve was apparently the one who officially had all the worthwhile ideas, so when Sarah had a serious thought she'd switch to a singsong. Translation: "I have an idea to express but I know that isn't my role, so I'm going to pretend I don't feel strongly about it and am just tossing it out for someone smarter to evaluate." All her vocal traits were emphasized by a high, breathy, Marilyn Monroe–style delivery.

Sarah must have learned that Steve would be more responsive to her needs if she played the helpless little girl and let him come to her rescue. The high-pitched tone was probably elective, but she had been using it for so long that it was second nature. I couldn't help but wonder what she sounded like when she became really angry.

Nonelective, involuntary traits should be evaluated carefully. How a person exploits them—or compensates for them—may be very telling. For instance, a man with an unusually high or "feminine" voice may adopt a coarse manner of speaking to come across as more masculine. Someone who stutters may speak very slowly to overcome that trait and ease his self-consciousness. A woman with an exceptionally beautiful speaking voice may be more outgoing than a woman whose voice is harsh and unpleasant. Someone with a thick foreign accent may become unusually quiet in a room full of strangers. None of these people is being intentionally manipulative. Rather, they're reacting to an involuntary condition in the way that serves them best.

As you read about the various vocal characteristics described later in this chapter, and as you apply this information to your life, always ask yourself whether the vocal qualities you hear are elective or nonelective. If they're elective (intentional), there is purposeful communication—and maybe even manipulation—going on. But nonelective (involuntary) traits that are purely physical in nature—a raspy or breathy voice, for example—may not have any relationship to the emotions of the moment.

Looking for Vocal Patterns, Deviations, and Extremes

This book has repeatedly emphasized the importance of identifying patterns. Only when a certain characteristic—for example, extravagance—crops up consistently in a number of different areas can you be confident that the person really is extravagant, and from that draw conclusions about how he will probably think or behave. In considering vocal traits, just as in considering any other characteristics, remember that deviations and exaggerations in someone's normal patterns are especially significant.

Deviations in Vocal Traits

We've all seen a normally calm person explode in anger. After he leaves the room, the rest of us glance at one another, grimace, and say something like, "Boy, he must really be mad. I've never seen him like that before." On the other hand, we all know a hothead who flies off the handle at the slightest provocation. When he leaves the room, people glance around, shrug, and say, "There he goes again." Because we're familiar with his normal behavior, we know not to take the outburst too seriously.

You may not be able to familiarize yourself with a person's vocal style in one meeting, but during your first encounter, try to notice her general tone, cadence, and other basic vocal traits. Once you've identified her fundamental vocal pattern, stay alert to any deviations from it. Somebody who is naturally even-tempered, with a calm vocal delivery to match, may express anger by becoming uncharacteristically quiet or breathing heavily, not by raising her voice and speaking more quickly, as many others might. *Everything is relative to the person's normal behavior.*

It's equally important to keep in mind that someone who may seem unusually emotional the first time you meet him may appear very different the following day or week. Don't make snap judgments unless you absolutely have to. Let a pattern develop over at least three or four meetings, longer if possible. That way you'll be able to accurately assess whether the vocal clues you notice reflect a temporary state of mind or a permanent character trait.

In assessing someone's character, determine whether you're seeing an isolated deviation or part of someone's normal pattern. For example, if I was asked to select a jury in a case in which it was very important that the jurors be compassionate and forgiving, I might not give too much weight to a single comment delivered in a somewhat harsh or sarcastic tone by a juror who otherwise appeared compassionate. However, if the same juror consistently maintained that tone, even if it was not extreme on any particular occasion, I'd assume she was sarcastic and critical—not compassionate—and I'd reject her.

Extremes in Vocal Traits

Pay special attention to any exaggerated characteristic. A slight tremor in a person's voice does not indicate nervousness as strongly as a bad stammer. There is a difference between someone who has a rather loud voice and another who sounds as if he's warning ships away from a rocky point. *The significance of a vocal trait is often a matter of degree.*

As I just mentioned, I don't usually give much weight to an isolated comment spiced with a particularly expressive tone—unless the tone and content are extreme. Recently, I was helping pick a jury in a case involving alleged insurance fraud. Jury selection went slowly, and many of the jurors had to wait in the hallway for what must have seemed like ages before they were called in to court to be questioned. A bland-looking middle-aged woman was among the last to be called. As she sat down in the jury box, she slammed her book onto her lap and announced *to the judge* in an angry, frustrated tone, "It's about time; I was falling asleep out there." Her level of irritation, coupled with the disrespectful tone of voice, and the fact that she spoke that way to the judge, left an indelible impression. Even though she quickly composed herself and did not take that tone again during her lengthy examination, that one comment, coupled with her body language, was all it took. I thought she would be quick to judge and uncompassionate. Confident that I'd seen her *real* personality slip out during that instant, I suggested that she be excused.

Extreme vocal characteristics such as these are easy to notice but can be rather difficult to interpret, especially when the speaker isn't someone you know well. The exaggeration may indicate the intensity of his emotions: Is he happy or ecstatic? Is he sad or in the throes of a serious depression? If you notice the extreme trait over several encounters, there's a pattern; it may point to a permanent condition, and you'll have to evaluate it accordingly.

Extreme vocal characteristics are also meaningful because their "owner" is usually aware of them. Many vocal clues sneak in and out of conversations without the speaker noticing, but when someone's voice is cracking with excitement or sobbing with despair, she usually knows it. This, of course, doesn't mean the tone has been adopted intentionally; expressions of extreme happiness, sorrow, fear, and anger often can't be repressed. In fact, if the person would prefer not to reveal an emotion, she might well be sorry it has crept out through her voice. Recognizing when an emotion is being expressed against the speaker's will provides the astute people-reader an opportunity to respond appropriately. For instance, if a woman is trying to appear confident in front of her boss but her voice begins to quiver, she'll probably be embarrassed. Recognizing that, her boss may want to make a special effort to put her at ease. Or, if she's usually upbeat but on this occasion her voice is entirely flat and lifeless, she may be, sad or depressed. Alert to that, her boss may decide that this isn't a good time to place additional burdens on her.

Regardless of the actual words exchanged, any vocal characteristic that is extreme compared with the speaker's usual manner should give you pause. Often people consciously choose to broadcast their feelings through their tone of voice, like the woman mentioned earlier in this chapter who sought permission to ask for sympathy. And often people who are crying out for help do so not with words but with tone of voice. This is particularly true when someone is depressed, hurt, or angry. She may insist that she is "just fine," but her tone will reveal that all is not well. By being sensitive to these subtle vocal clues, you will not only be able to understand people in a way that will help you achieve your goals, you will also be in a better position to offer your support to those in need.

Compare the Voice with the Person's Body Language and Words

Feelings are seldom revealed by tone of voice alone. However, by comparing someone's tone of voice with both body language and words, you can usually determine his or her true emotions.

When a person's tone of voice, words, and body language are in sync—when they all fit a consistent pattern—it's fairly easy to interpret how he's feeling and predict how he'll react to various situations. When the tone of voice and body language are at odds with each other or with the person's words, that's another matter. Then you must consider which elements form a more consistent pattern, and draw your conclusions appropriately.

How body language, tone, and words can be interpreted together was important in a case I worked on recently. During jury selection, the lead attorney's wife had a miscarriage. The attorney asked the judge for a one-day continuance so he could be by his wife's side. The judge refused because the delay would have inconvenienced the many prospective jurors who were still under consideration. The lawyer had to leave jury selection in the hands of his associate and me while he tended to his family's personal crisis. In his absence, the judge asked us to pass on his best wishes to the attorney and his wife.

If all I had to go by was the printed transcript, the words would have suggested the judge's compassionate concern. However, they were spoken in a perfunctory and unemotional way, with neither warmth nor compassion. As he spoke, his face did not change its expression. He continued to look down and shuffle papers on his bench, as if more concerned about the next motion to be heard than the loss of the attorney's unborn child. His tone of voice alone was certainly a powerful clue, and in conjunction with his body language it created the impression that his words were not heartfelt.

Later in the same trial, the judge revealed more of himself through a slightly different combination of words, tone, and body language. A juror asked to be excused from what was sure to be an eight- or ten-week trial, claiming it would be a hardship for him to attend. "I want to know what your hardship is," the judge barked in a sarcastic, aggressive, and almost mean-spirited tone. Again, his words taken alone would not have suggested any particular emotion or state of mind. This time, the judge's tone could best be characterized as angry or hostile. His body language, however, provided the most telling clue to how he was really feeling. His facial expression wasn't angry. On the contrary, it was impassive. Nor did other aspects of his body language reflect anger—he didn't lean forward, gesture, or flush, for example. Here, an analysis of the entire picture—words, tone of voice, and body language—suggested to me that the judge was simply using an angry tone as an intimidation technique to get the juror to confess that there really was no compelling reason to excuse him.

These two exchanges revealed a pattern. The judge was concerned about moving the trial along. He was determined to keep his courtroom efficient and to make sure everyone, attorney and juror alike, participated to his satisfaction. Personal issues took second place. In both instances, the judge's apparent motivations were revealed only when I compared his words, tone of voice, and body language. Once we recognized his characteristics and priorities, we had a basis for predicting how he would respond to various events through the balance of the trial.

The same process can be used by the boss whose employee complains of the flu in a low, halting, pained tone of voice yet walks to his car with the usual spring in his step; by a customer talking with a salesman who speaks confidently, loudly, and unhesitatingly about his product yet immediately stops making eye contact when asked questions about its warranty record; and by a woman whose boyfriend professes his undying and committed love in the most sincere tone while glancing over her shoulder as a good-looking woman walks by.

Unless tone, body language, and words all match, something may be amiss. Take a second look to find out what.

Consider the Environment

If I notice that someone seems nervous on the witness stand, I take into consideration that the courtroom is a very stressful environment. Of course, *any* environment has some impact on the way a person sounds. A loud voice, for example, may be a meaningful clue to a person's character and state of mind, but only if it is consistently or inappropriately loud. In fact, the significance of almost any vocal trait may be diminished or eliminated entirely in certain environments.

I wouldn't draw the same conclusions about someone who speaks in a loud, booming voice in a library as I would if he were at a crowded party. Nor would I draw the same conclusions from someone's rapid speech if she were warning me about an oncoming car as I would if she were trying to sell me a vacuum cleaner. A person may talk rapidly because she is happy, nervous, excited, or afraid. Knowing which often requires some assessment of the environment. This is particularly true if you're encountering someone for the first time. When people feel comfortable in a given setting, their tone of voice is a fairly good indicator of their mood or personality. If they don't feel comfortable, their tone may reflect little more than their uneasiness.

Decoding Vocal Clues

Understanding the messages encoded in vocal traits takes some practice and requires that you pay close attention. More than other traits, tone of voice shifts from second to second, depending on environment and circumstances. If you're not alert, you can miss something critical. While permanent traits such as a loud, booming voice may be fairly straightforward and easy to interpret, other, more transitory characteristics such as pitch, pace of speech, and stammering can be harder to peg. A given tone can sometimes have opposite meanings, like many other traits. Look for patterns, as always, and pay special attention to whether the tone matches or conflicts with the person's body language and words.

There are far too many different voice traits to discuss them all; these are the most common and most telling:

- Loud voice
- Soft voice
- Rapid speech
- Slow speech
- Halting speech
- Pitch
- Intonation and emphasis
- Flat, unemotional voice
- Pretension/snobbery
- Whining
- Breathiness
- Raspy voice
- Mumbling
- Accents

Loud Voice

From time to time we all encounter someone with an exceptionally loud voice—a big, booming baritone or a loud, shrill soprano that you just can't miss. That's the idea. People with loud voices usually have acquired them for a reason. The key to evaluating the significance of a loud voice, therefore, is to assess when and how the person uses it and what he is attempting to accomplish by it.

CONTROL A loud voice is often used to control the environment and those in it. Loudness is authoritative and intimidating, so those who are seeking to dominate or control others often cultivate high-decibel voices. In some instances, loudness is coupled with the practice of "speaking over" others, another probable attempt to control, and one that suggests insensitivity and rudeness as well. Excessive domination of the conversation may also reflect egotism and impatience. Most people assume those with loud, booming voices are displaying confidence. That may be the case—but some people shout because they're afraid no one will hear them if they whisper.

PERSUASION Some people have discovered that a loud voice is a terrific tool for persuading others, or at least forcing them into submission. They have learned that if they speak loudly and stridently enough, many people will interpret their tone as confident and fall in line. Even if they think the speaker is dead wrong, they may not want to argue with him. In my profession, I have seen more than my share of blowhards who use volume to intimidate the weak, fool the feeble-minded, or control the insecure or lazy who would just as soon have someone do their thinking for them anyway.

COMPENSATION FOR A PERCEIVED FLAW I have also seen many instances in which volume compensates for other perceived deficiencies, such as small stature or a physical disability.

I was involved in a case where we examined a prospective juror who was a very small, rail-thin middle-aged man. He sat, as rigid as if he were wearing a back brace, throughout the examination of the other jurors, his hands carefully folded and perfectly still on his lap. He looked like a heavily sedated Don Knotts. The first time he answered a question, his response nearly knocked us all over backward. I have seldom heard a louder, more booming voice. It had to have been purposely acquired. I concluded that he compensated for his diminutive stature and rather bookish bearing by developing a voice like a foghorn.

REACTION TO HEARING LOSS This usually occurs among the elderly, in which case the problem is usually obvious. But be alert to hearing loss among younger people as well.

INEBRIATION Drunk people sometimes get loud, but their volume won't be the only sign of intoxication. If you're meeting someone for the first time at a hard-drinking Christmas bash, withhold judgment about his or her loud voice until you meet again under calmer circumstances.

When you're evaluating what category the loud-voiced person falls into, keep these questions in mind:

- Is the voice appropriate for the occasion?
- Is the loudness constant, or does it vary according to the number of people in the group?
- Is the voice used aggressively, to control, intimidate, or speak over others?

Generally speaking, I have found that people who have a loud, dominant voice but use it courteously and appropriately are confident. Those who abuse others with their loud voice, like a bully with a big stick, are often insecure.

Soft Voice

A soft voice can be used to manipulate others, or it can indicate a person who himself is easily swayed. While a low tone may initially suggest that the speaker lacks confidence and assertiveness, don't be fooled. A soft voice may well reflect calm self-assurance: the speaker feels no need to dominate a conversation. There also may be an element of arrogance: "If you want to hear what I have to say, you'll just have to listen more closely."

When evaluating the significance of someone's muted tone, you'll first need to determine whether he or she always has a soft voice or whether it has dropped on this particular occasion. If the latter is the case, ask what has occurred that may explain the decrease in volume.

- Has there been a confrontation from which the person is withdrawing?
- Is the person in an uncomfortable situation in which he feels nervous or intimidated?
- Do you see indications of grief or sorrow?
- Is there some sign that the speaker is lying, and acting on the natural preference for lying quietly if she must lie at all?
- Is the speaker attempting to force someone else to come within earshot? This is a power play.
- Is the speaker intentionally lowering her voice to limit who can hear it?
- Does the speaker seem tired?
- Could the soft tone be the result of illness?

You will almost always find an explanation if you look for one when low volume is not characteristic of the speaker's normal tone. The speaker's demeanor will probably provide confirmation.

When you evaluate somebody with a consistently soft voice, focus on the appropriateness of whatever modulations do exist. Does the person make an effort to speak louder when it is clear some of those present may not be able to hear him? If not, he may be unobservant, inconsiderate, or arrogant. If the volume is low but he makes good eye contact and his body language is relaxed, the soft voice has little significance. If, on the other hand, the consistently low volume is combined with body language that reflects discomfort, such as lack of eye contact, turning the body or face away, or fidgeting, I would "read" the voice as a symptom of discomfort and lack of confidence.

Two attorneys with whom I've worked illustrate how differently a soft voice can be perceived. The women are about the same age and have the same number of years' experience. Both are bright and articulate. Both are also extremely soft-spoken. One, however, exudes confidence and control, while the other does not.

The confident one sits very still in her chair as she speaks with me. Her hands are usually relaxed on the desk in front of her unless she is writing notes, which she does only when appropriate. We always have excellent eye contact. Her voice, while quiet, has no hesitation and incorporates appropriate emphasis, although subtly.

The other attorney, while equally intelligent and insightful, often speaks haltingly and uneasily. There appears to be no pattern to the emphasis she places on various words, which gives me the impression that she stresses one word or concept over another because of anxiety rather than as a conscious choice. The low volume and other vocal traits are mirrored by her body language, which includes frequently downcast eyes, nervous fiddling with her pen or paper, and a hunched-over body posture. All of these point to a lack of confidence, the opposite of the impression given by the other soft-spoken attorney.

Rapid Speech

We've all heard the phrase "fast-talking salesman." It usually refers to somebody who is not only speaking quickly but lying quickly. Rapid speech does sometimes indicate untruthfulness, but that's only one of several possibilities.

There's a difference between fast-talking all the time and fast-talking in reaction to specific situations. People who always speak quickly may have grown up in households where they had to talk fast to get a word in edgewise. Other fast-talkers are type A personalities, tightly wound from the get-go. Regardless of the cause, I have found that consistently fast-talkers are often as quick to assess and judge a situation as they are to express themselves. As a result, they are often not cautious, but impulsive and judgmental. I usually don't like them to sit as jurors when I'm working with the defense in a criminal case because they tend to jump to conclusions quickly rather than carefully evaluate the evidence.

I've also found that many fast-talkers are compensating for a basic insecurity. These fast-talkers will show signs of poor self-esteem, such as a generally nervous personality and inappropriate efforts to gain attention.

The occasional trip into the verbal fast lane by someone who usually speaks at a normal pace is typically caused by one of the following:

- Nervousness
- Impatience

- Anxiety
- Insecurity
- Excitement
- Fear
- Drugs or alcohol
- Anger
- Desire to persuade
- Being caught in a lie

Most people have experienced the unpleasantness of being caught in a lie. Someone's chatting along at normal speed, then realizes there's an inconsistency in her tale. Suddenly, she switches to fast-forward as she tries to explain herself. The more she lies, the faster the words spring from her lips. I saw a prime example of this a few years ago in the form of a reluctant juror.

This man desperately wanted to be excused from jury duty, so he told the judge his wife was sick and he had to take her to the doctor. When the judge suggested scheduling a late-afternoon appointment, the juror, talking faster and faster, explained that he actually had to take his wife to the doctor *a lot,* and he didn't think he'd be able to get late-afternoon appointments. When the judge suggested he call the doctor, find out, and report back to the court that afternoon, the juror added that he also had to take his dog to the vet (I'm not kidding). Finally, he told the judge his roof needed to be repaired. Half of us in the courtroom could not restrain at least a chuckle, if not outright laughter, as the excuses mounted and his voice sped up.

I'm always alert to the possibility that a fast-talker is trying to obscure the truth in a barrage of words—but it's much more likely that he's just nervous and insecure, and speaks quickly out of anxiety, or a desire to mask his lack of confidence or to make his point. We recognize this in our kids: childhood excitement often gets translated into fast speech. Usually, it's not much different with adults.

Slow Speech

People who speak slowly tend to fall into one of two categories: those who sound and appear comfortable and relaxed; and those whose slow speech is accompanied by other physical and vocal clues suggesting discomfort. By determining which camp the person belongs in, I can make an educated guess about the causes of the slow speech.

Some people who consistently speak slowly have a physical or mental disability. In the latter case, the slow speech will be coupled with an inability to express ideas. Physical ailments are also fairly obvious once you've spoken with someone for a few minutes. People who are unfamiliar with the language may also speak slowly, as might those who are self-conscious about their level of education. And there are common regional variations in the speed of speech—for example, Southerners typically speak more slowly than people from New York City.

Teachers, the clergy, and others who frequently speak to large groups sometimes adopt slow speech to be sure their audience gets their drift. The technique then sometimes bleeds into everyday conversation. Occasionally, slow speakers are being condescending, in which case they'll usually adopt a noticeably sarcastic tone.

If someone usually speaks at a normal pace, slow speech on a given occasion may mean he is

- trying to make a point that is very important to him
- anxious
- confused
- lying
- sad or grieving
- fatigued
- deep in thought
- ill
- under the influence of drugs or alcohol

To decide which, consider the speaker's body language and the content of his speech.

Halting Speech

Halting, hesitant, or broken speech is different from slow speech. A stop-and-start pattern is usually caused by insecurity, nervousness, or confusion. On occasion, it may reflect untruthfulness, as when someone struggles to come up with an excuse. But it can also point in the opposite direction: the speaker wants to be very accurate and is searching for just the right words. Or she may pause to give you an opportunity to interject something.

To determine whether someone's halting speech signifies insecurity, nervousness, confusion, untruthfulness, or an attempt at precision, look at the entire pattern of his speech, words, and body language. People have to be pretty uptight about what they're saying for the tension to cause broken and halting speech. Other signs will nearly always appear, too. Someone who's fibbing will lose eye contact, inadvertently cover his mouth or other parts of his face, or fall prey to one of the other body-language tip-offs we discussed in chapter 5. A nervous person won't just speak haltingly; she'll also shift in her chair, tap her fingers, and so forth.

Assuming the speaker isn't lying or nervous, you can often chalk up halting or broken speech to an honest struggle to articulate thoughts. A woman I've worked with is an excellent example. She's an extremely bright and very precise attorney, but has a sometimes disconcerting habit—she'll stop mid-sentence, pause, and then continue again, sometimes in a slightly different direction. She shows no signs of nervousness, dishonesty, evasiveness, or insecurity. Rather, her body language reflects thoughtfulness and focus. Her gaze is fixed, and the volume of her speech doesn't vary significantly. She is clearly concentrating on what she's saying, and is trying to be precise.

You should distinguish such an attempt at precision from scatterbrained chatter—when someone appears to lose his train of thought, heads off in another direction, seems to bounce off an invisible wall, and careens back and forth, with his mouth obviously preceding his brain by several seconds. Halting, hesitant, broken speech coupled with disjointed content indicates confusion or a lack of concentration and focus. It can also mean the person wants attention even if he has to ramble on to get it.

When halting speech dissolves into actual stuttering or stammering, it's usually because of nervousness. Of course, there are also people who stutter because of a physical condition. Notice whether the stuttering is consistent over several conversations, or whether the speaker stutters or stammers only when he or she seems nervous or tongue-tied. The chronic stutterer is not necessarily chronically nervous. Severe stuttering is a vocal condition that's not yet fully understood.

Pitch

People's voices range from the calm and soothing to the shrill and irritating. Vocal pitch is largely nonelective: if you were born with Fran Drescher's fingernails-on-a-chalkboard voice, you pretty much have to live with it—or develop a routine and head for Hollywood. But within the range that is normal for each of us, we raise and lower our pitch for a few standard reasons.

Most people's voices will rise in pitch when they're especially scared, joyful, agitated, excited, and so on. If the feeling is intense enough, their voice will crack. In these cases, the cause is usually clear from accompanying body language, words, and actions.

Some people noticeably lower their voice from its normal range when they're trying to seduce someone. They tend to come across like the late-night deejay on a local jazz station or the sultry temptress in a 1940s detective flick. Pitch may also drop when someone is sad, depressed, or fatigued. Once again, the meaning is hard to miss if you pay attention to all the available clues.

Intonation and Emphasis

In many languages, words take on completely different meanings depending on which syllable or word is stressed. While English doesn't rely as heavily on intonation and emphasis as some languages, we all communicate different emotions and meanings by altering our speech pattern. Pay attention to this, and you'll catch important clues.

We've all asked someone whether he or she would like to go somewhere with us, and been told in response, "I'd really love to go." Sometimes as we heard the words we knew immediately that our invitation had been accepted. On other occasions, as the person completed the phrase "I'd really love to go," we knew the next word out of his or her mouth would be "but."

If you listen carefully to intonation, pauses, and emphasis, you can recognize "incomplete" sentences. Even if you can't make an educated guess about what words might complete the thought, at least you'll be able to detect ambiguities and follow up with appropriate questions.

Not surprisingly, vocal emphasis is usually also accompanied by physical emphasis. While stressing a word, the speaker may lean forward, nod, or gesture. As a result, even subtle changes in intonation or emphasis can be easier to recognize if you listen for them while watching for changes in body language.

Flat, Unemotional Voice

Remember the judge who offered condolences to the attorney whose wife had just suffered a miscarriage? The judge's apparent insincerity was revealed not by his words but by his flat, unemotional tone of voice. A flat voice can also tip you off to boredom, anger, resentment, frustration, depression, and some physical ailments.

If you tell a friend you just received a big promotion, you expect her response to reflect some level of excitement and happiness for you. There should be some bounce in her voice. Perhaps she'll offer a warm and sincere "Congratulations." You don't expect a flat, quick "That's nice." When you get an unexpectedly unemotional response, you should go on the alert. Look first to body language to help you determine whether the person is distracted, bored, or depressed. Or is the flat voice an attempt to camouflage more intense feelings, such as jealousy or resentment? Those, too, will probably leak out in her body language. Depending on what you learn, you can proceed accordingly, either pursue the matter then and there or file away the response for later reflection.

Pretension/Snobbery

As a kid, I watched *Gilligan's Island.* The "millionaire and his wife" spoke in an overstated, pretentious way, which my sisters and I loved to mimic. Thirty years later, I hear my young son ask, "Pardon me, do you have any Grey Poupon?" in that same tone. Pretension and snobbery aren't usually revealed so dramatically in someone's voice, though to my amazement I do occasionally meet someone who has a bit of Mr. Howell in his vocal delivery.

If I admit that I am unfamiliar with a particular current event, my comment may be met with the response "Oh, really," said in a tone suggesting surprise that anyone could be so ill-informed. Or someone may describe his new house or car in a voice more suited to the narrator of *Lifestyles of the Rich and Famous.* It's difficult to capture a snobbish tone in writing, but (to paraphrase what U.S. Supreme Court Justice Potter Stewart said of pornography) "You know it when you see it." The question is, what does it signify?

Many people adopt a snobbish tone or other pretentious mannerisms to present an image of success, sophistication, intelligence, wealth, or upper-class values. Those characteristics may not be at the core of their personalities. Instead, the apparent snob may just be insecure and seeking approval and recognition.

Many other snobs really, truly believe they *are* better, more intelligent, and more worth listening to than the rest of us. They're not at all insecure. They're confident. And try as you might, you will not be able to persuade the snob to respect "lesser" folk or their ideas or lifestyles. Such a hard-core snob usually comes from a family that's upper-class or thinks it is. Since socioeconomic background is a key predictor of how people think and behave, don't assume you'll ever change the way a true snob sees the world. That view usually has been set in concrete.

Whining

Whining is not always a singsong lament coupled with a screwed-up face and hand-wringing. It can be much more subtle. But whether it's underplayed or obvious, whining is a technique used to manipulate others without forceful words. It's often an effort by someone to get what he wants without asking for it outright. A sentence whined is a sentence that says, "I really feel strongly about this, and I am going to moan and complain until you do what I want."

Over the years I have watched thousands of mock jurors deliberate. I have seen my fair share of whiners among these men and women. They complain there's not enough ice for the Coke, but they don't go get more themselves. They whine that the lawyers' presentations were confusing, but they seldom exert the effort to sort through the evidence. If their views are rejected by the majority, they withdraw and pout.

Whiners are usually followers—on juries as in life outside the courthouse. They don't have the courage or confidence to lead. They want others to take care of them. They feel helpless and out of control. If you want to know whether someone is truly a whiner, try to get a sense of her human environment—in other words, meet a few of her friends. How does she behave with them? How manipulative is she? If she's married, pay particular attention to her interaction with her husband. Whiners whine because it works for them. And whining is a difficult trait to overcome, even if the whiner wants to change. The whiner's behavior toward others will give you a preview of what your relationship with her might be like. It's up to you to decide whether you feel up to the challenge.

Breathiness

"Happy Birthday, Mr. President," Marilyn Monroe cooed in her tribute to JFK, a classic example of breathy seductiveness. Voluntary breathiness can usually be chalked up to seduction. Involuntary breathiness is caused by other equally important emotional states or by illness or fatigue.

Since we normally don't hear significant audible breathing (like Darth Vader's), whenever I do, I wonder why. Is it physical or emotional? People afflicted with emphysema, other lung diseases, or any number of debilitating illnesses may have difficulty breathing, in which case the breathiness is only an indication of the illness.

If I can rule out illness (by looking at body language or asking tactfully about the person's health), I consider the other conditions that commonly cause breathiness:

- anger
- sexual interest
- excitement
- frustration
- exercise or fatigue
- disbelief
- nervousness
- stress

During trials, I often detect changes in the breathing patterns of jurors, witnesses, and even lawyers. Given the circumstances, it's usually fairly easy to eliminate several possible causes, such as sexual interest or exercise. Most frequently, audible breathing in court is the result of frustration, surprise, disbelief, or nervousness. Even the most experienced trial lawyers will sometimes get nervous and begin inhaling and exhaling in an unusual manner. By the time the trial actually starts I've usually seen and heard them speak many times, so I'll pick up those subtle changes instantly. Normally, people reveal such nervousness not just by deeper or less rhythmic breaths, but also by body motions like drinking water or making exaggerated hand movements. I also listen carefully for the quick, audible bursts of air exhaled by jurors (and sometimes the judge, lawyers, or witnesses) as signs of surprise, disbelief, or exasperation. Again, these vocal clues are usually accompanied by shakes of the head or other visual signs. The key is to notice the characteristic, identify its various possible causes, and then see which of these causes matches the person's body language, behavior, and words.

The Raspy Voice

A raspy voice is often a sign that the speaker smokes, but it can also be caused by a cold or bronchitis, or by a permanent physical condition. It also could be that the speaker has recently stressed his voice in some way. Ask about it. If he frequently sings, or gives speeches that leave his voice tired and rough, you have a good starting point for a conversation that could reveal a lot about him. Often people's voices get raspy from yelling at sporting events or elsewhere. Again, ask: Was he cheering on his son at peewee football, or shouting encouragement to the hometown baseball team? If he yelled so much he made himself hoarse, I know he's an avid fan, and I suspect he may be fairly aggressive and controlling. (On some level, he may believe that if he yells loud enough he can influence the outcome of the game.) If nothing else, I'm confident that he's outgoing and excitable. Few quiet, shy, reserved people will yell until their voices give out.

Mumbling

Some mumblers speak so softly they're inaudible. Others habitually cover their mouths with their hands when they talk. Still others avert their heads or look down. Some mumblers will speak more clearly when asked to, but others seem virtually incapable of clear speech, even though there is no physical explanation for the phenomenon.

The mumbler who responds to a request to speak more clearly may have been distracted, tired, chewing, under the influence of drugs or alcohol, or otherwise straying momentarily from a normal pattern of clear speech. The chronic mumbler (one who doesn't respond to the request to speak clearly, at least not for more than a few minutes at a stretch) often reveals

- lack of confidence
- insecurity
- anxiety
- an inability to articulate thoughts
- self-consciousness
- preoccupation
- fatigue
- illness

Mumblers seldom demonstrate significant leadership ability or even any desire for such control. Often mumblers also appear depressed or sad. I have seen very few animated, upbeat, happy mumblers. And this is usually reflected in their body language: limp, passive motions, a weak handshake, and a tired demeanor.

Accents

We live in an increasingly diverse world. I hear the accents of at least six different nationalities and as many regions of the United States on any given day. A person's accent can provide you with valuable clues about how he might think or act.

If I meet a man who speaks with a heavy foreign accent, I watch to see if he has any language limitations that might affect his speech or behavior. I'm also alert to the possibility that he may have an unusual cultural background, which may have an impact on his vocal mannerisms. For example, some cultures are more verbally expressive and uninhibited than others.

Someone who does not feel comfortable with the language he's speaking may also be self-conscious about his lack of fluency or preoccupied with his search for the right words. He may feel frustrated or nervous because of this difficulty. If I didn't consider his accent, and the possibility that he may communicate very differently in his native tongue, I could misread his personality completely. I might wrongly assume he is passive, shy, or nervous; in fact, he may be very aggressive and confident when language doesn't present a barrier to communication.

To a lesser degree, the same applies to those from different areas within the United States. General attitudes about appropriate manners, social decorum, and self-expression vary from region to region. In large metropolitan areas, such as New York City, people generally learn to speak faster, louder, and more aggressively than they do in small towns in the South or Midwest. There, the New Yorker's speech patterns might be considered rude. Unless you are very familiar with the region or country reflected in someone's accent, you won't know how her particular cultural background may affect her vocal mannerisms. So ask her about where she's from. It's a great way to break the ice and learn more about her.

KEY POINTS

Learn to hear between the lines: Two dialogues take place in every conversation. One uses words, the other relies on conscious or subconscious vocalization techniques. Sometimes the two match; often they don't. When in conflict, vocal variations are usually a more reliable indication of the message someone is really sending than the words he uses.

Listen for emotional hide-and-seek: When we're feeling emotions or thinking thoughts that we don't want to discuss for some reason—embarrassment, insecurity, fear—we often ask others for permission with vocal signals.

To hear the unspoken message:

- Focus on the voice, not the words, in short spurts from time to time during a conversation.
- Consider whether the vocal characteristics are voluntary (often manipulative) or involuntary (usually reflecting true emotion).
- Look for patterns, extremes, and deviations from the person's normal voice.
- Compare voice to body language and words.
- Consider the context and environment in which the words are spoken.

SEVEN

Communication Style— Why Did You Put It That Way?

Finding the Hidden Meanings in Communication Style

Some conversations, particularly those about delicate subjects, remind me of scenes from the nature programs my kids watch: A small bird is sitting in a nest on the ground. As a predator approaches, she feigns a broken wing and hobbles off, leading the predator away from her young. Or a snake lies frozen in the grass—except for the twitching tip of its tail, which irresistibly attracts its next meal.

There are many parallels between how people interact and the dynamics that occur in the animal world. We humans advance and withdraw, distract and lure, as all creatures do. We lead others away from subjects we want to avoid, or pull them in the direction we want them to go. We accomplish this by using an arsenal of communication techniques developed for the sake of social survival: words and tone, actions, and even silence. Some are instinctive; others are conscious maneuvers.

As helpful as it is to know how to ask questions and listen to answers, not all questions are welcome and not all answers are forthright. We often tackle subjects that are unpleasant, humiliating, and even threatening. We steer conversations away from topics that would reveal our weaknesses or mistakes and usually try to avoid embarrassing others. We're socialized not to brag or lie. And most of us try very hard to respect those and other similar unwritten rules.

If we don't want to admit our shortcomings, openly boast about our accomplishments, or lie about our misdeeds, how do we handle situations in which we need or want to do just that? We rely on our stockpile of verbal and behavioral maneuvers. In this chapter you'll learn to recognize and interpret these maneuvers. The topics discussed here range from manipulative answers and other fairly straightforward verbal traits to typical conversational detours and more complex habits. Like all other traits and behaviors, these conversational maneuvers should always be viewed alongside other characteristics as you try to establish a pattern.

Communication expert Linda McCallister, author of *I Wish I'd Said That!*, has identified six different communication styles. People can be Reflectives, Nobles, Socratics, Magistrates, Candidates, or Senators. Although no one fits completely into any one category, all of us have a tendency to use one particular style more than the others. Recognizing that different people impart their information in markedly different ways, noticing the way they communicate can earn you valuable insight into their personalities and priorities and consequently help you understand them better.

At one end of the spectrum are *Nobles*. These people believe communication serves one purpose and one purpose only: to exchange information. That's what they do when they come into your office, and that's what they hope you do when you come into theirs. Nobles seek to discuss relevant data with as few words as possible. They will not ask you how your weekend was or how your son did in his hockey tournament. And if you ask a Noble how his weekend was, he may reply "Forty-eight hours long." Even if you have been working together for years, all a Noble will ask you on Monday morning is the time and location of the next meeting.

On the other end of the spectrum are *Reflectives*—the "touchy-feely" people. To them, communication is all about building relationships. Despite how busy these people may be, the first thing they want to know when they walk into your office on Monday morning is how your son did in his hockey tournament or how your daughter's dance recital went. And they can't wait to tell you what they did over the weekend. You may also be able to peg Reflectives and Nobles through watching what people do when they arrive at work in the morning. A Noble, as you might imagine, makes a beeline to her office to get right to work, while a Reflective makes the rounds, greeting and socializing with everyone else before finally settling in at his desk. Problems arise, as you can imagine, when a Noble works with a Reflective. The Noble may read the Reflective as inefficient, spacey, and distracted, while the Reflective may think the Noble is rude.

For a *Socratic,* the purpose of communication is to talk. Many of the lawyers I work with are Socratics. They love discussion and debate. These people may seem like they are running at the mouth or being unresponsive, when in reality, they just like to talk things out and exchange ideas.

Magistrates display some of the characteristics of Socratics, and some of Nobles, and as such, these people are often opinionated, argumentative, and difficult to deal with. Their goal is to explain to you why they are right and you are wrong. You will likely read these people very negatively, even if you don't realize it, because you can sense that they are not listening to you; they are merely selling themselves. At first they may seem to enjoy the exchange of ideas, but as the conversation progresses you will notice that they don't seem to care what you have to say.

Candidates don't want to upset anyone, so they seek to communicate along a path of least resistance. They are people-pleasers whose goal is to avoid conflict. They may sometimes seem evasive, but if you recognize this communication style you will understand they are not trying to be dishonest; they just don't want to displease anyone.

A *Senator* chooses whatever communication style works in the situation. Senators go out of their way to respond warmly to Reflectives, and respect the austerity of Nobles. They apply whatever communication style works under the circumstances. If a Reflective walks into a Senator's office, he will ask about the Reflective's weekend, and tell the Reflective about his. If a Noble comes in and asks, "What time is the meeting, and where?" his response will be, "Two o'clock, conference room."

Knowledge of these different communication styles is critical to accurately reading people. Just because someone answers a question with a short and terse response, it doesn't necessarily mean she dislikes you or is being evasive or dishonest. She may simply be a Noble, and that is the way she communicates. Identifying these communication styles may allow you to put other traits you have observed in context. And because most of us are fairly consistent, always pay attention to changes in communication style. If someone is usually a chatterbox but clams up in response to certain questions or suddenly communicates differently when certain people come into the room, you may be correct in assigning significance to the change in his demeanor and communication style.

So how else can you use this information about communication styles? As with your observations in the other Colors, use it to "win friends and influence people," to quote the title of Dale Carnegie's bestseller. If your boss is a Reflective, take the time and go say hello in the morning. If your husband is a Noble, answer his questions responsively and with clarity, and without taking offense! By deciphering someone's communication style, you will be able to tailor your interaction accordingly and make communication not only effective, but also a positive experience for the both of you.

Look for the Motive

When I realize someone may be trying to direct or control a conversation, I always ask myself what he's trying to accomplish. By examining a person's behavior in the context of the broader conversation, I can usually identify his objective. When it isn't crystal clear from my observations alone, a few questions will generally bring the answer to the surface.

Even if there is no apparent reason for a person to manipulate a conversation, just the fact that he communicates in a particular way—volunteering information about himself, bragging, criticizing, or whatever—may have implications about his personality. If someone drops a name for a specific reason, for example, it may not say much about his character. But if he routinely name-drops, even when the name has little to do with the topic at hand, that points to insecurity, a need for acceptance, and a desire to call attention to himself.

People try to manipulate conversations for many different reasons both positive (to avoid embarrassing or hurting another person) and negative (to cover up a lie, to trick someone, or to pull someone into an argument). When you notice that someone is attempting to steer a discussion, ask yourself why. What does he have to gain? Does his behavior reflect an attempt to achieve a specific goal, for instance to gather facts or protect someone's privacy? Or does his maneuvering indicate low self-esteem or a need for attention? Pursue the conversation until you're fairly certain of the answer. You may have to watch and listen closely to spot some maneuvers; they may come and go quickly. Other techniques are easy to see, but their motivation is not as obvious. Whichever is the case, try to identify both the method and the motive. Once you do, you will gain tremendous insight into a person's character.

Manipulative Answers

No matter how skillful you are at formulating questions, you're bound to run into people who are just as adept at sidestepping them. Some answers seem designed to avoid revealing anything, while others force unrelated information into the conversation. When you know what to look for, you can tell when someone is leading you toward or away from a particular topic, and why.

Nonresponsiveness

There are a number of ways to avoid responding to a question, from changing the subject to clamming up altogether. But before you place too much significance on someone's nonresponsive answer, make sure she heard and understood you.

I've seen many well-meaning and candid witnesses initially appear evasive, only to demonstrate later that they were trying their best to respond. Some people don't want to admit they don't understand a question, which is very often the case. Others are so preoccupied with another issue that they go off on a tangent without even realizing they haven't answered the question. Still others misunderstand the question, and sincerely believe they've provided an answer. Language and cultural differences can also make a person misconstrue a question and appear evasive or nonresponsive. In situations like these, nonresponsiveness is usually nothing more than a bump in the conversational road. With a few more questions, you'll be able to get the information you need.

However, if someone avoids answering several open-ended follow-up questions, you're probably on to something. He might be avoiding embarrassment, conflict, the truth, or an emotionally difficult subject. He might also be intent on talking about something totally unrelated, in which case his nonresponsiveness usually isn't an evasive tactic. Chances are, once he says what's on his mind, he'll be happy to discuss what's on yours. To determine what's going on, ask leading questions or, if necessary, pointed ones. If that still doesn't work, you'll have to try to get the information elsewhere, or abandon the search altogether.

Before you launch into a full-scale assault, however, try to make an educated guess about the reasons for the person's reluctance to answer. Without having at least some sense of his motives, you'll be forging ahead at your own risk. Many people find it insensitive and rude when someone insists on discussing an issue they have plainly tried to avoid.

During jury selection, it's not uncommon for a lawyer to encounter this pitfall as he bores in unmercifully on a juror who is clearly embarrassed by a particular subject. In a recent breach-of-contract case, the attorney representing the man who filed the lawsuit was examining an elderly juror who obviously did not want to talk about his son. The attorney wanted to know why. His unrelenting and very public inquiries quickly became offensive. Initially, the man revealed that his son was "incarcerated." Further probing established that the son had been convicted of burglary. That should have been enough for the plaintiff's attorney to make his call regarding the juror, but he continued to pry, asking for details about the conviction, the length of the sentence, where the son was incarcerated, and the nature of the relationship between the father and the son. With each question, the father's answers became shorter, until finally he stopped replying altogether. He knew he'd be excused from the jury, so why bother responding? Throughout this scene I was acutely aware of the man's humiliation and distress, and wondered why the lawyer persisted in the examination, especially since these issues had nothing to do with a breach-of-contract case.

I later realized that the attorney was so curious about the man's reluctance to talk that he couldn't help but probe; his urge to know the facts got the better of him. In suggesting that nonresponsiveness should excite your curiosity and prompt follow-up, I'm not urging you to do it thoughtlessly. As much as you may want or need a certain piece of information, recognize when further questions will only alienate the other person, and try another approach later.

Not Denying or Explaining When It Would Be Expected

Just as people can protest too much, they can also fail to deny an accusation or explain an event, leaving the truth hanging there in the silence for anyone who cares to hear. The behavior is similar to nonresponsiveness but can be even more revealing.

Most of us are quick to deny any hint of wrongdoing and happy to explain ourselves if we have nothing to hide. That's why, in nearly every courtroom, judges instruct juries that they may draw a negative inference if one party has a chance to explain an important issue but doesn't. Keep this instruction in mind as you deliberate about people outside the courtroom as well.

Imagine a woman asking her boyfriend, "Did you have a good time last night?" after he's stayed out unusually late one evening. If he's normally talkative and quick to volunteer details about his evening's activities, but this time he averts his eyes and says simply, "It was okay," hoist the red flag. The more communicative a person normally is, the more significance you can place on his failure to explain or deny unusual behavior. To be absolutely sure he didn't misunderstand, raise the issue again. If he once more fails to explain or deny, it's time to consider possible motives.

Avoiding a topic by failing to explain or deny is especially significant because most of us want to be loved, respected, and understood. We also want to spare our loved ones any unnecessary worry or heartache. When we deviate from these expected patterns, it's usually because honesty would hurt someone we love, or would cost us their respect, approval, and affection. We hope that if we just ignore the issue, it will go away.

But people aren't always hiding something when they fail to explain or deny. Someone may be defensive about an issue or angry because you keep pressing it. He may want to avoid confrontation, believing you're going to scoff at any explanation he does supply. He may be playing games, wanting you to be jealous or insecure. Or he may be trying to control you by keeping you off-balance. He might even be offended by your suggestion of impropriety and not want to dignify it with a response.

All of these are possible motives, but they're also the excuses typically pulled out of the hat by someone who really is hiding something. Whenever I hear them, I am suspicious, just as I would be if my teenager came home at two A.M. and, when asked where he'd been, replied, "What's the matter? Don't you trust me? I can't believe I have to explain my every movement to you!" That sounds like guilt. Don't let someone's aggressive response distract you from what you should be hearing.

Short Answers

There's nothing inherently suspicious about short answers. They're often refreshingly frank and to the point. Still, the person who constantly offers only very brief responses is rather unusual—and leads me to ask myself whether my questions called for more information than he provided. If open-ended questions that call for a narrative response are repeatedly met with a brief yes or no, my eyebrows go up.

To investigate, I look at the person's body language and listen to his tone of voice. An honest but succinct reply typically doesn't look the same as a dishonest one. By the same token, someone who gives short answers because he is nervous, afraid, defensive, or embarrassed won't use the same body language as someone who is no-nonsense but basically at ease. Short answers are just an early warning signal—what they mean must be checked against other clues. An excellent example is the prospective juror I mentioned earlier, whose son was doing time for burglary. The man's answers were very curt, his body language extremely defensive. I could clearly see that he was honest, but he sure wasn't happy about being forced to publicly discuss such a sensitive subject.

Long Answers

Long answers are more challenging to interpret. There are plenty of long-winded people out there with no motive except to get attention, and lots more who just have a hard time expressing themselves. But sometimes a long answer hides or distorts the truth. *People who want to avoid lying outright often try to spread the truth around in a long an-*

swer so that, in order to discover it, you have to pick out a piece here, a piece there. The person may tell himself, "I'm not lying; all the pieces are there. If he can't find them, that's not my problem."

Don't place every person and response under suspicion, but you'd be foolish not to be on the lookout for possible hidden meanings in extra-long responses. To test an unusually long answer, first ask yourself if it's appropriate under the circumstances. Did it answer the question, if in a roundabout way? Or did the person respond like a politician, answering the question he *wished* had been asked? Did he reveal much of himself in the answer, in a candid manner? Did his body language and voice reflect honesty and openness? Suppose you *had* asked for a five-minute response. Would his answer have been appropriate?

Next, ask yourself whether the answer was coherent, or rambling and disjointed. If it was incoherent, that might be a result of nervousness, social ineptitude, insecurity, or confusion. An answer that's coherent but seemingly uncalled-for may be meant to hide the truth, to control the conversation, to keep the floor in an attempt to push a specific agenda, to buy time to think of what to say, or to impress others.

Bear in mind that some people are simply more articulate than others. Someone who isn't used to speaking publicly may have more difficulty expressing herself, and as a consequence may take longer to do so. This doesn't mean she's insecure, confused, or lying. As always, look at the pattern that has developed before you draw any conclusions. A rambling and disjointed answer from a slick-talking salesman would suggest one thing, the same answer from a nervous recluse quite another.

Answering a Question with a Question

"So, what do you think of the new sales guy?"

"I don't know. What's your impression?"

"Well, didn't you have lunch with him yesterday?"

"Why do you ask?"

When someone doesn't want to commit himself, he will often answer a question with a question. He's waiting for more information from you so he can tailor his answer accordingly. Is it safe to admit you think the new sales manager is terrific, or does your colleague disagree? What will he think if you confirm that you went out to lunch with him?

I often see this dynamic played out in the courtroom: "How do you feel about the death penalty?" "What do you mean, how do I feel?" The juror may want more information before committing herself. She may want to know how we think she *should* feel, or she may want to get some hint as to the most socially acceptable response. When she finds out, she can give the answer that will make her feel comfortable.

When someone answers a question with a question, stay alert. It doesn't necessarily mean she's being evasive; although sometimes that's the case. She may also be insecure, embarrassed, or eager to please; or she may just want clarification. The motive may be sinister or innocent. For example, assume an employer says to an employee, "I called the store yesterday afternoon and you were gone. When did you leave?" If the employee responds, "When did you call?" he may want to know so he can say he left as late as possible. On the other hand, he may have come and gone several times during the afternoon and have a perfectly good reason to ask for clarification. Don't be too quick to judge the answer harshly.

Another common reason people answer a question with a question is to redirect the conversation. "Want me to get two tickets to the ball game on Friday?" a man may ask his wife. "Did you know the Wilsons are going to be in town this weekend?" his wife might reply. A response like this usually means one of three things: the other person didn't hear you; she's trying to answer in a roundabout way, by giving you new information with her question; or she just doesn't want to answer. If she doesn't want to answer, it may be that she's avoiding something, such as the fact that she already made plans for Friday without consulting you. Or it could be that she hates ball games and wants to avoid a fight. You'll find out which with another question or two.

Some individuals with good people skills have figured out that by answering a question with a question they can get others talking and break the ice. These born socializers are naturally curious about other people; they shouldn't be viewed with suspicion. However, if someone consistently turns the conversation to other people and never reveals anything about herself, I usually assume she's secretive.

There are, then, a number of possible motives for answering a question with a question. To focus on the most likely, first ask yourself whether the information sought in the second question was necessary to answer the first—for instance, to clarify a point. If not, the person is probably probing for information so her answer won't seem stupid, trying to find out what you know so she can plot some sort of strategic response, or fishing for clues about what will win your approval.

Next, consider whether the second question is an attempt to redirect the conversation. If so, the other person either didn't hear you or wants to avoid responding. If she's trying to avoid a response, you've probably hit a sensitive issue. Cautious follow-up is definitely in order.

Once again, look for patterns. Review the exchange in the context of the entire conversation. If the person responding to your question with a question is otherwise candid, there's no reason to conclude she has an ulterior motive. If she consistently avoids responding by asking you questions, consider the possibility that she may have something to hide.

Conversational Detours

The best discussions aren't laid out like train tracks across the plains. They take interesting twists and turns as information is exchanged and opinions expressed. Detours such as pregnant pauses, interruptions, and rambling are usually just a part of the flow. But sometimes, such detours aren't so much the natural product of conversation as conscious efforts by one participant to change the subject. When this happens, it's worthwhile to pay extra attention; what people *don't* want to discuss can be extremely revealing.

The Pregnant Pause

You're in the middle of a free-flowing and spontaneous conversation. You say something, perhaps something provocative, threatening, or off the subject. There is no response. The rhythm of the conversation has been broken—whatever you just said caught the other person off guard. He's derailed and taking a moment to get centered again.

Pregnant pauses are often accompanied by the "deer in the headlights" look: someone freezes and panic or anxiety sweeps across his face. He doesn't blink. It's as if something in his brain has shorted out momentarily and he's thinking, "Oh God, what do I do now?" When this occurs we often assume we've caught him in a lie, but the reaction also could signal that he is surprised or offended by what you've just said. When I see this look, I immediately ask myself what may have prompted it. Was it the question about why he left his last job? Was it the mention of lipstick on his collar?

Not all pauses are so dramatic. Brief pauses can reflect anger, frustration, or even disgust. Frequently, someone who is upset will take a moment to regain control of his emotions before he responds. If this is happening, you'll see a quick look of anger, accompanied by a tightening of the jaw, a grimace, or a shake of the head. If he's frustrated, he'll show it by exhaling air, shrugging, turning his head, or exhibiting some other sign. And it's possible that the pause simply means he had a completely unrelated thought; he may have realized suddenly that he forgot to lock his front door or turn off his stove. If that's the case, you'll probably see a look of distraction, a faraway gaze, and a slacking of the facial muscles.

When a pregnant pause occurs, don't try to fill the void with another question or comment. Instead, look closely for clues in the person's face, eyes, and mouth. Think back to the flow of the conversation that was interrupted by the pause. What were the last words spoken, the ones that knocked this person off balance?

Interruptions

As the previous chapter pointed out, interruptions are often fatal to good conversations. Most of us want our companions to listen carefully when we speak, with their attention focused on our every word. But some interruptions are inevitable. It's natural for someone to interrupt when she's excited about what you're saying and wants to jump in, or when she senses you're groping for words. However, someone who interrupts consistently or at particularly annoying junctures not only derails the conversation but also reveals a lot about her own state of mind or personality.

Consistent or poorly timed interruptions may be motivated by impatience or boredom—you may be going too slowly for the other person, or pursuing a topic that doesn't interest her. You might be tempted to chalk up her behavior to intentional rudeness. But it may point to a family background in which conversations were highly charged and competitive, or rules of conversational conduct weren't very strict. If someone grew up in a big, vocal family where every dinnertime conversation was a verbal free-for-all, the habit will be hard to break.

People eager to push a specific agenda also often interrupt to steer the conversation their way. They want to persuade you, not listen to your point of view. These interruptions are often argumentative. The more heated and frequent they are, the more likely you've touched a nerve with the person, especially if she doesn't usually interrupt.

Chronic interrupters may also fall within the general category of attention seekers. They want to take the floor away from you so everyone will focus on them and what they have to say. People who have this habit are usually insecure and self-centered and will do whatever is necessary to direct the conversation. They may not hesitate to bring up an entirely unrelated topic in order to control the discussion, or they may be content to stay with the existing topic as long as they're the ones talking. If the interruption leads to an entirely different topic, it may signal that the person is uneasy with the subject at hand.

Sometimes it isn't clear whether someone has interrupted in an effort to control the conversation or seek attention, or simply because she's excited about the topic. If someone's body language speaks of enthusiasm, and an interruption contributes to the dialogue, there's probably no harm meant. But if someone interrupts with a comment that is completely off the topic, he is usually trying to control the conversation, either to avoid an uncomfortable issue or insert his personal agenda, or because he is bored, impatient, or anxious to move on to another topic or end the conversation altogether.

Rambling

It's important to distinguish between the rambler and the person who changes topics to control the conversation. Ramblers bounce from topic to topic and thought to thought, almost at random. Their conversations consist of many detours. Sometimes they seem incapable of pursuing an orderly line of thought for more than a few seconds.

I've found that most ramblers can't control their habit. They also don't usually have a conscious motive for rambling, except in the rare case when they may be buying time while they think of something else to say. Rambling usually reveals nervousness, confusion, insecurity, a need for attention, or a lack of mental or emotional focus. It's unusual for someone whose speech is normally coherent and organized to lapse into rambling. When that happens, look for signs of intoxication or severe fatigue or distraction. If you suspect that someone's rambling is nothing more than nervous chatter, look for the associated body language to confirm your theory.

Changing Subjects

We don't possess Mr. Spock's flawlessly logical Vulcan mind. Our conversations meander a bit—which keeps them interesting. But occasionally someone will completely change directions in the middle of a discussion. A sharp turn is usually no accident.

When you spot someone changing the subject, ask yourself whether he was previously open to the topic but suddenly went cold on it, or whether he avoided it from the moment it was first mentioned. For example, assume a young woman asks her husband when he wants to start a family. He responds, "I'd love to have kids, but do you really think we're ready? Can we afford it? Is my job secure enough?" During the conversation that ensues, he brings up his problems at work. He has effectively changed the subject. The change, however, is a natural detour and relates to the original question, which he was willing to discuss. It's just that, in his mind, his job security is directly related to whether they are financially prepared to have children.

Compare this with how the wife might interpret the response if her husband doesn't even address the issue of children but instead responds, "Don't even talk about kids. It's all I can do to keep my head above water at work," and then launches into a detailed report on his boss, stalled projects, and staffing problems. Such an immediate shift sends a very different message. Here, his wife might conclude that her husband is actively avoiding the topic.

Whether someone is wandering innocently or with the intention of avoiding a topic altogether can usually be determined from the relationship between the original topic and the new one. Are the two connected, or has this person completely changed the subject? The only way you can find out is to listen for a while. Don't attempt to redirect the person immediately, but instead explore the new topic with him and see where the conversation carries you. He may eventually return to the original subject—revealing more information in the process.

I often see this in court. A witness will give what at first appears to be a completely evasive answer. When the attorney asks him to answer the question that was asked, the witness may express surprise, and even take offense, at the suggestion that he was trying to change the subject. As the questioning proceeds, it becomes obvious that he's being candid, but felt it necessary to preface his response with an explanation, which at first blush seemed irrelevant.

If someone is allowed to answer however he chooses, and still never returns to the topic at hand, he may be trying to avoid the original subject. There's also the possibility that he is so focused on an issue of particular importance to him that he has forgotten what he was asked in the first place. If you're talking to someone who wanders, gently nudge the conversation back in the original direction and see if the resistance continues. If it does, you know the detour wasn't accidental.

Revealing Habits

People use a variety of techniques to get their points across or sidestep delicate subjects, but certain maneuvers seem to be much more common than others. Maybe it's animal instinct; maybe we come equipped with only a limited number of tricks. The habits described in this section are those that crop up most frequently in everyday exchanges. Sometimes they're unconscious, but more often they are intended to provoke a specific response. Once you familiarize yourself with them, you'll start noticing conversational nuances you were never aware of before.

Defensive Behavior

Chapter 1, "Reading Readiness," described how defensiveness can hinder our attempts to view people objectively. We can learn to curb our own defensiveness, but what do we do when we encounter it in others? Defensiveness is extremely common and can put an end to a conversation in a matter of moments. If you see someone starting to get defensive, quickly try to diffuse his anxiety if you hope to keep the conversation going.

Defensiveness arises in a number of ways, some passive, some very aggressive. Most defensiveness is entirely understandable—if you're being attacked or criticized, it's natural to defend yourself. But even so, the defensiveness has to be dealt with before a meaningful discussion can continue.

The type of defensiveness that's most difficult to identify is defensive withdrawal. Someone who withdraws when she feels attacked will usually just grow silent. Withdrawal is hard to read; it can reflect not only defensiveness but also boredom, preoccupation, pensiveness, or even agreement. Usually, the only way to find out which is to ask. The tone and content of the response should provide the answer.

On the other end of the spectrum are people who aggressively attack when threatened or challenged. "The best defense is a good offense," goes the old sports cliché, and many people live by it. The person who has adopted this coping mechanism has usually found that she can intimidate others into submission with the threat of a confrontation. A typical part of this tactic is to blame you or someone else in an effort to deflect the focus from herself. She may also try to make her "attacker" feel guilty by pointing out how hardworking she is, how much she's sacrificed, or how much personal pain she's endured on his behalf. "Where's the customer suggestion file? You said it would be on my desk by noon," a manager might ask his assistant. "Neither Susan nor Linda is in today, and I've been covering for them," the defensive assistant might reply. "I skipped my break and had to answer the phones, too. Plus I've got a cold. I dragged myself out of bed to come to work. I shouldn't even be here!" The assistant is hoping that her good deeds will outweigh the neglected file, or, at the very least, that her manager will back off rather than get into an argument.

Withdrawal and aggression are common defensive behaviors among animals. If cornered, most animals will either freeze or lash back. We humans use these strategies but have also developed a few more sophisticated methods of handling perceived threats. One of these is to profess our religious beliefs, our family values, or our high morals and ethics. Politicians are famous for this. Richard Nixon, accused in 1952 of taking illegal campaign contributions, declared on national television that the only thing he'd received was his dog, Checkers. "The kids, like all kids, love the dog, and I just want to say this, right now, that regardless of what they say about it, we are going to keep it." Nixon was trying to deflect criticism by professing the family values of a devoted and loving father.

The courtroom is a natural forum for such protestations. People accused of unethical or criminal behavior often retreat behind their religious commitment as a first line of defense. They are also loyal friends, devoted fathers, and loving husbands. They've recently found the Lord and are born again. We hear it all the time, even when the defendant is guilty of unimaginably brutal crimes.

Another uniquely human defensive behavior is to emotionally disarm the attacker by flattering him. The person on the defensive will respond to criticism by declaring, "You're really important to me, and it makes me feel awful that you're so upset about this. I value your opinion more than anyone's. I'm sorry you're so unhappy with me. If it weren't for your support, I'd be lost"—and so on until the critic is swept away on a wave of compliments. How can he criticize someone who is so fond of him? If he doesn't realize he's being manipulated, the guilt-stricken attacker may even end up apologizing for his criticisms.

Yet another sign of defensiveness is the unprovoked protestation of innocence. This is the tactic that elicited Shakespeare's "The lady doth protest too much, methinks." It's natural, and even expected, for someone to deny or explain accusations against him. But when someone launches into a long excuse for his conduct even before it has been called into question, he's acting defensively. Likewise, even if someone's conduct has been questioned, his response may be so overblown that you should wonder why.

The most common causes of defensiveness are embarrassment, anger, guilt, or being caught in a lie. But specific events aren't al-

ways to blame; some people are defensive about their very existence. Consider the stay-at-home mom who refers to herself as
"just a housewife," or the corporate employee who calls himself a
"wage slave." Even if these people believe they're doing the right
things with their lives, they apparently don't feel that the rest of the
world respects them for it. A sort of free-floating defensiveness
seeps into their personalities. The housewife may express her political opinions defensively because she fears no one will take her seriously; the wage-earner may get snippy with a car salesman who,
he thinks, isn't treating him with enough respect. If you didn't know
about their defensive streak, you wouldn't understand their behavior.

When you recognize the signs of defensiveness, ask yourself what
the cause might be. If the person is probably reacting out of guilt, embarrassment, or anger, or to cover up a lie, stick to your guns. Don't let
someone's various defensive maneuvers distract you. If she seems to
have no obvious reason to behave defensively, consider the possibility
that her attitude has more to do with her basic insecurity than with
anything you said.

Volunteering Information

Throughout, this book has made a point of how important it is to reveal information about yourself. Self-disclosure makes others feel
comfortable, encourages them to open up, and leads them to trust
you. But there's a difference between being open during the give-
and-take of a conversation and forcing information about yourself
into the dialogue, particularly at inappropriate times. Whenever
someone volunteers information, listen carefully. What they're telling
you is significant to them and should be to you as well.

It's one thing for someone to tell me she is a recovering alcoholic
if I ask her why she doesn't drink. It is quite another for a virtual
stranger to approach me at a cocktail party and volunteer that she's
drinking soda water because she's a recovering alcoholic. Likewise, if
I ask someone whether he played sports in college and he tells me he
was on the football team, I don't draw the same inferences as I would
if he volunteered this news out of the blue.

People commonly volunteer information to make a connection with you by telling you what they think you want to hear or what they believe will impress you. During jury selection, we're always on the alert for people who talk at length about how fair and unbiased they are. They're clearly trying to sell themselves, which is always cause for concern. Maybe they really are fair, but if so, it's going to be revealed in their attitudes about a host of issues. We're not just going to take their word for it. The fact that they volunteer the information only excites our suspicions. Anyone that eager to serve as a juror may be saying whatever he thinks we want to hear, not what he really thinks.

People also volunteer information as a way to cover up what they don't want to reveal. If the saleswoman volunteers how religious or ethical she is, take note. She may be proffering the information to disarm you. Anytime someone touts any aspect of their character *without being asked,* I wonder why. Volunteered personal information about someone's beliefs or habits is often inaccurate or exaggerated. These self-disclosing statements are like flashing neon arrows pointing to areas you should watch carefully.

Often people will volunteer personal information about their accomplishments. When they do, it's usually because they're feeling a bit insecure and need to brag to boost their ego, or maybe they're hoping to influence your opinion of them. There's always the possibility, too, that they're just trying to get the conversation rolling.

Another reason people volunteer information is to gauge your reaction to a sensitive subject. They want to avoid investing their energy in the relationship if whatever they volunteered is going to create a problem. Several years ago, when the AIDS epidemic was most highly publicized, a friend revealed to me that he was HIV-positive. As he did this, I watched him closely. He was not glancing down or trying to avoid my gaze; rather, he was studying me intently. It was clear he cared very much how I responded; he was testing me. Would I judge him or withdraw from him? Similarly, I've known a number of single mothers who very early in a new relationship with a man reveal that they are divorced and have young children at home. They broach the topic at the start because they know there's no future in a relationship with someone who isn't sympathetic to the burdens of single parenthood.

A similar tactic can work in business situations. For example, when meeting with new clients I frequently volunteer that I have young children at home. When I disclose this, I usually learn more about the client, who will almost always reveal whether he or she has children. I also communicate my need to schedule meetings in advance since the demands of parenthood sometimes keep me from dropping everything on a moment's notice. If I make this clear up front, the client and I can establish rules that work for both of us.

People may volunteer information about themselves to set limits, gauge your response, sell you, or create intimacy. Always keep your ears open for these statements, and give them special attention.

KEY POINTS

Identify the person's communication style: Although no one fits completely into any one category, from Noble to Reflective to Senator, all of us have a tendency to use one particular style more than the others. Noticing the markedly different ways people impart their information can earn you valuable insight.

Always ask why someone is leading you toward or away from a topic of conversation: Is it a noble effort not to brag, criticize, hurt, or embarrass you or another? Or is it an attempt to cover up a lie, self-promote, or grab attention? Or is it just a coincidence?

Be on the alert for common ways people use their answers to direct conversation:

- *Nonresponsiveness.* An isolated occurrence doesn't mean much, but if there's a pattern, there's a reason.
- *Failure to deny or explain when it would be expected.* If you're certain she heard you, her silence usually means your concerns are well-founded.
- *Short answers.* The consistent lack of a normal amount of detail should make you question "why?"
- *Long answers.* They're often used to disguise the truth, by deflection and distraction.

- *Answering a question with a question.* Unless more information is really needed to answer the question, someone who uses this technique is usually probing for information from which he can tailor a response.
- *Pregnant pauses.* Something derailed the person. It's usually the last thing you said.
- *Interruptions.* The motive may be to control the conversation, get attention, or just excitement or enthusiasm.
- *Rambling.* It's usually a nervous habit or lack of focus.
- *Changing subjects.* Watch to see if the person is abandoning the subject or just approaching it from a different direction.

EIGHT

Content

The Proof Is in the Putting

What a person *says* is always a good place to start. And once someone reveals information, if you pay close attention to what he says, you can compare and contrast it with the rest of the information you glean from the person by applying the other six Colors. The key here, of course, is getting people to open up, as discussed in chapter 2, "Learning to Ask the Right Questions—and Listen to the Answers." Once you elicit content, consider the language used and how much more word choice and topics reveal about the person.

Verbal Calling Cards

The words we choose to express our thoughts always do double duty. In addition to expressing our ideas, they reveal our perception of the world and our place in it. Certain verbal traits are particularly reliable as "calling cards," telegraphing basic data about a person's background and beliefs. Our use of slang, word themes, and titles may be so ingrained we're rarely conscious of them, which makes them all the more telling. Profanity, the final category in this section, is a more obvious and equally revealing trait. Each of these four verbal calling cards provides easy access to important information.

Slang

The term "slang" has a relatively broad meaning. It can include colloquialisms, bad grammar, and even the latest trendy sayings.

Colloquialisms can reveal whether someone was raised in a rural or urban setting and shed light on his cultural influences and socioeconomic background. Whenever I hear a particularly vivid colloquialism, I ask about its origin. The answer usually broadens my understanding of the person's upbringing and gets him talking about his past.

Rural slang is filled with colorful metaphors, whose meanings might not be instantly obvious to you if you're from another part of the country. I know a man whose parents were raised on a cattle ranch in Wyoming and who sprinkles his conversation with cowboy colloquialisms. To folks unfamiliar with ranching terminology, his slang sometimes comes across as a bit odd, if not offensive. During one business meeting with a woman senior executive, he described a harsh and disheveled woman as looking as though she'd been "rode hard and put away wet." Seeing the shock on the executive's face, he was quick to explain: the idiom refers to the appearance of a horse that has been run until it sweats, then put into its stall without being brushed. Judging by her expression, the executive understood him to mean something else entirely.

Bad grammar, also an aspect of slang, can reveal much about a person, but never assume that because someone has bad grammar he isn't smart. Poor grammar more frequently reflects someone's socioeconomic and educational background. Some of the shrewdest people I've ever known were not brought up using the Queen's English. When I encounter someone who is obviously intelligent but ungrammatical, I'm fairly comfortable concluding that his parents were not well educated and that he himself has probably had little formal schooling. But having said that, I must add that there are many exceptions to this rule. You can usually spot them by tuning in to the context in which the bad grammar is used.

First, take a look at the person's human environment, the men and women with whom he surrounds himself. Some people consciously use poor grammar so they'll seem to be just one of the guys or blend in with a certain peer group. For others, reverting to slang with family or close friends is a way of relaxing or showing familiarity.

If someone can clean up his language at will, he may be intentionally using slang to convey a particular image. Is he trying to play the

part of a good old boy or a street-smart hustler? Is he in an environment where he doesn't want to reveal his level of education or sophistication? Does he lapse into slang when he's excited and has perhaps
lost some control? The circumstances and context, coupled with the
degree to which slang is used, will reveal interesting shades of character.

Word Themes

The English language provides us with an immense menu of words
to describe what we're feeling or thinking. Most of us order up our
words from many different sections of the menu, but some people
routinely express themselves in themes.

For example, many lawyers habitually use terms of combat or aggression. Their vocabulary is sprinkled with terms like "won," "battle,"
"aggressor," "destroyed," "confronted," "maneuvered," "outflanked,"
"strategize," "in the trenches," and so on. Lawyers and nonlawyers who
use the language of battle reveal their aggressive, competitive, and
often combative nature. Nonconfrontational people do not usually use
these terms to describe a trip to the grocery store or the purchase of an
automobile.

Other people describe life in sports terminology, peppering their
speech with words such as "score," "goal-line stand," "touchdown," "at
bat," and "bottom of the ninth." Sports analogies frequently reveal a
competitive or aggressive nature. Sports talk might also reveal a person's avid interest in sports.

Every so often I encounter someone whose speech is laced with
sexual innuendo and who is quick to point out any sexually suggestive
meaning that might be given to what someone else says. Usually, this
type of person is trolling to see the other's reaction; it's an extreme
form of flirtatiousness. And it's not limited to men. While most of
the men and women who engage in this practice would be quick to
profess innocent intentions, in my experience their word themes are a
good gauge of their intentions. They use sexual innuendo because
that's exactly what's on their mind. People who are comfortable with
their sexuality, and not interested in yours, don't constantly inject sexual innuendo into a conversation.

The "honesty" word theme can also be very enlightening. People who use it preface their remarks with terms such as "frankly," "to be completely honest," or "to tell the truth." I'm always suspicious of someone who feels the need to tell me when he's telling the truth. Am I to infer that when he *doesn't* say "frankly" I can't trust him?

As always, be on the lookout for deviations and extremes. The more a person relies on word themes, the more strongly he relates to some aspect of those favored words.

Use of Titles

The way a person uses titles can reveal his geographic background, life experience, and upbringing. For example, most lawyers refer to the "ladies and gentlemen of the jury," but I work with one who always refers to the "men and women of the jury." This usage reflects his military background: military officers, who are used to addressing the troops, don't refer to them as ladies and gentlemen but as men and women.

Many Southerners address women as "ma'am" and men as "sir"; it's a characteristic of that culture. If I heard someone I knew was from southern California consistently address men as "sir," I'd assume he'd been in the military. If I knew he was from the South, I wouldn't automatically make that assumption.

A title may also be used sarcastically or to show respect—or it may be purposely ignored. I came face-to-face with this technique the first time I was asked to testify as an expert witness in a trial. The issue was whether it would be possible to select an impartial jury from members of the community where the case had received substantial media coverage. The lawyer who called me as his expert referred to me as Dr. Dimitrius throughout my examination. But when the opposing counsel began to question me, he called me *Mrs.* Dimitrius. When I'm referred to as Mrs. Dimitrius at my sons' PTA meetings, I don't conclude that the speaker is trying to downplay my professional qualifications. In the courtroom, however, that is exactly what the opposing lawyer was trying to do.

Whether the use of titles reflects cultural background, respect, or some other state of mind is usually fairly obvious if you ask yourself: "Does he routinely refer to everyone in the same way?" If so, his use of titles probably reflects his cultural background. But if not, he is probably using titles on a particular occasion to convey a particular attitude—respect, disrespect, or sarcasm. Look to the context and his accompanying body language and tone of voice to see which.

Profanity

Several years ago, I worked with a very well-respected jury consultant who by all indications but one was as prim, proper, and highly professional as you can imagine. The exception was her frequent and colorful use of profanity—she swore like a sailor. This was particularly remarkable coming from such an attractive and well-educated young woman, who socialized almost exclusively with other highly educated professionals. Profanity is more frequently used by those who are less well educated, come from a lower socioeconomic background, or work and live with others who also swear a lot. Language is greatly affected by peer pressure since we all tend to conform to the behavior of the group with whom we spend most of our time. My colleague's use of profanity, a deviation from her normal behavior, proved key to predicting her independent and rebellious nature.

Profanity is much more common in the media today than it was fifteen or twenty years ago, but it is still usually perceived as a deviation from normal polite conversation. If someone curses frequently, especially on particularly inappropriate occasions, it suggests he is socially inept, insensitive to the reaction of others, or excitable. It's not unusual for someone who uses profanity when agitated to be aggressive and have a volatile temper as well. Excessive profanity is threatening. Those who indulge in it often are aware of the effect it has on others and may use it as a method of intimidation.

Of course, most of us swear every now and then. Even someone with tremendous self-control might shout an off-color word or two when he hits his thumb with a hammer, wins the lottery, or feels some other sudden, intense physical or emotional stimulus. But when someone uses profanity regularly or inappropriately, it doesn't signal a temporary loss of control. Rather, it likely reflects more deeply upon his background and personality. *To gauge the significance of profanity, consider how often the person uses it and under what circumstances.* Don't be too quick to judge someone who occasionally lets loose with a curse word or two; rather, try to determine what inspired the outburst.

Recently, I met with an attorney whom I've known for some time. She's a petite, extremely well spoken, and very gentle person. Yet she let fly with a few choice expletives on this occasion, while describing an opposing attorney. As soon as the words escaped her mouth, she stopped and apologized. We both laughed and went on with our conversation. Her lapse told me that her anger and frustration were intense enough to have temporarily overrun her social graces. That was a significant observation because it helped me understand her intense feelings about the case and those involved with it.

The attorney's outburst also revealed that she was becoming more relaxed with me. Those who usually avoid profanity will be more inclined to let dicey words slip once they have become comfortable with you. When two people are first dating, they'll typically avoid the use of profanity like the plague. Once the couple becomes more comfortable with each other and less wary of being judged, curse words might start slipping into their conversations.

Braggadocio

"I'm not bragging—it's really true." Whether it is or not, someone who inserts self-glorifying comments into a conversation is usually doing so for a reason. Braggadocio typically takes the form of interjecting one's accomplishments when they're not relevant, name-dropping, or exaggerating one's successes.

To recount your accomplishments or mention someone's name for a good reason is not braggadocio. During a job interview, for example, it's appropriate to stress your achievements and offer impressive references. Similarly, there's nothing wrong with responding truthfully when asked "How much do you earn?" or "Were you a good student?" If you make a million dollars a year and were a straight-A student, so be it. You didn't volunteer the information but merely answered a question—so you're not bragging.

Before we examine jurors in open court, we often know a tremendous amount about them from their questionnaires. But we have few clues about who will be a braggart because the questionnaires usually don't give the jurors much chance to boast. It's always telling when, during oral questioning, someone launches into a self-aggrandizing speech about his fairness, superior intelligence, or stunning accomplishments.

Bragging is a color- and class-blind trait. It occurs in people from every walk of life and at every level of success. Sometimes they have a lot to brag about. Sometimes they don't. Sometimes what they brag about is true. Sometimes it is clearly fictional. *But over the years I've noticed one consistent trait among braggarts: they nearly always lack true confidence.* They boast because they need approval and recognition. Confident, secure people who are satisfied with their position in life don't need to steer the conversation to themselves and their achievements.

When you see this occurring, first ask yourself whether the horn-blowing was called for, as in a job interview, or volunteered out of the blue. If it was called for and handled appropriately, I wouldn't attribute any significance to it. If the boast was gratuitous, try to determine whether it was true, exaggerated, or totally false. If it was true but inserted at an inappropriate moment, you can usually interpret the behavior as a sign of arrogance, lack of confidence, or need for approval.

Claims that are greatly exaggerated or altogether false shed a very different light on the person. Someone who falsifies her achievements reveals deep unhappiness and dissatisfaction with her life, as well as an obvious lack of candor. This behavior points to a sense of inadequacy far greater than that of the person whose boasts are gratuitous but true. In rare instances, the fabrications are so extreme I have to wonder whether their maker is delusional, if only because she actually thinks people believe what she's saying.

I recently conducted a mock trial in a case that involved the design of a piece of machinery. Among the jurors was a fifty-five-year-old man who had been one of thousands of engineers with a large aerospace company for many years. He was asked about his job, and one could have inferred from his answer that he had been a key player in the development of the American space effort over the past two decades. For a number of reasons, I got the impression that he was grossly exaggerating.

After the presentation of the evidence, the jury began its deliberations. The aerospace engineer was extremely opinionated and egotistical. He quickly rejected opposing views and constantly reminded the other jurors of his vast experience with product design. Everything from his words to his body language reeked of his dissatisfaction with his life. He cut people off in mid-sentence, was sarcastic toward those who disagreed with him, and shook his head and rolled his eyes in frustration and contempt if someone voiced a view different from his. Without a doubt, this was a man who had not achieved the degree of professional success he had hoped for. The bitterness in his voice led me to believe that he would be quick to blame his lack of success on someone or something other than himself.

Ultimately, as I would have predicted, this man's opinions swayed most of the other jurors. They allowed his aggressive, boastful approach to intimidate, subdue, or persuade them. Had they been reading him correctly, they would have realized he was the last person whose lead they should have followed: he was motivated by his need to be important, not by the desire to listen to all points of view and reach a fair decision.

Exaggeration

Imagine a conversation between Little Miss Sunshine and Eeyore, the gloomy donkey of the Winnie-the-Pooh stories. Little Miss Sunshine's statements would be laced with words like "wonderful," "the best," "perfect," and "fabulous," while Eeyore's would be loaded with "awful," "horrible," "disgusting," "depressing." There would be no room for shades of gray.

We all encounter Little Miss Sunshines and Eeyores in life. Sometimes we run into someone who gets equally worked up about positives and negatives. This sort of exaggeration often signals the person is insecure and trying to be noticed. If you had a bad experience at the dentist's a few years back, she had an even worse one. If you know a great Italian restaurant, she knows the world's best. Besides being insecure, people who engage in this sort of exaggeration are often trying to control the conversation and the behavior of those participating in it. If a group of friends is pondering which restaurant to try, aren't they likely to choose the one that's "absolutely the best"? Who wouldn't shy away from a movie that is "the worst piece of junk I've ever seen"?

Some people express themselves in extremes not because they want to control others' behavior but because that's how they see life. The positive thinkers include those who are sincerely thrilled to be alive and who express their enthusiasm at the drop of a hat. But there are also people who adopt a jovial attitude in an attempt to disguise a deep disappointment with life, or in an effort to change, or at least ignore, their fate through sheer force of will. "If I act as if I'm happy, I'll be happy," they tell themselves. It can be very difficult to distinguish between the person who is truly joyful and the one who has constructed a sunny façade. Occasionally, someone who's overcompensating will let down her guard, revealing her anxiety or sadness in a passing comment or facial expression. But often, only time will tell. By watching and listening to her and perhaps asking questions, you'll eventually learn whether her cheerful disposition is genuine.

More distressing are people who are intensely pessimistic and critical. They're not happy with life and are quick to let you know it. What's worse is that they often seem to want to infect everyone around them with their own misery. There's a natural inclination to recoil from these naysayers, but I try not to. When I'm speaking with someone like this, I try to be sensitive to why he has chosen this form of communication. Is he reaching out for me to soothe his misery? Has he recently been overwhelmed by a tragic loss?

As this book has emphasized throughout, the benefits of reading people aren't limited to protecting yourself in a sometimes harsh, competitive, and dishonest world. These techniques also enable you to make the world a little better for those around you. When you understand what motivates people and learn how to listen to them, you'll be a better friend, a more effective boss, even a more compassionate stranger. So although your instinct may be to run from the Eeyores in your life, try to connect with them at least once or twice. At the very least, you'll learn a little bit more about human nature.

Ingratiating Behavior

Ingratiation is generally interpreted as blatant manipulation. The many colorful nicknames for this trait—"kissing up," "sucking up," and "brownnosing," to cite three of the tamest—testify to the contempt in which the behavior is commonly held. But there are times when people ingratiate themselves with others out of innocent motives. So before you judge someone a brownnoser, consider the context.

Someone may try to please out of a desire to make you feel comfortable, intelligent, and accepted. Sympathy is another possible motive. If you've recently gone through an ordeal, your friends may offer such utterly unconditional support that it seems they're yessing you to death. Whether or not you like the behavior, their intentions are good.

People who lack confidence in their own ideas sometimes offer unwavering support to those they admire. They are followers, too timid to make their own choices. Their actions may resemble brownnosing, but they aren't truly manipulative.

Then there are real brownnosers—the ones who *are* manipulative. They typically fall into two categories: those who ingratiate to gain a personal advantage, and those who do so to win your approval.

I recall an interview I held with a candidate for a research position at my office a few years ago. She had excellent qualifications, a pleasant appearance, and an engaging manner. But as the interview progressed, I started to get the uncomfortable feeling she was too good to be true. When I told her the job involved a lot of fieldwork, overseeing mock trials, conducting community attitude surveys, and so forth, she assured me the tasks I described were exactly what she wanted to do. When I asked how she felt about working in a small company, she said it was perfect given her temperament. No matter where my questions headed, she followed with enthusiastic answers. Either this was a match made in heaven, or the woman would say anything to get the job. I decided to find out which.

Having already established that what this young woman supposedly longed to do more than anything else was assist me with my fieldwork, I asked how she felt about the clerical responsibilities that came with the job. She was quick to respond that she loved to type, organize files, and handle phones. When I asked how she felt about the prospect of my small company merging with a large national firm, she apparently forgot that just twenty minutes earlier she'd said working in a small, informal office was extremely important to her. Now she gushed that the merger was "an incredibly exciting possibility";

she "looked forward to the opportunities it would present." She did not get the job: her ingratiating behavior was clearly a means to an end.

To determine whether an apparent brownnoser is trying to manipulate you for her own gain or just seeking approval, take a close look at her other traits. People who use ingratiation to control or manipulate will usually demonstrate some of the other controlling, manipulative traits discussed in previous chapters. They'll show signs of self-centeredness that will be absent in the person who just wants your approval. That person will tend to be quiet and unassuming, perhaps even nervous. If his demeanor, appearance, and other clues point to a passive or timid nature, he probably isn't trying to control you in the strict sense, but to gain your acceptance.

Self-criticism

The ability to poke fun at yourself is an admirable quality. We all do it from time to time. Extremely self-deprecating behavior, however, makes a powerful statement about a person's self-esteem. Whenever you hear somebody make more than one or two self-critical remarks in the course of a conversation, you should wonder why.

The first question to ask is whether the comments are meant as icebreakers or good-natured social gestures. "I'd forget my head if it weren't screwed on" is clearly a casual remark, unless the person repeats similar sentiments so often you feel compelled to respond to them. However, when an obese person says, "I'm such a pig, I can't say no to a meal," there is a lot more going on than lighthearted self-mockery.

In my experience, people who make biting self-critical remarks are very insecure and (obviously) have low self-esteem. Their motives are often complex. They may be hoping you'll disagree with them, or they may be looking for encouragement, support, help, or sympathy. Some self-deprecating comments are an effort to deliver the first strike: by addressing the topic themselves, they don't have to worry that someone else will bring it up. Some people even use self-critical remarks to put their companions at ease. By laughing at a flaw of their own, they hope to send the message that it's not a big deal to them and shouldn't be to anyone else.

How someone responds to others' remarks about her is a good test for whether she is harmlessly poking fun at herself or is truly sensitive about a particular subject. For example, if a man bristles whenever someone comments on his receding hairline and also makes self-deprecating jokes about "pitiful old bald guys," that tells me this may be a very touchy issue for him. While it may not point to overall low self-esteem, it probably indicates he feels uncomfortable about his appearance.

If a person doesn't handle others' criticisms well, but criticizes himself when you're around, it is a safe bet he's reaching out to you. People who repeatedly make such comments want a response. They are watching carefully to see whether you agree or disagree, whether you approve or disapprove of them. There are many ways to respond, but be aware that avoiding the topic altogether is in itself a response, which will probably be interpreted by them as your agreement with their self-criticism.

The Broken Record

We all have favorite conversational themes, chords we like to strum over and over again. We have stories we like to tell, good times we like to recall. Now and then, however, you'll encounter a person who returns to one particular topic with tiresome regularity, until you want to cry out, "Enough, already! I get it." Unless he's repeating himself because of a mental condition such as senility, such repetitiousness usually means one of two things. Either he is nervously trying to fill space in the conversation rather than suffer through awkward silences, or he's sending a loud, clear signal that something is on his mind, and he wants you to acknowledge it.

I saw a glaring example of this during jury selection in a case in downtown Los Angeles. One of the jurors, a middle-aged and significantly overweight woman, mentioned early in her questioning that at the tender age of eighteen she had become a grand master in a card game similar to bridge. A few minutes later, she let us know her IQ was at the "genius level." It wasn't long before we heard about her prowess at the card game again, and then another reference to her high IQ. The topic of someone's IQ rarely comes up during jury selection, and when it does, it doesn't come up half a dozen times. This woman was clearly trying to impress us with her repeated references to her intelligence. The repetition, especially when coupled with such blatant braggadocio, revealed she was obviously insecure, probably as a result of her weight, and was seeking acceptance and respect.

Whenever you encounter somebody obsessed with a particular matter, look for the reason. What is causing her anxiety, bringing her joy or satisfaction, or striking her as funny? Whatever it is, it weighs so heavily on her mind that there's no room for anything else. If you ignore it, it usually won't go away. No matter how unimportant the subject may be to you, she's crying out for you to acknowledge it. And until you do, don't expect her to focus completely on anything else.

Gossiping

"I really like Diane, but . . ." "Did you hear that Jim got fired?" "Could you believe how Joe and Mary behaved at the party last night?" Gossip is the tool of the insecure, unhappy, vicious, and manipulative. Whenever someone tries to draw me into a gossipy conversation, I wonder what she says about me behind my back.

People who love to gossip are seldom comfortable admitting it, so they often disguise their rumor-mongering as concern for others or idle chitchat. No matter how it's packaged, gossip has a few distinguishing characteristics. First, gossip is nearly always negative. Even if the person begins on a positive note, the conversation will soon degenerate into a critique. Second, the person who gossips usually wants to persuade you to her way of thinking or ferret out your opinion about the gossip's victim. Finally, the person who instigates the gossip session is often trying to boost her own ego by demeaning someone else.

The best way to figure out the motives for gossiping is to consider the target and the context. If the target is a social or job-related competitor, jealousy and resentment are frequent motives. If the topic is a mutual acquaintance, the gossip may want to learn how you feel about her, or to influence you to dislike her. Occasionally, the person who is gossiping is strictly hunting for information: gossip usually begets gossip. It's also a way for the person who knows a juicy tidbit or two to feel important and get attention.

Humor

Humor has many faces. It can be biting and sarcastic, subtle, slapstick, genuine, or insincere. It can be used to bring people closer, or to maintain distance. Scores of books have been written on the topic, and still some aspects of humor are too subjective ever to be explained fully. But a basic understanding of how it's used in communication is essential to accurately reading people.

Humor can be employed as a weapon or a shield. It can be a powerful tool of aggression, used to hurt and humiliate. It can be used to deflect criticism or defuse a crisis. People frequently use humor to disguise their true feelings; if they don't dare lodge a serious complaint, they'll toss off a humorous but pointed remark instead. As with self-criticism, humor can also be a means of self-protection. The woman who jokes about her height may be introducing the topic to guard against someone else bringing it up, or to suggest to others that she is comfortable with it.

Always ask whether humor is directed at a particular person and, if so, whether it has a critical element. If the employee who arrives late is met by a supervisor who says, "I'm glad you could join us," he should take that comment seriously, no matter how lightheartedly it was delivered. Similarly, whenever I hear someone follow a critical but humorous remark with the phrase "Just kidding," I take note. Usually, they're not kidding at all. They're just trying to disguise their message.

If I decide the humorous remark wasn't a veiled criticism, I look to the other most likely motivations:

- Does the humor redirect the conversation? If so, it may be the speaker's preferred method of getting control or attention. Or perhaps the person is trying to distract you from a subject he would prefer to avoid.
- Does the humor take a serious topic and attempt to turn it into a casual or lighthearted one? Consider whether the joke is an attempt to avoid confrontation.
- Does the humor reflect a compassionate attempt to show empathy or understanding?

- Does the humor disguise emotions the person may not want to reveal—fear, disappointment, jealousy, anger?
- Does the humor add meaning or enjoyment to the conversation? People who are happy and comfortable with life often just naturally use humor. They have no particular motive. But if this is the case, the joke will not be at someone else's expense.

By evaluating the nature of a joke (harsh or warm, for example) and gauging its impact on the dialogue, you can usually figure out the motives behind it.

Sarcasm

Sarcasm is one of the most powerful ways to communicate. Like humor, it can take various forms, but unlike humor it is rarely harmless. Nearly always, people use sarcasm to express a strongly felt opinion, belief, or emotion when they don't want to come right out and say it.

Whether I'm selecting a jury or choosing a friend, I'm always very alert to sarcasm. Cutting and harsh, or mild and funny, sarcasm says a tremendous amount about a person. It speaks of anger, hostility, bitterness, jealousy, frustration, and dissatisfaction with life. Someone who resorts to sarcastic remarks, no matter how charmingly they are delivered, is saying, "Watch out, I bite." He almost always ends up at the hard end of my personal "hardness scale."

No matter how confident they may appear, people who make sarcastic remarks rather than communicate more directly are often insecure. Confident people usually express their feelings directly. They don't need to attack from the flanks. The sarcastic person is also usually manipulative; he attempts to influence the action from the sidelines instead of approaching it head-on.

Sarcasm can be extremely hurtful. It's usually aimed at an individual rather than a group or event, which means that for nearly every sarcastic remark, there's someone who feels its sting. With very few exceptions, sarcasm is a cruel and insensitive way to get a laugh or make a point at someone else's expense. Always be alert to someone who favors this method of communication.

KEY POINTS

Watch for verbal calling cards and revealing habits: They're usually laced with meaning.

- *Slang.* Colloquialisms, bad grammar, and trendy sayings are good indications of personal background. But before you reach any conclusions about someone, look to see if she can turn it on and off at will.
- *Word themes.* Our interests, values, and temperament are revealed by the word images we favor.
- *Use of titles.* Sarcastic, respectful, or just the way someone was raised, there's often meaning behind their use.
- *Profanity.* To gauge its significance, consider how frequently it is used and under what circumstances.
- *Defensiveness.* Remember the best defense is often thought to be a good offense. Don't be knocked off the scent by someone's aggressive behavior.
- *Braggadocio.* Unsolicited boasting reflects not just the obvious arrogance, but an insincere streak as well.
- *Exaggeration.* Watch for other signs of dishonesty and low self-esteem, as one of those traits is usually at the core of this behavior.
- *Ingratiating behavior.* Brownnosers want approval, but don't assume evil motives.
- *Self-criticism.* Humility is great. But in the extreme it reflects deep insecurity.
- *The broken record.* Whatever warrants obvious repetition by someone is very important to her. Don't ignore it.
- *Gossip.* Consider it the tool of the unhappy, insecure, mean-spirited, and manipulative.
- *Volunteering information.* Unsolicited self-disclosure, especially in large doses, signals an attempt to connect, impress, persuade, brag, test, or deceive.
- *Humor.* As a sword or shield, it's a powerful tool. Identify whether it is lighthearted or cutting, and you'll be well on your way to discovering what it says about the jokester.
- *Sarcasm.* With few exceptions, sarcasm is a way to get a laugh or make a point indirectly—usually at someone else's expense.

NINE

Actions Speak Louder Than Words

Recognizing the Revealing Nature of Behavior

The McMartin Preschool trial taught me many things about human behavior. Oddly, one of the lessons that has stayed with me the longest has nothing to do with the defendants, the children, or the media circus that surrounded that trial for years. Instead, it has to do with one of the jurors, a quiet, analytical Asian man with a college degree in engineering. When we first interviewed him, he seemed the very essence of the anonymous engineer: nondescript, neat, clean clothing; bland hairstyle; quiet voice; controlled, precise mannerisms. As I watched him in the jury box and listened to his calm, intelligent responses, nothing about him suggested he'd be anything more than a quiet follower type once he got on the jury.

But his behavior toward the other jurors cast a whole new light on the man. As they entered and left the courtroom, he graciously held the door for them. He organized groups for lunch, and on Monday mornings was always the first one to ask how everyone's weekend had been. In addition to being smart, he was clearly a caregiver. Intelligent caregivers take charge. He became the foreman.

This experience reinforced just how closely we have to watch the way people behave toward others if we want to get the fullest sense of who they are. All the other factors covered in this book—appearance, body language, environment, voice, even the words people speak—must be viewed alongside their actual behavior in the real world. Life isn't just a series of one-on-one interviews between you and other individuals. In order to understand people well, you must see them in action and learn to recognize when their actions are speaking louder than their words.

Character is ultimately revealed by what a person does, not what he says. A few of the most highly evolved among us may achieve perfect consistency between what we say about ourselves and how we behave, but with most of us there's a gulf. This is by no means always sinister. Sure, there are times when people pretend to have good qualities that their actions prove aren't there. But there are also diamonds in the rough whose real beauty is hidden beneath their modest, self-effacing ways. Very often the people least likely to blow their own horns are the most loyal friends, the hardest workers, and the most dedicated parents. And it's their actions that prove it.

Honesty, compassion, confidence, egotism, commitment, and many more key personality traits can be seen in people's behavior toward you and others. Sometimes the *only* way you'll learn of certain traits is by observing people's behavior. This chapter will cover some of the most common ways important traits are revealed by actions. If the behavior matches the pattern you've already seen develop, you'll know you're on the right track. If the behavior points in a far different direction, I suggest you believe the behavior.

How People Treat Others

Unless you live in a remote farmhouse, you encounter dozens of people every day. The encounters can range from a three-hour heart-to-heart with your girlfriend to a friendly wave to the guy who lets you merge in front of him on the freeway or a nasty gesture to the one who doesn't. A bit of our character is revealed in each of these exchanges. To a remarkable degree—over time, and through the hundreds of encounters we have each week—most of us are consistent. We may put on an especially genteel face for a first date or a job interview, but eventually our real character peeps through the curtain, then boldly steps out.

As you meet new people and try to get a better sense of your older acquaintances, you have lots of opportunities to watch the way they treat other people, not just you. Three groups are especially revealing: coworkers, children, and "everyday" people.

Interaction with Coworkers

Whether it's an office tower or a gas station, the workplace is like a mini-kingdom. There's his highness the boss, the knights of the realm, and the serfs. Which is to say that unless you're at the very peak of the pile or its extreme bottom, you deal daily with superiors, coworkers, and subordinates. Those dealings are often political, and always delicate. The way people handle them reflects many facets of their character.

How a supervisor treats his employees is tremendously telling. Power is intoxicating, and many people handle it poorly. The supervisor who is kind, respectful, and friendly with his employees tends to be self-confident, compassionate, generous, outgoing, and concerned about the way others perceive him. The supervisor who treats her subordinates like servants is typically insecure, domineering, insensitive, and uncaring, not only in the workplace but in every aspect of her life. People don't flip a switch and consistently treat their employees in one way and their spouse or friends in another.

When we select jurors, one of the most important questions we ask is whether they are supervisors at work and, if so, how many people report to them. People who spend much of their time in a position of control and responsibility over others typically take those workplace attitudes home. Not surprisingly, they also often become the foreperson of the jury.

An employee's attitude toward his boss is just as revealing as the boss's attitude toward her employees. Some employees are sullen and bitter, resentful, dissatisfied with their lives, angry, frustrated, and even jealous. Others are eager to please, sometimes to the point of kissing up; that points to insincerity, a manipulative character, and a need for approval. Still others are respectful, responsive, and cooperative; that reflects security, high self-esteem, and comfort with their role in the workplace. Usually, those who are at ease with their position at work are also comfortable with their lives in general.

Pay particular attention to how people treat their peers at work. Some are supportive, helpful team players. Others seem to believe that their success at work depends on their coworkers' failure. They are unsupportive and critical; they typically don't socialize with their coworkers. The better the relationship between a person and his coworkers, the more likely that he is self-confident, comfortable with his situation in his life, and considerate. On the other hand, if he's competitive, unsupportive, jealous, and selfish at work, why should you expect him to behave any differently at home?

Interaction with Children

Children are unique objects of our attention. Some people are instantly at ease with them, while others, even if they themselves are parents, never quite get the hang of communicating with kids. It would be unfair to assume that the latter type is uptight or uncaring; to a great degree the rapport one has with youngsters is a nonelective trait. But the way people treat, and train, their own children can be very helpful when you want to gauge their values and their attitudes toward others.

I have friends whose two young sons are always included at the beginning of any dinner party. Their parents introduce them to each of the guests, who are met with an exceedingly polite "Good evening, Ms. Dimitrius," or "Good afternoon, Ms. Mazzarella." When it's time to eat, the adults withdraw to the dinner table. Meanwhile, the children enjoy something special apart from the grown-ups, who can then engage in lively, uninterrupted conversation. My friends are proud of their children and sensitive to their need to be included— but equally sensitive to the fact that many adult guests will enjoy the evening much more if dinner isn't dominated by squirming youngsters, tipped glasses, and incomprehensible descriptions of the latest video game.

I know another couple whose three young children are allowed to run wild not only through their own dinner parties but at homes where they are guests. This insensitivity to guests and hosts alike reflects egocentricity and a lack of consideration for others. It also reflects a failure to take personal responsibility.

Between these two extremes lie the rest of us. Do we caution our children not to touch objects in a souvenir shop? Do we ask them to be quiet at the movie theater? Are we playful with them? Do we include them in our conversations, rather than follow the "speak only when spoken to" approach? Affirmative answers to these and similar questions may reveal consideration, thoughtfulness, sensitivity to others, compassion, patience, and even playfulness and good humor. A negative response may reveal just the opposite. There's so much to learn, it's well worth paying attention.

Interaction with "Everyday" People

I recently went out to dinner with a friend and her new beau. She had been raving for weeks about what a kind, considerate, and engaging person he was. He had truly swept her off her feet. Within minutes of meeting him I thought, "Boy, has he got her fooled." At the restaurant, he curtly announced his reservation to the hostess without so much as a glimmer of courtesy. He proceeded to interrogate the waiter about the menu, as if he were conducting a criminal investigation, then glared at the busboy who brushed against him as he served his water. Meanwhile, he was exuding charm and grace to those of us at the table, whom he obviously deemed worthy of his attention and good humor. It was clear to me that he was a nice guy only when it served his purposes. The "little people" obviously didn't rate.

I have made the same observation about many jurors during the course of my career. It is not unusual for a juror to be polite, solicitous, and respectful to the lawyers and judges, then downright rude to his fellow jurors and to court personnel. He may let the door to the courtroom close behind him even though a fellow juror is right behind, or push through the crowd as he enters or exists the courtroom, or bump thoughtlessly against other jurors' knees as he heads for his seat in the jury box. Since assessing a person's position on the "hardness scale" is so important in evaluating character, every time I see someone act thoughtlessly or rudely, I take note.

As for the lawyers in the courtroom, very frequently they display completely different attitudes toward the judge and other court personnel. Sometimes they will be respectful and friendly to the clerk, court reporter, and bailiff when the judge or jury is present, but rude when no one "important" is watching. A lawyer's mistreatment of court personnel reveals his arrogance, controlling nature, and possibly even insecurity. It also reveals his poor judgment: in most courtrooms the judge has an excellent relationship with his staff. They are quick to report to him any abuses by the attorneys—usually during the very next recess.

Whenever I'm evaluating someone's character, I pay careful attention to how she relates to the clerk at the grocery store, the teller at the bank, the gas station attendant, the waitress at the local diner, and whoever else she meets. Does she always walk past the Salvation Army volunteer without reaching into her pocket? Is she the type of person who always writes thank-you notes and sends get-well cards or thoughtful gifts? Does she glare at the clerk who's having trouble with the cash register, or give her a comforting smile?

Truly kind, thoughtful, and confident people do not treat others in dramatically different ways depending on their mood or their perception of what someone can do for them. As a result, *watching how someone acts toward "everyday people" can give you a pretty good idea how he or she will act toward you once the bloom is off the rose of your relationship.*

Reading the Group

Certain situations are tailor-made for people-watching. In these settings you can observe how someone deals with people he likes, people he can't stand, family, coworkers, and strangers. You've been a participant in scenes like these many times, but the next time you're there, take a moment not only to watch the people around you but to read them.

The Family Dinner

In many famous films, the crucial scene takes place around the family dinner table. It's the perfect forum for drama, and it's fun and informative to watch, especially if the family isn't your own.

The family dinner can be extremely revealing, especially if it's attended by someone's parents, spouse, siblings, and children. For one thing, you can get a good feel for the person's background. As was noted in chapter 2, someone's background is a key predictive factor. How someone was raised, and by whom, will have a tremendous influence on the type of person she is. Psychologists often point out that when it comes to child-rearing, what goes around comes around: those who are raised with criticism become critical, those who are raised with love become caring, and those who are raised with encouragement become supportive. By watching how someone's parents treat her and her siblings, and how she treats them, you can get a good feel for the way she was raised and how she's likely to treat others.

A person's relationship with his spouse is also very telling. Does he expect to be waited on, or is he quick to offer to fill empty glasses, set and clear the table, and wash the dishes? Does he lead the discussion, or passively sit by and watch? Is he affectionate or distant?

The dinner table is also a good place to watch how a person treats her children. Does she draw them into the conversation? Does she keep an eye on their manners? Is she warm and affectionate? Is she relaxed and comfortable around her kids, or critical and tense? Patient or quick-tempered? Take note of the subtleties, and how the children behave toward their parents. Are they timid or confident? Polite or disrespectful?

If you spend time with the family before or after the meal, keep your eyes open. Is there laughter and playfulness in the home? Does the family sit motionless in front of the television until dinner is served, or do they chat? If so, what about? Can you spot evidence of family projects—a jigsaw puzzle, art projects, a plate of kid-decorated cookies? Are there any pets, and if so, how do the family members interact with them?

The first time you have a meal with the family of someone important to you—a prospective mate, a new friend, a business associate—you're often too nervous about the impression you'll make to notice much of what's going on. If you can summon your concentration and really look around, you'll get a priceless preview of what's in store should your relationship grow.

A Workplace, Not Your Own

I love going to my dentist's office. It's not that I have a masochistic streak that attracts me to Novocain and dental drills. It's just that I always feel uplifted in that environment. My dentist and his assistant, hygienist, and receptionist have all been together for years. There is constant laughter, joking, and friendly inquiries about the events in one another's lives. I'm inspired by the competence, good cheer, and kindness with which the people in the office interact with one another and with patients. This is how all dentists' offices would be in a perfect world.

Even before I learned more about the individual personalities in my dentist's office, I could guess a lot about them just because of the environment they have created together and the way they treat one another. The laughter tells me they're friendly, open, and don't take life too seriously. It also suggests that they're content with their jobs and with life in general. I've never heard any of them gossip about anyone. While all of them are very professional and competent, no one appears oppressed or fixed, nose to the grindstone, at his or her station. The overall feel is one of ideal equality, respect, and teamwork. In fact, if I didn't know that in a dentist's office the dentist is typically the boss, I would probably pick the receptionist as the one in charge since she's always directing traffic.

What can I tell from a workplace like this? The person whom it reflects most strongly is the dentist. He picked the staff, and he nurtures the environment. While the other members of the team are equally dedicated and cooperative, he gets credit for creating and maintaining this atmosphere because he has the most control over it. The fact that his staff has stayed with him for many years indicates not only that he's a nice person and good manager, but also that he probably pays them a fair wage. He's generous not only with his praise but with his pocketbook—an all too uncommon trait.

You can learn several important things when you enter someone's workplace. First, the atmosphere will tell you what kind of person is running the show. This can be an important clue about the person you're evaluating: Why did he choose this workplace, and this boss? Does he enjoy the atmosphere, or dread coming to work each day? Are the other workers cheerful or grouchy? Are they tired and overworked, or energetic? After sizing up the atmosphere, take a look at how your "readee" fits in. If it's a healthy atmosphere, does he appear to be contributing to it, or cynically staying on the sidelines? If it's a tense, unpleasant atmosphere, does he seem to notice and mind, or does he shrug and say, "That's life in the big city"?

When someone is willing to work in a tense, high-pressure atmosphere, it's essential that you look for reasons. For instance, many large law firms have reputations for being sweatshops. The attorneys, particularly the young ones, work incredibly long hours and have little time for themselves or their families. If the only thing I know about someone is that he works in one of these firms and is happy and satisfied there, I know he is probably aggressive, hard-charging, confident, intelligent, and strong-willed. I can also reasonably assume that his family is not his highest priority; he's ambitious and probably self-centered. Once again, there are always exceptions, but this is my bias, and it has been borne out many times as I've gotten to know people who thrive in this environment.

The Company Picnic

A company party or picnic is an excellent occasion to watch your coworkers. Maybe you see them every day at the water cooler or in staff meetings, but larger events can give you a different, and often more revealing, view. Frequently, those in attendance are so busy partying they don't spend much time people-watching. But where else can you see someone interact with his boss, colleagues, subordinates, friends, spouse, and children (other people's as well as his own)?

Watch to find out who organizes games and who joins in. Who are the socialites and who are the recluses? Do people spend their time mingling comfortably with superiors, coworkers, and subordinates alike, or do they keep to their own? How do they relate to the children present? How do they treat their spouse? Who spends time with his mate, and who abandons her in favor of other pursuits?

If you apply what you've learned from previous chapters, you'll be able to pinpoint the leaders, the followers, and the loners. You'll find out who is confident and who's insecure; who is happy and who's discontented; who is friends with whom, and who is no one's friend. So don't back out of the next company event. Go to it, watch, and learn.

The Crowded Room

If you've never gone to a party, wedding, or other big event where you don't know most people, and played the observer with the intent to read them, try it. A bash like this is a great opportunity to try to peg different types.

Find the person with the loudest voice and watch how he moves around the room. How closely does he approach the people he talks to? How frequently does he sit down with them? Does he dominate discussions? Observe the observer. Watch how she reacts when someone approaches her. See how she holds her drink, and whether she sips it nervously or takes long, slow sips as she peers over the glass across the room. Watch the line at the bar or the buffet table, and see who pushes in and who graciously makes room for others. Identify who's taking the lead by organizing activities, making toasts, introducing people, or assuring that everyone's needs are met.

This is, in essence, what we do as we pick juries. We don't just observe physical appearance, ask questions, and listen to the answers; we watch how people interact. An excellent example comes from a case in which the defendant was charged in a murder-for-hire scheme involving the Hare Krishna religion. The juror was a middle-aged, heavyset white woman. There was nothing in particular about her appearance, background, or answers during jury selection that suggested she would be sympathetic to the defendant or the Hare Krishna movement.

But she frequently looked at the defendant almost maternally with warm, kind eyes, and smiled gently whenever he looked toward her. Unlike most of the jurors, while walking in and out of the courtroom she did not give the defendant the widest berth possible, but instead seemed almost to try to engage in contact with him by walking close by.

This woman's actions told me loud and clear that she somehow connected with the defendant. And as it turned out, she was an excellent juror for the defense. In fact, after the trial she befriended the defendant.

Practiced observation like that will reveal much about the personalities you study in a crowded room. Some people will seem intent on dominating the group. They will position themselves at the head of the table, or wherever the most people are. They will be loud and control virtually any discussion in which they participate. These people, while seemingly confident, may actually be the most insecure. Undeniably, they are seeking attention.

There are also observers. They will typically position themselves at the edge of the room, where they can watch everything. They usually speak with people one on one, and while talking they continue to survey the environment. Observers may withdraw to their observation posts because they are uncomfortable in large groups. It's just as likely, however, that they are perfectly comfortable but would rather sit on the sidelines. I can usually tell which: If an observer is approached and withdraws at the first opportunity, he reveals that he's uncomfortable and has staked out his observation post for that reason. If, on the other hand, he engages in conversation for a reasonable period of time, but then graciously excuses himself to find another secluded post, he shows that he is not particularly uncomfortable with large groups but for whatever reason has chosen on that evening to remain on the sidelines.

Those who are generally uncomfortable in large groups will typically shift nervously and change locations frequently. They will avoid contact with others. They will resist when someone attempts to draw them into whatever activities are under way. I know a man who frequently seeks out a television to watch, even when he's a guest in someone else's home. Others will disguise their retreat as an excursion to look at the art down the hall or check out the landscaping in the yard. This type of reaction in a group environment may reveal a number of different things. Perhaps the person is preoccupied with other matters and simply wants to be alone for a while. He may also be very uncomfortable and trying to escape.

I know one very well-known attorney who has the disconcerting habit of looking over people's shoulders as he greets them in a crowded room. He's scanning for anyone more worthwhile on whom to focus his attention. This obviously reflects arrogance and earns him a poor score on my personal "hardness scale."

Other people will quickly attach themselves to someone and spend hours without mingling at all. Maybe these two have a lot of catching up to do. But if not, they probably feel uncomfortable in groups.

Still others will work the room, going from person to person as if prizes were being awarded to whoever shakes the most hands. Generally speaking, more confident and outgoing people will be much more sociable in large groups but won't feel the need to flit from person to person.

You never need to evaluate these interactions in isolation. The general observations I've offered here may be confirmed by physical appearance, body language, voice, and other clues. But if those other clues persuade you that the person's interaction in a crowd doesn't fit his overall pattern, you may choose to give it little weight. But make sure you add it to the mix.

Is What You See What You Get?

We'd all like to believe other people when they tell us how honest, caring, and committed they are. We may even feel a little guilty for doubting what people say about themselves, especially if they are close friends or family. Personal experience has taught us, however, that we can't always take people at face value.

A few basic characteristics are important no matter what your relationship is with someone. Honesty is usually at the top of the list. Whether you're looking for a mate or a repairman, you want to know that what you see is what you'll get. Here are a few areas to keep in mind as you're assessing what someone's really like.

Consistent Honesty

It's amazing how often a person who professes to be honest, and maybe even believes it herself, will reveal a certain level of "candor flexibility" in her everyday actions. It's easy to spot a lack of basic honesty if you keep your eyes and ears open.

Does the person call in sick when she wants to take the day off to go shopping or extend her weekend? Does she stretch the facts when she's trying to make a point? Does she acknowledge that she's late because she misjudged her schedule, or does she tell a little lie about bad traffic, car trouble, or alien abduction? Does she fabricate stories about her past accomplishments to impress others? When the clerk at the market gives her too much change, does she bring it to his attention? I watch for these behaviors, and I watch for them very carefully.

Just as we all want other people to believe we're honest, we want to believe others are honest with us. But why should we think that someone who lies to others when it's convenient or profitable won't behave the same way with us? *True honesty, like other character traits, is marked by consistency.*

If someone is dishonest with you, she'll go to some lengths to disguise the fact from you. But, astonishingly, she often won't bother to hide her dishonesty toward others! It's as if dishonesty doesn't count if it's directed elsewhere. Don't be foolish enough to think you're so different and special that no one would dream of fibbing to you. *Assume someone's exactly as honest with you as she is with others.*

Talk Is Cheap: Recognizing People's Values and Priorities from Their Choices

Life is full of choices: free time versus career success, family versus friends, commitment versus freedom. Someone's choices normally carry more weight with me than his professed beliefs. If his choices are inconsistent with his stated values, I'll go with the values reflected by the choices. *Choices reflect what a person's values are; words reflect what he wants you to believe his values are—or what he wishes they were.*

Talk is cheap. It should be tested against actions, if possible. If you want to know whether your spouse really places your marriage before his or her job, you might ask yourself how frequently dinner plans, trips to the movies, vacations, or watching the kids' Little League games are sacrificed to the demands of work. If you wonder whether you're really on your most important vendor's "preferred customer" list, don't rely on what the salesman says, recall what happened the last time a product was in short supply and he had to decide which of his many customers were going to receive a shipment. If you want to know whether your best friend still feels as strongly about your relationship as you do, set aside what she says and ask how frequently she gets in touch. Does she invite you to join her in the activities she once did? Is she now spending her free time with others?

Before you begin evaluating any given action, make certain there were no extenuating circumstances. People *usually* make choices on the basis of what they want, need, or value, but sometimes they act under duress, or out of fear, anger, or misinformation. If you hold someone strictly accountable for her choices without taking circumstances into account, you may judge her too harshly, or even be completely off target.

One, Two, Three Strikes—You're Out

How many chances do you usually give your friends and loved ones? Do the second chances really amount to tenth or eleventh chances? If so, you're not alone. But this habit can leave you involved with people who are never going to live up to your expectations. Everyone makes mistakes, but when someone does the same things over and over again, they are no longer mistakes; they are conscious choices reflecting probable future behavior. You might be justified in overlooking a single questionable action, but when the odd behavior repeats itself, that's not a coincidence. It's a compass, and it should guide your decisions.

Not long ago I couldn't suppress my urge to tell a friend just how incredibly naive I thought she was. She was dating a man who professed to want a committed relationship and assured her he was not seeing anyone else. She wanted to know whether I thought he was cheating on her.

When she told me he never allowed her to answer the telephone at his house, and that he screened calls privately while she was there, I thought, "This doesn't sound good." She then added that he'd changed his phone number several times during the four months she'd been dating him. "Even worse" was my reaction. Then I found out he often went for long walks alone—except for his cell phone! I thought: "It's getting worse all the time." She added that he was always careful to pick up his mail and tuck it away before she could see it. When she told me that he frequently went off in the evenings and declined to tell her where he'd been, I thought: "What next?" There was one more thing: when he traveled alone, he'd put the telephone in his hotel room on "Do not disturb" mode at night.

This guy was either seeing someone else, or he was a criminal. Whatever he was up to, it wasn't good. Any one or two actions might have been understandable, but there was no innocent explanation for the whole pattern.

Likewise, it may be possible for an industrious, responsible employee to sleep through his alarm once, or even on a couple of occasions. But if an employee shows up to work late several times a month, it's fair to assume that he's the opposite of industrious and responsible. If you want to effectively incorporate a person's actions into your analysis of his character, at some point you have to acknowledge what you're seeing and say, "Enough is enough."

What's in It for Me?

The interview goes something like this:

> BOSS: What I'm looking for is a team player who is going to spend his time at work worrying about the company and not focused on himself.
>
> APPLICANT: I've always been a team player. I believe if you remain focused on what's best for the team, everything else will take care of itself.
>
> BOSS: Do you have any questions about the company or the responsibilities that come with the job?
>
> APPLICANT: Well, I was curious about how long it would be before I'm eligible for a vacation, and how many weeks of vacation I would get each year.

Putting aside that the boss hopelessly tainted the first response with very poor questioning, this applicant has revealed a "What's in it for me?" personality. The true team player wouldn't have focused immediately on himself. There is nothing unusual about wanting to look out for your own interests; we all have a natural instinct for survival. In fact, someone who constantly sacrifices her own interests for others and becomes a doormat is showing very little self-esteem. But some people take self-interest too far, steadfastly pursuing their own goals to the exclusion of everything and everyone else.

This type of person keeps track of favors and never gives one without expecting at least as much in return. He pursues personal opportunities at the expense of family, friends, and coworkers. Frequently the "What's in it for me?" type is critical of others and jealous of their success. Oddly, he is often the one who most loudly proclaims his commitment to the team. The last thing he wants to do is admit to his selfishness: to do so would defeat his primary goal, which is personal gain. Moreover, many "What's in it for me?" types seem oblivious to the fact they possess this trait, or else they write it off as assertiveness.

Spotting a "What's in it for me?" person is relatively easy. Does the individual ever give up something important to him without exacting some kind of payment in return, emotional, financial, or other? When he hears of a good opportunity, whether it's tickets to a play or a chance to become involved in an interesting project at work, does he try to hoard or trade on the information, or does he attempt to include others in his good fortune? Is he always looking for an angle, asking questions that relate to how he might benefit from a situation? If you notice a pattern like this, you're probably dealing with a "What's in it for me?" personality.

Remember, level of compassion is among the key predictive traits. "What's in it for me?" people are not usually considerate or compassionate. They may pretend to be, in order to achieve their objectives, but their concern is usually only for show. The "What's in it for me?" person tends to be selfish, jealous, insecure, petty, excessively competitive, and egocentric.

When I am selecting a jury, I make note whenever one of the jurors expresses inordinate concern about such things as the number of days he'll need to be off work, whether he can get a note for his employer excusing him for a full day even if he served only half a day, and whether lunch is provided. This person is not focusing on his opportunity to participate as a citizen-judge. He's concentrating on what's in it for him. As a juror, he's likely to be closed-minded and opinionated. I almost always suggest he be excused.

Performance Under Fire

It's relatively easy to be kind, generous, gracious, and witty when all's right with the world. It's a lot more difficult when you're in crisis, under stress, ill, or otherwise tested physically or emotionally. Some psychologists believe that only a thin layer of socialization prevents our id—the animalistic, instinct-driven child within us—from grabbing what we want and throwing tantrums when we don't get our way, just as we did as little children.

Working in the judicial system has given me the chance to see how people react under extremely stressful circumstances. Some rise to the occasion, the internal animal reined in by self-control, manners, and strength of character. Others break down, go ballistic, or lose all sense of ethics and become abusive and dishonest. You don't know how someone will take the heat until you see her perform under fire.

In the military, those who perform well under fire are recognized and promoted. In business, the dispatcher who calmly meets the crisis presented by a large and unexpected order is equally revered by her boss. In private life, the man who suffers financial or personal loss without blaming others and with honesty, dignity, strength, and a resolve to overcome adversity and move forward should also be respected and admired. Most of us don't weather the storm so nobly.

It's tempting to excuse bad behavior by attributing it to stress, illness, or temporary anger. Sometimes these excuses are valid. But by the same token, it's life's highly charged situations that reveal a person's strength of character. If you have the opportunity to be with someone who is in a state of crisis, stress, or illness, watch him carefully. His actions may not tell you exactly how he'll behave in everyday settings, but you *will* learn how he's likely to react when similar pressures surface in the future. That's invaluable information if you'll be depending on the person either at work or in a personal relationship. My friend's mother used to tell her, "Never marry a man until you've seen what he's like sick, stressed, and angry." It's good advice.

"That's Not Like Him"

This book has emphasized throughout that any deviation from the norm is worth noticing. People are creatures of habit: they develop routines, have a certain repertoire of responses to life's daily challenges, and tend to act the same way over and over again. When someone's behavior deviates dramatically from usual, there is almost always a reason. Occasionally, the deviation can be chalked up to one of the exceptions to the rules discussed in chapter 11. But more often the deviation has specific significance. Even if the person denies its importance, you should take note. The deviation may be the first sign that a major change is about to take place.

For example, let's assume a coffee salesman always calls on Le

Coffee Beanery on the first day of the month and receives its order on the spot. Then one month when the salesman shows up, the manager says, "I'll get back to you." While it may be tempting to take the manager at his word, chances are that something's up. Is the Beanery having financial problems? Is the manager talking to another supplier? Is he thinking about leaving the company and thus not tending to business as usual? Whatever the explanation, the fact that there has been a deviation from the norm is significant, even if the manager says, "Don't worry, everything's fine."

I'm not suggesting there's a sinister reason whenever someone's behavior deviates from normal practice. Perhaps when your close friend declines to go on your customary Saturday morning walk, it's because she's just not feeling well. So don't be paranoid—just alert.

People Do Change—Sometimes

An entire generation of hippies in the 1960s transformed itself into the yuppies of the 1980s. The pot-smoking free-love flower children put on their three-piece suits and Rolex watches and jogged to their Wall Street offices.

People change, particularly over long stretches of time. But there's a difference between the decades-long evolution of a personality and the sort of dramatic changes we often wish we could inspire in certain friends or acquaintances. In the typical situation, someone fervently wants his or her mate to change overnight—to be more committed to the relationship, a better parent, more romantic, or harder working. Many psychologists will tell you that anyone can change "if he really wants to." But how can you tell whether someone really has changed, and whether that change is permanent?

First, consider how long someone has behaved in a way that reflects specific beliefs. Back to the hippie-to-yuppie example: a person who spent four years in a hippie phase at Berkeley is less likely to retain those values than someone who spent twelve years living in a commune. *The longer a person engages in a particular type of behavior, the more likely it reflects a core belief or quality, not just a temporary phase or mind-set.*

Another important criterion is how recently the person exhibited the behavior. If I find out that thirty years ago a juror helped his fellow students take over the dean's office, but that since then he's lived a fairly "establishment" life, I don't conclude he'll be antigovernment. But if I find out he picketed the governor's mansion last year, I'll assume he still feels a certain amount of hostility, or at least suspicion, toward the government. *The further in the past an action took place, the less significance you should give it when predicting future behavior.*

If a person's past actions conflict with the way you're reading him today, you should consider how long it took the change to occur and why. Some people really do change their behavior practically overnight, but there's usually a compelling reason: alcoholics stop drinking, abusers quit abusing, some sinners really do find religion. Most often, however, genuine change is an evolutionary process. It takes time. For that reason, when you evaluate someone who has dramatically changed his behavior, try to find out why he changed and how long the process took.

It's natural to want to give people the benefit of the doubt and believe they won't repeat whatever unpleasant deeds they've done. But such generosity can be costly. If you want a clear-eyed view of somebody, temper your goodwill with a little healthy skepticism. Ask yourself:

- How long did he engage in the behavior?
- How recently did he engage in the behavior?
- If he changed his behavior, did he do so overnight or was it an evolutionary process?
- Why did he change?

Why Did You Do That?

Most traits and behaviors are fairly easy to understand once you start paying attention and have learned what to look for. Those discussed in this section are no exception. Why does your girlfriend make promises she doesn't keep? Why is your assistant avoiding a simple task that someone with half her abilities could polish off in an hour? What should you make of "preachers"—those annoying folks who feel compelled to lecture you on everything from exercise to parenting to financial planning? What about people who make a big deal out of every act of kindness they perform? Why does money sometimes inspire grand gestures—acts of stunning generosity or appalling chintziness? Finally, what about excuses? Is it possible to tell a sincere apology from an empty one? All of these actions command your attention, and all of them can teach you something useful about a person.

Unkept Promises

We all make commitments we don't keep. We say we'll follow up on that customer order we missed yesterday, and we don't get around to it. We promise to call someone back later in the day, or to stop by and visit soon, and somehow it just doesn't happen. Most of the time we have every intention of following through on our promises, but life interferes. A child gets sick, the car breaks down, or we simply forget. That's normal, and if it happens only now and then, it doesn't mean much.

However, when someone consistently forgets, has "something come up," or neglects commitments, it does mean something—usually, that she says what sounds good at the moment without thinking or caring about whether she'll be able to deliver. This doesn't necessarily mean she's dishonest or has some evil motive. She may just not consider what it will take to keep her promise. But whatever her motive, you can't count on her—and you shouldn't expect her to change.

Some promise-breakers do have an evil motive. They tell you whatever will get them what they want, then keep the promise only if it's convenient or beneficial. Sometimes they have no intention of following through. They're just saying what they need to as part of some larger strategy to achieve their personal objectives. The trick is knowing the difference between the person who makes a promise without thinking it through and the one who makes a promise with no intention of keeping it.

When evaluating a promise-breaker, I find it helpful to ask four questions:

• Did something unanticipated happen that explains why the person didn't follow through?

- Was the promise made quickly—perhaps too quickly for the person to think it through?
- Is this the type of promise the person has made and broken frequently in the past?
- Did this person have any reason to pacify me with a promise he or she had no intention of keeping?

Someone who breaks her promises frequently but seems to have nothing to gain by it is probably just a people-pleaser who finds it difficult to say no. Once you realize this, don't expect her to keep her promises, but don't judge her too harshly. But if you can identify some selfish reason for her to have made a commitment and failed to keep it—and again, if it happens frequently—watch out. Such consciously misleading behavior points to a self-centered, insensitive, and dishonest character.

Sometimes What You Don't Do Speaks Louder Than What You Do

If you've ever gone to one of the many clinics on how to reduce stress in your life, you probably received the following advice: make a list of all the tasks you've been avoiding and, one by one, complete them. It's very stressful to avoid duties or neglect your commitments. People normally put up with the stress of putting things off only when they find the task even more unpleasant than the stress.

The things people avoid can be extremely revealing. Of course, there are a lot of chronic procrastinators around who put off virtually everything. But when someone who's usually reliable stalls like a mule over a particular job, especially when it would make a lot more sense for him to simply do it, it's important to look for the cause.

First, before you assume that someone is purposefully avoiding a task, make sure there is no other explanation. Maybe she's just approaching the job in a roundabout way or is overwhelmed by other tasks and not specifically avoiding anything. If, however, the circumstances point toward intentional avoidance, ask yourself what the reason could be. It is usually because she

- lacks confidence and fears failure
- is uncomfortable about doing the task but unwilling to acknowledge that

- is embarrassed
- is offended or put off by some aspect of the task
- is not getting along with the other people involved in the task
- is not personally interested or motivated
- is trying to avoid revealing something that will be disclosed if she acts
- is trying to avoid confrontation

In a fraud case I worked on a few years ago, the passive partner in a restaurant business suspected that the partner who was actually running the restaurant did not properly account for all income and expenses. He asked for an accounting and got a lengthy response detailing the history of the eatery and all of the managing partner's efforts. The response also recounted the restaurant's past successes, included glowing newspaper reviews, and predicted even greater glories in the future. But lo and behold, it did not include the only thing the passive partner wanted: an accounting.

The managing partner's evasiveness only increased the passive partner's curiosity and resolve. Why hide the ball? After a lengthy battle, the passive partner eventually obtained all the pertinent records. Not surprisingly, he found the managing partner had been skimming for years.

In court and in everyday life, I've found that if I know what someone is actively trying to avoid, I can learn much about how she is thinking and feeling. If an employee is putting off a project, odds are she feels overwhelmed or intimidated by it, does not want to deal with the other people involved with it, or is bored with it. But (unless she's a habitual procrastinator) there will be a particular reason. Likewise, if a man has promised his girlfriend that he'll ask his old flame to quit calling him, but he never seems to find the right time or opportunity, there's a reason. He may be embarrassed or offended by the request, or still attached in some way to the old girlfriend. In these cases, as in most, once you've realized the person is avoiding the task, you'll be on your way to unearthing the reason.

Preachers

Some people are quick to tell you what you should think, how you should feel, and how you should behave. They may tout a strong work ethic, aggressiveness, frugality, compassion, attention to detail, or just about anything else. They deliver their message with such intensity it seems reasonable to assume that they possess whatever value it is they're advocating.

Unfortunately, many people preach values that are totally foreign to them. Preaching goodness does not make someone good; preaching hard work does not make him diligent; and preaching compassion does not make him kind. His actions do. Regardless of the passion with which someone delivers a sermon, and despite the fact that he might genuinely believe he practices what he preaches, don't be fooled. When evaluating someone's character and attempting to predict his behavior, focus on actions, not words.

And whether or not someone seems to practice what he preaches, I always wonder why he felt the evangelical urge in the first place. Is he "selling" himself? Trying to control me? Or just rambling to get attention? What is important to keep in mind is that the preacher always has an agenda. If you want to understand him better, look hard for his motive. You'll usually find it, and when you do, you'll find another important clue about him.

Why All the Fanfare?

I was sitting in a small coffee shop one night when I heard a man proudly announce, "This one's on me." I looked up and saw a well-dressed couple in their early fifties. He had his arm rigidly around her waist in a nervous but excited way that indicated they were on a first or second date. Apparently afraid she hadn't heard his generous offer the first time, he turned to her again and with a reassuring nod of his head, repeated, "This one's on me." True to his word, he sprang for her coffee. I wondered, "Why all the fanfare over a cup of cappuccino?"

I see fanfare not just in personal relationships but in all areas of life—in the man who makes a big fuss when he picks up the check, instead of quietly slipping the waiter his credit card; the boss who parades around the office at bonus time handing out checks as if his employees, after kissing his ring, should bow deeply as they back out of the room; and the woman who is sure to let her friend know just how inconvenient it was to run an errand for her.

When someone insists on making a big deal out of something he does for you, he is sending a message: "I have just done something nice for you. I should be recognized for it. You should be grateful, and you should do something nice for me in return." It's a way to give with strings attached. In some cases, people aren't satisfied with the attention they receive at the time, and continue to remind you afterward of what a generous gesture they made or how much they sacrificed.

The person who insists on fanfare feels he needs to buy your affection, and thinks he has. He's insecure and doesn't believe you'll appreciate him properly if left to your own devices. To ensure your gratitude, he makes certain you realize you're indebted to him. When you repay the debt, you'll prove how much you care.

Now consider those unassuming people who quietly pick up the check, go out of their way to run an errand for you, fill in for you in a pinch at work, bring you chicken soup when you're ill—all without asking for any recognition, let alone payback. Even when you thank them, they're quick to remark, "It was nothing!" They are not trying to win or buy your approval. Their actions spring from a generous and caring nature, and they're confident enough of their own worth and their relationship with you not to worry about how much you appreciate them.

The next time someone does something nice for you or someone else, watch him. As a gauge of confidence, self-esteem, and a caring nature, the fanfare test is very reliable.

Big Spenders and Scrooges

A few years ago, I worked on a case in which a dispute arose between the beneficiaries of an elderly woman who had recently died. The woman was partially blind and lived a very isolated and simple life in the same small house she had called home for twenty-five years. When she went to the market, she bought what was on sale. If she could use a coupon as well, even better. Her friends and family knew she'd bought a few apartments over the years, and that after her husband died almost twenty years earlier she had managed the apartments herself. They thought this was more of a hobby than a profession.

She left an estate worth more than $33 million.

A much more common personality type is the big spender. Whatever the big spender does, he does first-class: buying expensive clothes, eating at expensive restaurants, staying only at five-star hotels, or always flying first-class. Big spenders are not always rich. People with modest incomes may be big spenders in relative terms. They're the ones who always buy the most expensive gifts, drive cars that cost more than their colleagues', and flaunt wardrobes and jewelry that likely eat up half their salaries.

What moves people to such extremes—frugality to the point of self-sacrifice, or extravagance to the point of financial ruin?

Most people who are frugal to a fault have been poor at some time. As was pointed out in chapter 2, socioeconomic background is a key predictive trait, likely to have a huge impact on a person's outlook and behavior. Many people saw their worlds, or their parents' worlds, crumble during the Depression. These people lived for a decade without any luxuries. For many of them, any personal extravagance is unacceptable. It violates their need to store acorns for the winter that is sure to come again. Some extremely frugal people also have very low self-esteem and don't feel they are worth spending money on.

The big spender often shares the frugal person's low self-esteem but expresses it in the opposite way. He has a need to impress people, and therefore when he does spend money he likes to make sure everyone knows about it. It's vitally important to him to be seen as a "first-class person" because, in his mind, being first-class buys him the credibility and respect that an unassuming lifestyle will not. Many big spenders cannot truly afford their extravagances but feel compelled to keep spending because they think it ensures them the approval of others.

A useful test in evaluating why someone is a big spender is to ask whether she pampers herself the same way whether or not others are aware of it. Most big spenders will be quick to explain that they simply enjoy the finer things in life and can afford them. If they quietly treat their mom to a trip to Hawaii every year, have an expensive coin collection no one knows about, or engage in any other pricey, but private, activity, their self-indulgence does not reflect a need to impress others. But if they spend only when others are looking, they are trying to buy more than just things. They're purchasing approval. Knowing that about them is a great asset when you're trying to predict their behavior.

"I Can't Help It—It's How I Was Raised," and Other Common Excuses

It's rare to hear an honest, heartfelt apology. What we most often get after someone has behaved badly is a halfhearted "Sorry," followed by an excuse: "I was angry" (or "drunk," "upset," "not myself," "confused," "hurt," "jealous"). "I didn't know any better." "It's just the way I am." "The devil made me do it."

Our behavior, including our bad behavior, is usually a matter of choice. When someone offers an excuse for what was clearly voluntary behavior, I always try to determine whether the excuse suggests that the behavior was an isolated incident that won't be repeated. It's often a very tough call to make. If you reject someone's excuse, there may be a confrontation; ultimatums may be issued, and conflict can erupt. So before you decide someone's excuse doesn't fly, ask yourself the following:

- Does the behavior reflect a lapse of judgment, a temporary loss of inhibitions, or a more deep-seated lack of fundamental values?
- Did the behavior continue for a long time?
- Did the person attempt to cover up the behavior?
- Was the behavior inconsistent with the person's usual pattern?
- Was the behavior entirely voluntary, or was there some other factor at play?

If someone has control over his behavior, his excuses are usually less persuasive. It's one thing for an employee to explain that he was late to work because an accident on the freeway closed the traffic lanes for an hour. He couldn't help that. It's quite another to blame his tardiness on running out of gas. He could have avoided that with a little advance planning. The same can be said of most excuses. Someone who fails to take responsibility for his own mistakes or bad judgment, hiding behind lame excuses, isn't being honest, either with you or with himself. Listen carefully. *The quality of a person's true character is often closely tied to the excuses he favors.*

The Golden Rule of Human Behavior

"Do unto others as you would have them do unto you." The Golden Rule, with a few minor modifications, is the last secret shared in this chapter. Here's the revised version: *"Others do unto you as they expect or want you to do unto them."* People want to see themselves reflected, and therefore validated, in those around them.

We all want to have a good image of ourselves. As a result, we tend to assign the most importance to whatever strengths we have and to devalue our weaknesses. Highly intelligent but less attractive people will generally value intelligence over looks. Athletes will value physical prowess. Artists will value taste. Those who pride themselves on being prompt will value punctuality in others. The hardest workers in the office will value effort over results, while those who are able to achieve their goals without much effort will place more importance on the end product and award little credit for how hard someone works.

In every aspect of life, the equation is remarkably reliable. If you know someone who loves to give flowers, you are probably safe in assuming the one gift she'd really like to receive is—you guessed it—flowers. If she likes to say "I love you" at the end of each phone conversation, she wants to hear you say it, too. Keep this simple principle in mind, and you'll be well on your way to understanding what others want and expect from you.

KEY POINTS

Remember, character is ultimately revealed by what a person does: How someone acts reflects his true values. His words, if inconsistent, tell only what he wants you to believe or wishes his values were.

Focus on how someone behaves toward others: True character is marked by consistency. People who are truly honest, compassionate, and kind won't just behave that way toward those who have something they want. Notice how they relate to "everyday people." And don't expect them to act any differently toward you once the bloom is off your relationship.

We all make mistakes: But repetitive behavior isn't a "mistake." Don't blindly accept excuses. Recognize repeat behavior for what it is—a clear sign of a person's character.

People do change—sometimes: To gauge the chances that change is real and permanent, ask:

- How long was the behavior set?
- How recently did it change?
- How quickly did it change?
- What motivated the change?

Look for patterns of behavior: Identify patterns such as:

- *Selfishness.* We all have needs, but someone who always asks first, "What's in it for me?" tends to be selfish, egocentric, jealous, insecure, petty, and excessively competitive.
- *Performance under fire.* We all have our breaking points. But remember, it's life's highly charged situations that reveal a person's strength of character.
- *Unkept promises.* Sometimes their motive is evil, sometime's it's not; but whatever the motive, don't expect to be able to rely on them.
- *Avoidance.* Sometimes what someone doesn't do is as important as what she does.
- *Preaching.* Preachers always have an agenda—persuasion, control, attention. But don't assume they always practice what they preach.
- *Fanfare.* It's a sure sign of insecurity. As a gauge of confidence, self-esteem, and a giving nature, the fanfare test is very reliable.
- *Spending habits.* Some people become scrooges, others big spenders, but any extreme in spending habits usually arises from deep-seated insecurities.

Question why someone has deviated from a set routine: The more consistent the habit, the greater the significant of a change in the routine.

Remember the golden rule of human behavior: "Others do unto you as they expect or want you to do unto them." People want to see themselves reflected, and therefore validated, in those around them.

TEN

Environment

Seeing People in Context

Imagine you're a contestant on *The Sherlock Holmes Show*. You and your fellow contestants are left alone in someone's office and given ten minutes to spot as many clues about him as you can. The object of the game is to test your powers of observation and deductive reasoning. When your time is up, you will be asked to tell the audience as much as possible about the man who works there.

From the photographs on the desk, you learn that he's married to a young woman and has two children, a boy about ten years old and a girl about six. You also notice that some of the photographs were professionally taken at a pricey studio. This suggests the man is a touch extravagant and is very proud of his family. In one of the other photographs, you see the family skiing. In another they're at the beach. He must be active and athletic.

You also see a diploma showing a degree in psychology from a local university. A small paperweight bearing the logo of the local chamber of commerce—this suggests that he is civic-minded—sits atop a tidy stack of papers. The rest of the environment is equally orderly. He is organized and neat. In one corner are several college social science textbooks. Maybe he's a college professor. Brightly colored modern artwork adorns the wall and tastefully complements the polished Danish modern furnishings. He is stylish, trendy, and cares about the impression he makes on others. By the time you have examined these and the dozens of additional clues available in the room—from the color of the walls to the type of pen he uses—you almost feel you know the man.

By the time you return to the studio, you have gathered so much information you're confident the audience will gasp with amazement at your incredible powers of observation and deduction. Surprisingly, each of the other contestants has performed at least as well. What is even more remarkable, all of you have reached very similar conclusions about the man. In this artificial situation, motivated by competition, you all paid careful attention. The results speak for themselves.

Now back to reality. How much information did you gather from the environment the last time you visited someone's home or office for the first time? Did you notice the photographs, their subject matter and quality, their frames? Did you note any distinctive characteristics of the knickknacks or furnishings? Did you give any thought to how the decor, the arrangement of the furniture, or other features of the environment reflected the person's personality, values, or life experiences? If you are like most people, you probably paid little attention. With today's heavy reliance on e-mail, some people don't even know where their coworkers' offices *are,* much less what they look like. It's just as likely that you haven't given much thought to the image your own home or office projects to those who walk through your doors. But to people who know what to look for, your environment is a rich source of information about your personality, values, and lifestyle.

A person's environment can reveal clues about her job, education, hobbies, religion, culture, marital and family status, political affiliation, friends, priorities, and wealth. Perhaps more important, environment can confirm, cast doubt upon, or deepen what you've already learned about someone from her personal appearance and body language—whether she is flamboyant or conservative, practical or extravagant, egotistical or humble, neat or messy, trendy or traditional, and much more.

Environmental clues are easy to see—they're just sitting there. And most of us enjoy exploring other people's habitats anyway. As children we may have been taught not to be snoopy, but curiosity is just part of human nature. Besides, you don't have to poke around in somebody's sock drawer to learn about him.

Because so much can be learned from someone's environment, try to stay focused when you enter it, particularly when you're first getting to know the person. Above all, you're looking for the patterns that will reveal his or her true nature. As always, pay special attention to deviations, extremes, and appropriateness.

We spend most of our time either at home or at work. It's not surprising that both environments can be extremely revealing. You will get the most complete picture of an individual only if you have some exposure to both and can compare them. Our workstation, office, company vehicle, or locker tells a story. But our home may say something very different since most of us have more control over it than over our workplace. A book on modern art would probably be a less revealing clue in your insurance agent's waiting room than it would be in his den at home.

Any disparity between the image someone projects in public and what is revealed in a more private environment can be an eye-opener. For example, you can learn a lot about a man if his car and the clothing he wears to work are expensive, stylish, and immaculately maintained. But you'll have a very different picture if you also know that his house is modest, messy, and not at all stylish. If you discover that he seldom invites people over, you might assume he places a high priority on impressing others: he has chosen to devote his money and attention to aspects of himself that other people will see regularly. The fact that he's perfectly comfortable spending his private time in a modest, disorderly home underscores the likelihood that he's concerned with appearances rather than just fond of the finer things in life.

You would learn even more about him if you met his wife and two children and found that their wardrobes weren't as snazzy as his. This would suggest that he prefers to spend his money on himself, not his family. You might conclude that he's self-centered and even selfish.

This chapter will describe how to learn more about someone from his workplace, his home, and even his car. It'll reveal which aspects of these environments are most meaningful. You'll also learn the potential significance of where someone chooses to meet with you. And you'll find out why the human environment—the company we keep—is so telling.

Reading the Workplace Environment

Knowing how to read your colleagues' work spaces can clearly help nurture your on-the-job relationships. From environmental clues, you can learn who has tastes and values like your own, determine which coworkers are most likely to be well-organized and reliable, and perhaps even conclude who is committed to the job and who is merely marking time there. But reading the workplace environment of those who are *not* your coworkers comes in handy, too. Many of our first encounters with people—your pharmacist, your mechanic, the principal of your child's school—occur in their place of business. What a person has chosen to do for a living, and what her environment is like, provide many clues about her personality, which you can evaluate along with her appearance and behavior.

The Workplace Neighborhood

If you hold a job, you don't usually have a say in where your company's offices are, but you do have a choice about where you live. Someone who buys a condominium downtown to be close to work may reveal a lot about himself, particularly if he has children and living in the suburbs is an option. In the suburbs, the children might have more opportunity to play outdoors and participate in other activities. But with a short commute, Dad can spend more time at work. If I knew nothing about a person except that he'd moved his family downtown so he could be close to work, I would wonder whether he is a workaholic; derives personal satisfaction more from his work than from his family; and is self-centered and ambitious. This is a very harsh judgment, and I wouldn't act on it in any way unless I was able to gather enough information from other sources to validate it. After all, it could be that he and his wife agree that the city's cultural opportunities are more important for their children, and that a shorter commute will leave more time for Dad to spend with his family.

If someone is self-employed, the location of her workplace can be much more telling. For example, most successful lawyers in large cities have offices on the top floors in downtown buildings. When I encounter one who has chosen an alternative, such as an old Victorian house in the suburbs close to home, my people-reading antennae begin to wiggle. I can't help but consider all the possible reasons she might have chosen this office location:

- The location is closer to home and family: family is important to her.
- She likes to renovate old buildings: she's active and creative.
- She likes the relaxed atmosphere of a smaller building in a less congested area: she's informal and unpretentious.
- She likes having an unconventional office: she's a freethinker who wants others to know it.
- Owning this small building is less expensive than renting space in a skyscraper: she's frugal and practical.
- She's looking for an investment, not just rental space: she plans ahead.

Before I spent too much time speculating, though, I would simply ask. Let's say she responded as follows:

I'm shifting my focus. I've decided to cut back on my general trial practice and devote a good portion of my time to representing parents and children in divorce and custody cases. This house is a lot more appealing to that type of client. There's a backyard where the kids can play, and a spare room with toys and videos. There's also plenty of street parking, so parents don't need to hassle with a big parking garage and elevators while they've got their kids in tow. It's casual; my clients feel comfortable here.

This would tell me a tremendous amount about her. It would reveal compassion and sensitivity to her clients. Moreover, it indicates a major shift in her life goals. What inspired this shift? Was she, or someone close to her, involved in a custody battle? Or had she reached some milestone that resulted in a reevaluation of her priorities? These issues are extremely significant when sizing someone up.

The neighborhood a person chooses for his or her work can be trendy, practical, inexpensive, functional, or showy. Often, the neighborhood reflects the business or clientele: a fledgling apparel designer would probably set up shop near the garment district, and a marine carpenter near the marina. In those instances, the person's choice of locale is primarily a practical one, but you can still make note of whether the establishment is strictly no-frills, or fancy and upscale, or somewhere in between. The person who has chosen the more luxurious route, particularly when he doesn't need fancy digs to attract business, is making a statement. Scenic views, spaciousness, or comfort may be important to him, but it's more likely that he's motivated by the image this more prestigious location projects. The choice indicates a certain level of success, but it also can reveal a person's need for approval, arrogance, self-centeredness, extravagance, or impracticality. On the other hand, the person who chooses a modest location, particularly if he could afford a more luxurious one, may be revealing confidence, practicality, frugality, and self-esteem that doesn't depend on outward appearances.

Office Props

Movie set designers add props to the background of every scene to provide context and emphasis to the actors' words and gestures. In real life, most of us select the props that surround us. And these objects are often much easier to read than nuances of body language or the cut and color of someone's hair.

Workplace props offer wonderful browsing for the attentive people-reader. Space is usually limited, so you're less likely to be overwhelmed with visual information than you would be at his home, and what you do see is more likely to be there for a reason. The workplace is sometimes a mini-replica of a home, with many of the same elements squeezed into a few revealing items. But someone's shop or office may also contain clues a home lacks. Away from the influence of spouse or family, some people more freely express themselves. This is especially true if the person's mate makes most of the decorating decisions at home.

The following list includes items most frequently found in someone's workplace. (It's not as long as it may seem—you'll need only a few minutes to visually register these items.) How often have you really thought about what such props might tell you about someone? If you make note of them the next time you visit someone's workplace, you will be amazed at how much information you'll accumulate.

WORKPLACE PROPS

artwork

blotter/desk set

books, magazines, and other
   reading material

bookshelves

business cards/holders

calendars

clocks

coffee/tea service

collectibles

computer

corkboards and the items they
   display

diplomas

display case and contents

exercise equipment/sports gear

fax machine

flowers

furniture

gym bag

hat stand

knickknacks

lamps

liquor bottles or flasks

mirrors

mugs (especially with logos or
   quotes printed on them)

musical instruments

paperweights

pen sets

phone

photographs

plants

plaques

posters

radio

refrigerator

Rolodex

television

tools

trophies

umbrellas

The Most Revealing Items in the Workplace

Although every item on the list can provide important information, certain objects consistently reveal more than others. Those described below can be found in most workplaces. You'll notice that they are all easily replaceable and relatively inexpensive. For this reason, they are usually a better indication of a person's current state of mind than permanent fixtures such as a desk, computer, chairs, and carpeting. Many people have no choice when it comes to those more expensive and permanent items anyway, and those who do frequently opt for the style associated with their job. For instance, an attorney may favor costly traditional furnishings at the office, and a hairdresser may select clean, functional, comfortable decor at the salon—even though both prefer Danish Modern furniture for their homes.

Office furnishings, then, usually won't reflect an individual's personal taste or priorities as well as photos, calendars, and the other items listed here.

These items have one other thing in common: they are all available in a nearly endless assortment of styles. Consequently, a person's choice is going to make a fairly specific statement. There's always the chance a particular item was a gift, but even so, people generally don't display gifts unless they like them.

CALENDARS Does a workplace boast a Sierra Club calendar, or one that features show cars, pinups, Norman Rockwell paintings, or *Far Side* cartoons? Calendars not only broadcast an individual's hobby or passion, they're great conversation pieces. Just ask the person about the calendar, and you're off and running.

PHOTOGRAPHS AND FRAMES The people or places in the photos, the number of photos, the type of frame (expensive or inexpensive, country craft style or black lacquer), and the type of photograph (snapshot, amateur photograph, professional portrait, or art photo) are all very telling. For example, photos of the person with celebrities, community leaders, or other famous types are a form of (often harmless) braggadocio. These, and all photos, are great conversation starters.

BOOKS AND OTHER READING MATERIAL The subject matter is important, naturally—a person with a stack of dog-eared science fiction paperbacks is probably a fan—but there are other factors to consider as well. Someone whose shelf is filled with unread leather-bound volumes by the "great masters" might just be pretentious. Are the shelves loaded with well-thumbed professional journals, or with magazines unconnected to the job? Is there a Bible or other religious book? What sort of reference works does the person have? Are there plenty of computer manuals, but little else?

The variety of reading material in someone's workplace may reflect more than the person's taste in books. It can also reveal his or her attitude toward the job. A pile of romance novels or a stack of parenting magazines on a desk suggests that this person's attention might often be elsewhere. Too many of them also point to a lack of judgment: the boss is sure to notice all the extracurricular reading material and wonder when the work is getting done.

ARTWORK Art—paintings, posters, even figurines—in someone's workplace, like art at home, reveals a person's tastes and often his or her sense of humor, hobbies, and interests, all of which indicate personality. But keep in mind that much of the art displayed in a workplace may have been chosen with a view to the nature of the business rather than according to the individual's personal preference. Your mechanic may like oil paintings of waterfront scenes but hangs posters of cars in the garage where he works. An oil painting might get dirty or be stolen, and also he may want to show his customers that he doesn't just work on cars, he loves them.

DESKTOP ITEMS At least some of a person's limited desk space has to be reserved for getting work done. What someone chooses to occupy the remaining area will often tell you what is most important to him. Is it a picture of his wife and kids? A golf trophy? A pen and pencil holder his son made in wood shop, or a marble and gold desk set he received when he retired from the Navy? Is everything functional—computer, telephone, Rolodex—or is there space on his desk (and in his workday) for family and hobbies? Does he opt for an expensive designer pen or the company-issue Bic? And is the desktop cluttered or neat?

Someone's desk can be a small collage of his personality. A messy, disorganized desk usually points to a messy, disorganized person, and never mind the standard assurances to the contrary. The person's home and car will probably look the same way. And someone who tries to impress office visitors with expensive pens and crystal paperweights will likely find the need to do so in all aspects of his life.

PLANTS AND FLOWERS The person who goes to the trouble of keeping fresh flowers or growing plants at work often cares a lot about beauty and nature in his environment. He's also likely to be somewhat artistic and health conscious. In addition, flowers and greenery are inviting, so they're a sign of a hospitable and caring nature.

I recently visited a courtroom before the trial of one of my cases began, as is my practice. I discovered that the judge routinely kept cut flowers in the courtroom. He had also made cushions for all the spectators' chairs. These special touches were very significant, particularly since they'd been provided by a male judge. Indeed, the judge's personality emerged during the trial as caring, considerate, open, unpretentious, and humane.

The Layout Tells a Tale

The way a person arranges the props in his workplace, as in his home, can also provide insight into his personality. Before you start tallying up sofas and chairs, however, find out whether the individual had a choice. If so, consider these points:

- Is the desk facing the door, a window, or a wall?
- Are there chairs for a guest to sit on, and if so, are they comfortable? (Remember that the office's occupant may not have chosen the chairs.)
- Is the space arranged so that guests and coworkers can talk comfortably?
- Is there a table with a coffeepot or coffee mugs?

Both at work and at home, the bottom line is that *any layout that removes barriers is significant.* If I walk into an office and see that its occupant has set up a conversation nook in one corner, I infer that he probably likes to speak with guests more casually and comfortably than he can when sitting behind his desk. He probably wants to put people at ease; he's informal and probably confident and not egotistical. On the other hand, the person who chooses to sit on one side of a large desk with his guests in smaller (and almost invariably more uncomfortable) chairs across from him is assuming a position of control and superiority.

Of course, most work spaces simply don't have room for such a setup. So look for items such as a coffeepot and mugs, bottled water, or other personal touches, which point to a person who cares about his guests. I can make some tentative judgments from these details about where the office's occupant might fit on my personal hardness scale.

Reading a Person's Home

Our home is our castle. It is usually the most private, personal, and permanent environment we enjoy. At work, others almost always control appearances to some degree; even when they don't, we may not reveal much of ourselves in such a public place. But home—that's different. Once you enter the space someone has created for her own comfort, you are in a position to find out some very pertinent information about her. If she shares her home with someone else, it may be more challenging to identify who is responsible for what features, but with close observation, a little time, and a few tactful questions, you can almost always find out.

Reading someone's home means looking around the "public" areas, not digging through the medicine cabinet. I mention this only because some people are terrible snoops, and I draw the line there. Privacy is sacred. Besides, if you're a good observer you don't need to delve into others' intimate territory. I consider "public" territory to be the neighborhood, the outdoor areas, the living room, the family room, the kitchen, and the guest bathroom. When you first visit and are taken on a "tour," you might get a peek at the bedrooms, too, but generally I'd consider them off limits.

Secret Lives

I've occasionally been surprised at how different someone's house is from the image he or she presents to the outside world. Sometimes the discrepancy is quite startling, though a dramatic direct conflict between someone's outer demeanor and home is unusual. Still, we all lead double lives to a certain extent. A stack of *People* magazines on the end table in the living room of a seemingly no-nonsense business-woman, or a collection of classical music CDs in the home of the rough, tough guy from work doesn't mean these people have split personalities—just that they may be more complicated than you assumed.

The point of this type of observation isn't to identify "deceivers" but to get a sense of the real person and compare that with his or her more public persona. If there are obvious and astonishing differences, something is off-kilter and you should proceed with caution. More often, by comparing the public persona with the person's home, you can learn how contented he is, whether he feels insecure or confident, what he spends most of his time doing, and in general what matters most to him.

The House Reflects the Person

Whenever you enter someone's home, be alert to public-private inconsistencies like those just described. If someone's home is entirely consistent with her public persona, you can usually presume that she is fairly comfortable with who she is and where she is. She has accepted herself and is not a "wanna-be."

If someone's home differs dramatically from the way he presents himself publicly, a red flag should go up. The first question you should ask is "Which is the more authentic presentation?" Time and again I've found that when there is a disparity between the person's public appearance and his home, the home offers more reliable clues. Home is where we literally and figuratively let our hair down.

Before passing judgment, however, make sure you're not seeing an inconsistency where none really exists. Take, for example, the issue of financial success. Our homes, like our wardrobes, may reflect not only our taste but our financial well-being. But what may at first seem an inconsistency between how a man's home and his attire reflect his financial circumstances might make perfect sense once you get to know him a little better. I have a wealthy client who wears jeans and a casual shirt to work every day (he owns the company). If you saw him on the street, you'd never think he was rich. But enter his house—an architectural gem perched high on a cliff overlooking the ocean—and you are instantly aware of his financial success. He doesn't feel like dressing the part, and he doesn't have to. He doesn't care what anyone thinks of his level of success; he's happy and secure with who he is. His home clearly presents a more accurate picture of his socioeconomic standing than his attire, but the two images aren't really inconsistent. The fact is, he loves his beautiful home, and can afford it. He also loves comfortable, casual clothing, even though he can afford to dress any way he chooses.

More often, though, blatant differences between the way a person dresses and the house in which he lives do signal that a choice has been made about where to spend money. When someone dresses elegantly but lives in a modest apartment with few trappings of wealth, the apartment probably represents where he actually is financially, while the clothes reflect where he would like to be. The bigger the gap, the more intense the drive to appear financially successful. The emphasis on appearance over creature comforts may indicate he's ambitious, driven, farsighted, and willing to delay gratification in order to achieve a long-term goal. But be on the lookout for other possibilities: materialism, insecurity, and vanity.

On the other side of the coin, the person who puts most of his income into his home and spends little on wardrobe and physical appearance is more likely to be comfortable with himself and less concerned about others' perceptions of him. He is probably more oriented toward family and friends than toward career.

Sometimes people will even pretend to have interests, hobbies, or talents that aren't supported when you visit their home. This unsettling information should always be considered carefully. Why, for instance, would a woman claim to be an avid chef if her kitchen looks as if it's poorly stocked and rarely used? If she has boasted of her cooking abilities to the whole office, it's probably because she believes others would admire that skill. The bare-bones kitchen has to make you wonder how insecure she is and question her truthfulness.

A person's home will rarely reveal "the key" to her personality all by itself. But sometimes a consistent, strong pattern will emerge from the clues you find there and will enable you to draw some fairly reliable conclusions. A friend of mine recently described her experience in searching for after-school day care for her youngest son. Ultimately, her choice was driven almost entirely by her evaluation of the environment.

In the first day-care provider's home, she noticed immediately that almost all the children were toddlers. Her son was in elementary school, and she wanted a person who would offer him activities he'd find challenging. Notwithstanding the care provider's assurances, the environment told her that wouldn't happen there. It was the middle of the afternoon, and the children sat clustered in front of a TV set in the family room. It was bad enough that they were staring at the TV like zombies; even worse, they were watching a talk show. My friend might have felt differently had the set been tuned to a Disney movie or a nature program, but a talk show for toddlers? She didn't need to see more.

Not long afterward, she found a woman who appeared to fit the bill perfectly. Again, the environment provided many critical clues. A tarp was spread under a tree in the backyard. There was a kiddie-size picnic table on the tarp, where children her son's age were painting. The day-care provider's assistant was actively involved with the children, who in turn were socializing with one another.

In the house were several items that indicated a strong Christian influence. This may have been a bad sign for someone with a different (or no) religious background, but given my friend's Christian beliefs and her interest in seeing her children grow up in such an environment, she found this even more comforting. The house was immaculate. There were safety plugs in all the sockets, rubber covers attached to the corners of the coffee table, and double sets of latches on every door, one at a height where none of the children could possibly reach it. Everything spoke of a very dedicated, careful, and caring woman—exactly who my friend was looking for.

Usually, it takes this sort of pattern building and attention to details to draw a reliable conclusion from a person's environment. So don't stop looking as soon as you've found what you believe to be one notable discovery. Keep searching.

The Neighborhood

The neighborhood in which a person chooses to live says much the same as her choice of work environment—but louder because there are so many more options. Our choices can reveal our financial status, our marital and family situation, our image-consciousness, and in some cases, traits that might not be expected. For instance, the black families who chose to move into all-white neighborhoods in the 1960s and 1970s showed courage, drive, and strength of character. And, like most people who choose improbable neighborhoods, they were strong-willed and independent thinkers. Our choice of neighborhood doesn't often reflect such resolve or commitment to our ideals, but it's often an important indicator of lifestyle and priorities.

The husband and wife who opt for a tiny apartment in an expensive area because it has topflight public schools have made a statement about the value they place on their children's education. The couple who give up vacations, piano lessons, and most other day-to-day luxuries to move into a more prestigious neighborhood show how much they value status and other people's impressions of them. Whenever someone chooses where to live, he must make trade-offs. If it isn't obvious, ask why he decided to live where he did. The answer may tell you a lot about him.

Indoors and Out

Frequently, the outside of a house looks very different from the inside. That disparity will often suggest what is more important to the inhabitants: outside appearances or their own comfort and aesthetic pleasure. When people move into a new place, that's a particularly good time to look for signs of their priorities. Most people have a limited budget for repairs and interior decoration, so they'll make a choice: fix up the inside or spruce up the outside. Their decision may offer some insight into what matters more to them.

The difference between inside and outside also underscores how crucial it is to wait until you see the whole picture before drawing any conclusions. A house that presents a very plain face to the street may look stunning on the inside. By the same token, a person who has put every last dime into buying the most expensive house he can possibly afford may be "house poor" and have only the most basic furniture. Both these people have made choices that may speak to their values. One may be more concerned with his own comfort and the other with outward appearances. But never forget, there are a host of possible motivations for most decisions. Perhaps the one who spends all his time and energy on landscaping just loves to garden and couldn't care less about what his neighbors think.

Usually, the first thing you'll notice when you enter someone's home is the decor. Style often gives clues about personality, although, as usual, there are exceptions. But by and large, traditional furnishings reflect traditional views on life, whereas more modern or unusual decor reflects more open, experimental views. Choices in furnishings may also reflect a person's background. If you were raised in the country, you may prefer country-style furnishings. Most of us associate our childhood home with feelings of security and love. It's rare that a person will divorce himself entirely from those feelings.

If someone has left home decoration to another, whether a spouse or professional designer, the decor is much less helpful in predicting character. While it's true that a designer's client usually has to approve his plans, often the client is either too busy to put much thought into the decisions or is willing to defer to someone with stronger feelings about the matter.

Using Your Senses

When you enter someone's home, your first inclination is to look around. After you've had a few minutes to absorb some of the visual information, concentrate on three other senses: hearing, smell, and touch.

LISTEN TO THE ROOM   Is quiet, soothing music playing, which might indicate the person who lives there is calm and serene—or wants to be? Or is the TV blaring? If so, what channel is on? Listen for wind chimes, dogs barking, children playing. If you hear rock and roll coming from a back room, are there teenagers in the home, or is the fifty-five-year-old occupant possibly stuck in the sixties? If you're not listening, you won't hear a lot of great clues that might provide you with valuable information—and point you in directions where you'll find even more.

SMELL THE ROOM   Notice any good or unpleasant odors, and try to identify them. Good smells may come from the kitchen or from an open window that lets fresh air flow through, or someone may have gone out of her way to make her home smell wonderful, or to mask the scent of medication, illness, or smoke. Sniff the air and try to identify smells associated with

- flowers
- food
- fireplace/wood smoke
- animals

- children/babies
- medication
- alcohol
- cigarettes, pipes, cigars
- cleaning products

Smells may tip you off to a person's interests (such as cooking or gardening), their use of tobacco and alcohol, whether they have a pet or young children, and even their health.

The odors someone introduces into his environment, or fails to remove, can tell you more than you might imagine. People with unclean homes tend to have the same traits as those whose personal hygiene leaves something to be desired. And those who create beautiful-smelling, inviting homes tend to be more socially adept, considerate, and sensitive to others and how others perceive them.

TOUCH THE ROOM   Don't put on white gloves and start feeling for dust on the fireplace mantel, but pay attention to items within your reach. Notice whether the furniture is cozy or stiff and inhospitable. Sofas upholstered in soft cotton might indicate a sensualist, while slick Naugahyde would point to a more practical nature. Are the floors slippery and highly polished, or carpeted and warm? Is the place comfortable or cold? Is it clean? All of this information will add detail to the pattern you are beginning to see develop.

House Props

A home contains thousands of items. When you visit, focus on those that may be most revealing. The list that follows includes many items worth noting, but it's not complete. You'd be amazed at how much can be revealed by even the most seemingly mundane objects.

One example of something to which you've probably never given a second thought is the type of facial tissue you find in someone's home. We all know people who splurge on the extra-soft, scented, flowery variety. And then there are those who buy whatever brand is on sale, even if it feels like newspaper. Almost everyone can afford the luxurious variety if they want to. Those who do are more likely to be sensual, extravagant, willing to pamper themselves, concerned about

HOUSE PROPS

alcohol

animal toys or bowls

artwork

ashtrays

books and other reading
material

candles

children's toys and furniture

clocks

collections

entertainment center

flowers and green plants

food

garden equipment

guns or gun racks

holiday decorations

items on the refrigerator
(magnets, cards, drawings)

items reflecting a physical
disability (cane, wheelchair,
oxygen tank)

knickknacks

mailbox

mirrors

musical instruments

pharmaceuticals

photographs

religious pictures, books, or
other paraphernalia

rugs

signs

special features (such as a wine
cellar, a darkroom,
a fireplace, a pool)

sports paraphernalia:
equipment, clothing,
trophies, posters, and so
forth

stereo system and record/CD
collection

television (size and location)

tools

vitamins

welcome mats

the comfort of others, and eager to be a good host. If they choose tissue decorated with flowers or pretty designs, they may also show their desire to surround themselves with beautiful things. Those who opt for the cheap, harsh, plain white variety are more likely to be frugal, practical, unconcerned about appearances, and unwilling to spend money on their own creature comforts or on the comfort of others.

Should you make a blanket assessment about someone based solely on the brand of facial tissue she prefers? Of course not. But you should consider it a useful clue in combination with others. Keep that in mind as you review this list of common house props.

The significance of many of these items is obvious if you take the time to notice them. A large-screen television located in the middle of the living room broadcasts a straightforward message about the person's priorities, as does a small TV tucked away in the corner. Records and CDs reflect someone's taste in music, candles may reveal a romantic or sensitive side, and vitamins an interest in health. Sports equipment, guns, musical instruments, and the like reveal the person's interests and hobbies.

As with everything else, individual features take on special significance if they create a pattern when combined with other features. If a home has security lights, bars on the windows, an alarm system, gates, a "Beware of Dog" sign, and several deadbolts or locks on the doors, it's a good bet that the person who lives there is very concerned about his security, perhaps even paranoid. Likewise, holiday decorations, swing sets, and children's toys suggest the person has a family-oriented lifestyle and values.

Most of these props are great starting points for a conversation about their owner's pastimes or interests. A few of the items listed deserve particularly close examination. Like those highlighted in the discussion of workplace props, these objects are chosen not because the person needs them but because he desires them.

BOOKS AND OTHER READING MATERIAL   What someone reads can be one of the most revealing items a home has to offer, particularly if it is unique. You won't learn much from the presence of the local newspaper, but you would from a copy of *Soldier of Fortune* magazine. However, not everyone displays her reading material in the living room, and not every avid reader reads magazines and owns a lot of books; some people go to the library. Others like to keep their homes uncluttered and keep their book collection in a back room or in boxes in the garage. If the house does have bookcases and tables that display books or magazines, take a close look at them. Look for patterns—mystery novels, cooking magazines, science journals. You'll be surprised at what you can learn. For example, someone who owns many books on health might only be a bit obsessed with the subject. But the presence of even one book on a specific serious illness may mean that the person or someone he knows suffers from the disease.

ITEMS ON THE REFRIGERATOR   Imagine a list of what is most important to someone tacked on a wall for you to review. That's what many refrigerators are like—they practically vibrate with life. Appointments, cartoons, magnets, photos, children's drawings, favorite sayings, poems, tickets, business cards . . . the list of what people put on their fridges is endless. And every item has been taken from a more obscure location and placed where it will be seen. Not everyone decorates her refrigerator, and I wouldn't draw any conclusions from a naked Amana. But when someone treats her refrigerator like a bulletin board, pay attention to what she posts on it.

COLLECTIONS   Collections are often passed from generation to generation. My mother collects beautiful porcelain teacups, and over the years my sisters and I have added to them. We know someday the teacups will be divided among us, and that we in turn will pass them along to our children. Collections can indicate stability, the importance of family, and a love of tradition. What someone collects is meaningful as well: rare and valuable coins say something different than an array of spoons acquired over years of family vacations. Someone's collections may reflect his or her socioeconomic level, trendiness, investment interest, hobbies, and life experiences. From baseball cards to Elvis paraphernalia, collections provide a wealth of information.

PHOTOGRAPHS   Photographs in the home can be more—or less— revealing than photographs in the workplace. There's usually more room for photographs at home, so you'll find a wider range of subject matter from which to gather clues. On the other hand, because space is less limited, the person doesn't need to be as selective, so the choice of photographs may not be as revealing. Still, look closely. There's almost always a lot to learn about—family activities, hobbies, travel interests, involvement in sports, cultural and religious background, and much more.

ARTWORK   Since we usually have complete freedom to choose the art in our home, it's a more reliable indicator of our taste than artwork in the office. If you are instantly attracted to something hanging on a person's walls, or if it reflects your sense of humor or interests, you may have encountered someone with whom you have a lot in common. If their paintings, posters, or photographs strike you as tacky or offensive, your worldviews are probably very different. Most people don't spend a lot of money on art, even if they could afford to. But whether someone buys poster art or original oil paintings, he will reveal his sense of humor, interests, traditional or untraditional values, and much more in his choices.

CHILDREN'S TOYS AND FURNITURE If there are children in a house, I always look to see how far their influence extends. Some families willingly turn over the living room to the kids, stocking it with toy barrels and indoor climbing equipment. These people probably also like family-oriented leisure activities. They're also more apt than some others to enjoy having your children around.

In other homes the kids' toys stay in the kids' rooms, and the parents reserve the rest of the house for adult-oriented activities. You may want to take that into consideration when you visit with your own children. Families fortunate enough to have separate family and living rooms can have it both ways.

ALCOHOL In the 1950s, 1960s, and 1970s, many new houses were built with wet bars, which were probably meant to supply a Frank Sinatra–Rat Pack look. These days, hard liquor has lost much of its glamour. When I find a fully stocked wet bar or any open display of liquor, I take notice, particularly if the resident is under fifty. Don't label someone an alcoholic simply because he has a well-stocked liquor cabinet, but nowadays it's unusual to find a lot of bottles prominently displayed. Their owner may be fond of drinking or of entertaining those who do.

FLOWERS AND GREEN PLANTS Flowers and plants require time and care. They make a house more comfortable, beautiful, and inviting. A person who is willing to devote time, energy, and money to their upkeep is likely to be sensuous, sensitive to beauty, and hospitable. (But because it's common, and easier, to keep plants at home, they're less significant here than they are in an office—unless, of course, the person has a *lot* of them.) On the other hand, unhealthy or dying flowers and plants may suggest their owner is unobservant, sloppy, or very busy. Usually, the rest of the house will be in the same state of disarray.

SIGNS Whether indoors or out, signs offer plenty of information. "Beware of Cat" indicates not only that someone is probably fond of cats but also that she has a sense of humor and wants to display it. "Beware of Dog," on the other hand, tells you the person has a dog and is concerned with security. Signs announcing security systems or organizational memberships are all useful clues to a person's background, beliefs, and priorities, as are symbols of religious affiliation. Any object in a person's home may provide extra material for your mental file. Each detail contributes to the overall pattern. If you notice anything that's unusual or that sticks out like a sore thumb, ask about it if you can do so tactfully.

My Wheels, Myself: Reading a Person's Automobile

"It Also Functions Like a Résumé," boasts the Lexus ad. Indeed, many people think of their automobile as a way to telegraph their financial success, masculinity, class, or style. Our cars do say a lot about us—not only our money, but also our priorities, interests, work, and personality. Cars are easy to read, although what they say may differ from region to region. However, if you spend more than a week in a town you'll quickly learn the regional "rules." Someone who drives a pickup truck in downtown Chicago probably uses it in his work. The same truck in Austin, Texas, may never be used for anything but show. A convertible in southern California is not nearly as extravagant or impractical as the same car in Seattle, where the top can come down only rarely. And don't fall victim to the stereotype that wealthy, successful, status-conscious people all drive expensive European sedans. In Detroit, they may drive Cadillacs and Lincolns, and in Tulsa, the wheels of choice may be big extended-cab pickup trucks.

When you're evaluating a car, keep in mind its practicality with respect to the region and the owner's work, family, and hobbies. Is it a sports car, a convertible, a "muscle car," a family car, a minivan, a truck? What did it cost? Does it get good mileage, and is it easy and cheap to repair? Is it practical, given the owner's family status and line of work? Every car says something very different about the person who picked it out. An expensive three-hundred-horsepower sports car tells me its driver is probably status conscious, aggressive, and a touch egotistical. The six-cylinder minivan speaks of practicality, frugality, and conformity.

Add-ons

Like the props in a home or office, the extras people add to their vehicles offer another glimpse of their interests, priorities, and values. Here we've listed only the more common items you might notice on someone's car.

- alarm
- antenna ornaments
- bumper stickers
- car phone (watch out if you also see a car fax)
- Club or other steering wheel lock
- customized license plates
- decorative painting
- floor mats
- hubcaps
- license-plate holders
- lights (ornamental/spot)
- mirror ornaments (dice, crosses, etc.)
- mud flaps (the silhouette of the Playboy Bunny may say a lot about the man driving)
- music system
- racks (bikes, ski, luggage, gun)
- raised or lowered height
- roll bars
- seat covers or cushions
- signs
- tires and wheels
- trailer hitches

Just how much can be learned from a car's accessories was brought home to me recently as I was driving down the freeway. I passed a small car driven by an elderly, white-haired lady. The license-plate holder read, "Timmy's and Julie's Nana," and the customized license plate "Nana N." From this I could tell not only that the woman had grandchildren named Timmy and Julie (obvious), but also that those grandchildren were extremely important to her.

Car Maintenance

How a person takes care of her car is often a clear sign of her priorities. I have an acquaintance whose mother, after interviewing prospective tenants for her rental house, always walked them out to their car. As she put it: "I may not be able to see how they take care of their house, but I can see how they take care of their car, and that'll tell me just as much." This isn't always true, but it's a sound notion to keep in mind.

The owner of a consistently filthy car is probably unconcerned about the impression he makes; not meticulous or detail oriented; very busy; disorganized; or lazy. Someone whose car is always immaculate probably exhibits the same fastidiousness in her dress and grooming; she's likely to be organized, orderly, concerned with how she appears to others, and attentive to detail. Children (and dogs) do weaken the equation, as it's very difficult to maintain a spanking-clean automobile when you're ferrying kids (or canines) around in it every day. If you meet someone who manages to accomplish this feat, you can probably assume that he or she runs a very tight ship.

Social Environments: Where Do We Choose to Play?

How many times have you heard someone complain about a spouse who drinks too much, only to learn the two lovebirds met in a bar? Where we choose to spend our free time is extremely revealing, yet we often overlook these environmental signposts. If abstinence from alcohol is important, why not try meeting people at alcohol-free functions? If you want to meet a religious person, your chances are best at church or synagogue. If you are looking for intellectual stimulation, check out a university or a library. Athletes can be found in the gym, and nature lovers at Sierra Club meetings. You find polar bears in the frozen north, not the tropics. Common sense, right?

It *is* common sense, but for some reason we frequently overlook how much the environments people choose tell about them. The more the choice is within their control, the more it reveals. If I meet someone playing softball with the kids at the park on a Saturday afternoon, I'd guess that she enjoys the outdoors, spending time with her family, and playing sports. But if she were doing the same at a company picnic, I wouldn't automatically draw this conclusion. Even if she's enjoying herself, I can't be sure that this is what she'd freely choose to do—only that she's adaptable enough to enjoy it when it has been chosen for her.

Before you place too much weight on a single encounter at the park, or anywhere else, you need to know how much time the person spends there. Most of us don't spend a significant amount of leisure time anyplace unless it fulfills our needs in some way. Church is probably important to someone who attends church most Sunday mornings, but religion may still not be a big factor in his life. However, it's a safe bet that his religious beliefs are central to his worldview and may even dominate how he thinks and behaves if he not only attends church on Sunday mornings but also goes to Wednesday night Bible study classes and Saturday church socials. The same is true of any environment, from health club to shopping mall to Little League fields. The more time a person freely chooses to spend there, the more that environment will reflect his beliefs and foretell his behavior.

Sometimes the choice of environment on even an isolated occasion can tell much about a person. If an old college friend is in town and calls to get together and catch up, her choice of locale for our chat can be a clue worth noting. Even the restaurant she selects can reflect her character, values, and lifestyle. Does she suggest we grab a bite at a fast-food restaurant, a family coffee shop, or a chic French bistro? Someone who opts for a very expensive restaurant for a casual lunch with an old friend may have moderate wealth—or an out-of-control credit account. Either way, she may be concerned with appearances and trying to impress. She apparently enjoys indulgences, and she may not be particularly practical. All that could reflect insecurity. I wouldn't necessarily draw the same conclusions if a businessman chose the same high-priced restaurant to meet his most important client. Perhaps he knows the client expects to be wined and dined.

On the other hand, someone who chooses a coffee shop is more likely to be frugal, practical, and either unable or unwilling to sacrifice financially for the sake of gourmet food or the image it presents. If my friend made that choice, I would assume that she just wants to talk, not to impress me with her success or status. If the businessman took his best client to a coffee shop for lunch, I would be inclined to believe he was very comfortable with their relationship and that neither he nor his client was concerned with showing off.

The person who suggests you meet at a bar also says something very different than the one who offers to meet you at an outdoor café or at your place for a cup of coffee. Even the type of bar sends a message—after all, bars run the gamut from topless joints to swank lobby bars at four-star hotels. The drinking habits of Americans have changed drastically over the past ten or fifteen years. To an extent, coffeehouses, restaurants, and clubs have replaced bars as popular places to get to know someone. Therefore, the person who suggests a first meeting at a bar may reveal that, to him, alcohol is an important social lubricant. If this is what you're looking for, fine. If not, keep an eye out for a pattern to develop.

I would never draw any final conclusions about someone on the sole basis of his choice of restaurant or bar, but I would notice and consider it. If he chose the same type of meeting place consistently, that would be even more significant.

Birds of a Feather: Evaluating the Human Environment

Let's go back to the example of the criminal defendant who came to court dressed in a conservative business suit. His true self may also be revealed by whom he brings with him to court. If the defendant has a companion, take a close look at him or her. If his girlfriend has stains on her clothing and looks like she just rolled out of bed, you may infer that is what the defendant looks like when he is not on trial. And if she has dilated pupils and can't stop fidgeting in her seat, you might not only suspect she might be under the influence of something but you might find the defendant guilty by association and attribute such habits to him as well.

"Birds of a feather flock together," goes the old saying, and it's a priceless piece of wisdom. The people we befriend, marry, hire, work for, and socialize with make up our human environment. They often reflect either who we are or who we'd like to be since to a large degree we have a choice about them. Most parents are acutely aware of this, which is why they monitor their children's friends so closely. Given enough time and contact, youngsters will begin to adopt the values and behaviors of their peers. An adult's crowd is very revealing as well.

The lawyer who has represented your sleazy brother-in-law for years is probably just as sleazy. He would have been fired long ago if he weren't willing to do your brother-in-law's dirty work. And that new boyfriend whose best buddy's favorite pastime is a ball game and a few beers must have something in common with him. Similarly, a woman tells you where her priorities are if her best friends are all mothers of children in her young son's play group.

As in the courtroom example, whenever you're reading someone, take note of his or her friends, confidants, business associates, and mates—especially if a person's acquaintances all seem to fall into the same category. Many people are skilled at disguising their personality and value system. If you can visit their home and workplace, you'll probably be able to discover more of their true nature. But if you have access to nothing else, *sizing up someone's friends and associates will give you a pretty reliable indication of his or her character.* While I hesitate to either damn or praise on this basis alone, association makes a very powerful statement.

Geographic Location as Part of the Environment

The conclusions I draw about someone's personal appearance may depend on geography. People with very similar personalities and values will look, dress, and act differently if they are from different locales. Expectations, norms, and cultural influences vary from town to town, region to region, and country to country. You can't hold everyone to the same standard. Before you draw any firm conclusions, make sure you've allowed for any unique geographical factors. If I see a young woman in Manhattan wearing heavy makeup, a severe hairstyle, and a trendy designer suit, I won't give her appearance much thought. She's probably style-conscious and conforming to what others in her environment deem appropriate. On the other hand, if I saw the same woman walking down the street in a small town in Middle America, I'd find that curious. Perhaps she's flamboyant, expressive, looking for attention by standing out. Maybe she's even bored and discontented with her life. Or maybe she's just visiting from New York.

Time of Day, Day of Week, and Season of Year as Part of the Environment

If I stopped by someone's house at five in the morning to pick her up for an early meeting, and she met me at the door bleary-eyed, moving slowly, and complaining of fatigue, I'd probably attribute that to the hour. But if she showed up at work at ten looking and acting the same way, I'd wonder why.

The day of the week can also be significant. A person says a lot about himself if he chooses to drink and dance until the wee hours on a Wednesday night. On the positive side, he is energetic and fun-loving. But—assuming he is due at work early the next morning—his behavior also suggests he is willing to sacrifice peak performance there. I wouldn't consider this an issue if I ran into him in the same club late on a Friday or Saturday night.

Even the time of year can be important. A man whose face is very red the day after a sunny Fourth of July weekend is probably sunburned. In December, after weeks of overcast and rain, I would look for other causes: fatigue, alcohol, medical treatment, or even embarrassment. If I met a man with a flawless tan in Seattle in December, and I knew he had not been on vacation in the tropics, I would assume he regularly visits a tanning salon. That would demonstrate vanity and concern for the way others perceive him. During the summer in San Diego, I wouldn't draw the same conclusion from a man's tan.

Is the Environment Friendly or Hostile?

A person's behavior can change dramatically when he is in an unfamiliar or hostile environment. You can't expect a lamb to act the same way when thrown into the lion's den as it would when grazing in a pasture, and the same is true of people. We typically show signs of anxiety, antisocial behavior, and lack of confidence when we are in a hostile environment. That doesn't mean we're all nervous, reclusive, and insecure by nature.

There are few environments in which people feel less comfortable than a courtroom. I've seen hundreds of people testify, ranging from professional experts to those who are on the witness stand for the first time. Often, someone I know to be completely truthful will come across as nervous and dishonest. His voice may crack; his eyes may be downcast or flicker from side to side; he may lick his lips, fiddle with objects in front of him, stutter, and even fail to recall recent events. It would be a grave error to conclude that he must be lying. By the same token, many expert witnesses have testified literally hundreds of times in court and are totally at ease. They know what they are doing and perform effortlessly and confidently. Many of them are in essence accomplished performers, and able to appear completely candid even if they're stretching the truth to its limits.

Outside the courtroom, people are no different. If I go to a party where I know everyone, I may be very outgoing, confident, sociable, and relaxed—I'll move freely from person to person. At a function where I've never met a soul, I may be more tentative, quiet, shy, or reserved. I may break the ice with one person, then spend a substantial amount of time in conversation with him rather than mingle freely with a crowd of strangers.

When you meet people for the first time and try to size them up, take into account how they may be feeling in that environment. Try to determine whether they are on familiar territory or feel like strangers in a strange land. If someone is on well-known turf and yet seems skittish and ill at ease, you might conclude that she's unusually shy or insecure; or perhaps she's suffering through some temporary personal difficulty. But if she behaves that way in a foreign or hostile environment, these conclusions would be unfounded—unless they were supported by further independent evidence.

Always Remember How Environment Might Be Influencing Behavior

From the first chapter of this book you've been reading about characteristics that can have virtually opposite meanings depending upon the circumstances. Someone who is loud may be confident—or inse-cure. Someone who wears mismatched clothes may be socially inept—or at the height of style within her peer group. Never lose sight of how a person's environment may be influencing her appear-ance or behavior.

I can offer a remarkable example of this from the federal prosecu-tion of the four police officers accused of beating Rodney King. The day after the jury was selected, one of the jurors, a middle-aged African-American woman, appeared in court wearing black gloves. She wore the same black gloves every day for the rest of the trial. It was driving me crazy. Was she making a racial statement? Were the gloves a political commentary? Did they have some other unknown significance? After the trial was over, I learned from her fellow jurors that she wore the black gloves simply because she found the court-room to be uncomfortably cold.

The importance of viewing every trait in the context of the envi-ronment in which it is found can't be overstressed. Like the animated characters in a Disney movie, our actions have little meaning absent their backdrop. Observe that carefully, and the rest of the details will come into sharper focus.

KEY POINTS

Read the environment with all your senses: Listen, smell, feel—don't just look.

See the big picture: Someone's work or home environment includes every-thing from the interior décor, to the lobby or yard, type of building, and even the neighborhood. Take it all in.

There are clues everywhere, but some tend to stand out: Calendars, pho-tographs, reading material, artwork, plants or flowers, and desktop or refrigera-tor door "props" are often the best place to start.

There's more to "reading" someone's home, workplace, or automobile than just identifying the "props": Notice how everything is maintained and where it is positioned; and always ask how much choice the person had about the matter.

Watch for distinctions between someone's private and public environments: Our work environments, to the extent we have a say in them, often speak most loudly about what we want others to think of us. The environment we create in the privacy of our homes usually tells more about who we really are.

Ask "where they choose to play":   Where people enjoy spending free time—the ball park, a jazz bar, the mall, expensive restaurants, the library—provides insight into both their interests and values.

Birds of a feather flock together: Our human environment—who we choose to work, play, and live with—is an excellent measure of our true values and character.

Remember, our appearance, speech, and behavior are affected by our environment: Hostile or unfamiliar environments; the time of day, week, or year; the weather; and many other factors all have an impact on us.

ELEVEN

Sometimes Things Aren't What They Appear to Be

Spotting Exceptions to the Rules

Josh was getting harder to handle each year. It began in preschool, where his teacher chalked up his behavioral problems to a low tolerance for frustration. In kindergarten things only got worse. He sometimes lashed out in anger at his teachers, and often ignored them altogether. He behaved better at home, but was also very short-tempered there. By the time he entered first grade, his distraught parents were ready to take him to a psychologist to be tested for learning disabilities. Luckily, the city's hearing program arrived at Josh's school in time to discover the real problem: Josh was hard of hearing. Who wouldn't be frustrated if he couldn't hear half of what was being said?

Even though teachers and parents today are more alert to signs of hearing impairment than they once were, this scene is still replayed thousands of times each year. It's a good example of what can happen when all the pieces but one fit a particular pattern, and that one critical piece goes unnoticed. Most of the people you meet who display a particular pattern of traits won't surprise you. But be careful not to leave out that one critical piece of the puzzle.

There are a few characteristics that can shed an entirely different light on what you thought was a crystal-clear image. I think of them as exceptions to the rules, because if you don't take them into account you may reach distorted or incorrect conclusions, even if everything else seems to fit.

I've found nine exceptions that occur more frequently than others.

Some are completely involuntary. Others are elective, and often an attempt to manipulate:

The "elastic" person who attempts to mold himself to meet your
   requirements
The person who has carefully rehearsed his presentation
The liar
The delusional thinker
The person who is mentally or physically disabled
The person who is ill, fatigued, stressed, or otherwise "not himself"
The person who is under the influence of drugs or alcohol
The person who is strongly influenced by his or her culture
Coincidences—they do happen

The Elastic Person

Engineers use the term "elasticity" for the tendency of a material to deform under pressure and then return to its natural state when the pressure is off, like a rubber band. People are naturally elastic, and from time to time, most of us consciously or unconsciously alter our appearance, behavior, or words to meet others' expectations or desires. But the person who consistently molds herself to be what she thinks you want her to be is, in essence, providing you with false information. If you're not getting the facts, you can't make a reliable judgment.

Slobs can be tidy, at least for a while, if the motivation is there. Lazy people can appear industrious—temporarily. Opinionated people can appear open-minded, and selfish people can seem giving. But these people will tend to "change" as time passes, relationships mature, and the desire to please decreases. The kind, considerate, understanding new boyfriend becomes insensitive, overbearing, and jealous. The hardworking, helpful employee becomes lazy and uncooperative as he settles in to the job.

In truth, the boyfriend and the employee were never really what they at first appeared to be. They always were insensitive and uncooperative. They were demonstrating the principles of elasticity: once the pressure or motivation that caused them to change eased, they reverted to their true form.

Don't assume that attempts to please always spring from a conscious desire to manipulate. They can be an unconscious and very well-meaning attempt to gain acceptance or approval. We naturally put on our best manners when we meet a new beau's parents for the first time or go out to dinner with the boss. But whatever someone's motives may be, it would be a mistake to see her under those unique circumstances and assume she always has impeccable manners. You need to see her over a period of time and in several different situations before you can tell which behaviors are real and which are elastic.

Once the bloom is off the rose of either a personal or professional relationship, the pressures that caused the elastic behaviors will subside, and the person will revert to her normal state, good or bad. Until then, it's wise to reserve judgment.

The Rehearsed Presentation

I have seen many witnesses who are articulate, forceful, and poised on direct examination by the lawyer who called them to the stand, only to crumble when the opposing attorney cross-examines them. Sometimes this is because a particularly skillful attorney has dished out a brutal cross-examination, but in many cases it's simply a matter of exposing the actor who has rehearsed his role. In daily life, if you're not alert to the rehearsed presentation, you run the risk of misjudging someone. You might find him more articulate and witty—or less imaginative, creative, or flexible—than he actually is.

Not surprisingly, you're most likely to encounter a canned presentation when someone is trying to sell you something. It doesn't have to be a car or a time-share. The "salesman" can be trying to persuade you to "buy" an idea, a point of view, another person, or himself. There is probably one "sales pitch" that he's found particularly effective, so he repeats it in order to achieve the best possible result.

Sometimes, too, people deliver a rehearsed story because they're trying to make a good impression and don't have the confidence to speak spontaneously. The insecure or nervous often find it easier to practice a speech in advance, like the high school boy who writes down a list of things to say to the girl he's about to call for the first time. People also tend to repeat the same stories if they've had positive experiences with them in the past. Others have laughed, been persuaded, or been charmed by the story. They hope you will be, too.

It isn't too difficult to spot this type of behavior. Often the presentation seems too perfect and utterly unspontaneous. When delivering a prepared shtick, people are in their comfort zone. If you want to find out how they behave when they haven't had the opportunity to prepare, take away the home-field advantage. Take them out of their comfort zone and put them in yours.

If someone is delivering a sales pitch, ask a pointed question that he'll have to respond to spontaneously. If he keeps dodging you, stay after him until he either answers or makes it clear he's unable or unwilling to, which in itself will tell you something. If someone you've just met is trying to wow you with her intelligence by discussing world politics, see if she's a one-trick pony. When the conversation allows, ask what she thinks about the latest movies. See if she knows anything about sports. What you choose to discuss isn't important. Your goal is to see how she reacts as you try to lead her away from her comfort zone. Does she speak willingly about other topics? Is she at ease and articulate even if she knows little about the subject? Does she ask intelligent questions? Or does she consistently try to lead you back to where she feels comfortable and in control?

Over the years I've seen some almost comical exchanges in the courtroom when lawyers, busy delivering a carefully prepared presentation of what they no doubt believe to be inspired arguments, are interrupted by a judge who wants answers to other questions. Even a casual court observer knows the courtroom is the judge's turf: whatever he wants to know takes precedence over whatever a lawyer might prefer to discuss. Even so, it's not unusual to see lawyers try to stay within their comfort zone by telling the judge they'll "get to that," or "That's not the point," or even "I don't think that's relevant." I can assure you that a lawyer's reluctance to deviate from his canned presentation doesn't bolster his credibility in the eyes of the judge. After all, if he were truly comfortable with his position, he'd be willing to examine it from any perspective.

In everyday conversations, we have to be a bit more careful about how we test someone outside her comfort zone. People try to stay with what they know because it's safe and familiar. It can be disconcerting to be forced off one's home turf, so your mission is to proceed gently. Make the transition with tact and diplomacy, not abrasively. The objective is to get to know the other person when she isn't just delivering a rehearsed presentation, and you won't achieve it if you alienate her. Instead, you'll see how she reacts when she's angry and offended.

The Wild Cards: Liars

If people were all honest with one another, reading them would be a lot easier. The problem is that people lie. I'm not talking about those who are wrong but sincerely believe they are correct, or about the delusional few who genuinely can't tell fact from fantasy. Rather, I'm referring to the one characteristic that is probably the most important in any relationship: truthfulness. And if we assume it's there when it's not—watch out!

Much of the information we gather about someone comes directly from the horse's mouth. If he is lying, the information is wrong, and we're likely to misjudge him. That's why it's so crucial to identify liars as soon as possible, and, if you have reason to doubt a person's honesty, to continue to test it until you're entirely at ease with your conclusion.

I have found that most liars fall into one of four basic categories: the occasional liar, the frequent liar, the habitual liar, and the professional liar.

The Occasional Liar

The occasional liar, like most of us, will lie now and then to avoid an unpleasant situation or because he doesn't want to admit doing something wrong or embarrassing. Also like most of us, he does not like to lie and feels very uncomfortable when he does. Because he's uncomfortable, he'll usually reveal his lie through his appearance, body language, and voice.

The occasional liar often gives his lie some thought, so it may be logical and consistent with the rest of his story. Because it's well thought out, you probably won't be able to spot the lie by its content or context, or by information from third-party sources. In fact, the occasional liar will seldom lie about something that could be easily verified. Consequently, when dealing with an occasional liar, you need to focus on the various visual and oral clues he exhibits.

The Frequent Liar

The frequent liar recognizes what she's doing but doesn't mind it as much as the occasional liar does, so she lies more regularly. Practice makes perfect: the frequent liar is much less likely to reveal her lie through her appearance, body language, and voice. Also, since it doesn't bother her as much to lie, the typical stress-related symptoms won't be as obvious. Any clues in her appearance, voice, and body language might be rather subtle. Often a better way to detect a frequent liar is to focus on the internal consistency and logic of her statements. Since the frequent liar lies more often, and tends to think her lies through less carefully than the occasional liar, she can get sloppy.

The Habitual Liar

The habitual liar lies so frequently that he has lost sight of what he is doing much of the time. In most cases, if he actually thought about it, he would realize he was lying. But he doesn't much care whether what he's saying is true or false. He simply says whatever comes to mind. Because he doesn't care that he's lying, the habitual liar will give very few, if any, physical or vocal clues that he's being dishonest. But because he gives so little thought to his lies and they come so thick and fast, the habitual liar doesn't bother to keep track of them; they are often inconsistent and obvious. So while it's hard to detect the physical and vocal clues in a habitual liar, it's easier to spot his inconsistencies. Listen carefully and ask yourself whether the liar is contradicting himself and whether what he's saying makes sense. Asking a third party about the liar's stories will also help you confirm your suspicions.

The habitual liar is fairly uncommon, so most of us are temporarily taken in when we encounter one. An acquaintance of mine told me she worked with a woman for several months before her suspicions that the coworker was a habitual liar were confirmed by an obvious and quite ridiculous lie. The liar, a brown-eyed brunette, came to work one day sporting blue contact lenses of an almost alien hue. When my friend commented on her lenses, the liar said, "These aren't contacts; they're my real eye color. It's just that I've always worn brown contact lenses before."

More than once, a client has told me that his adversary lies all the time and will undoubtedly lie on the witness stand. I counsel my client not to worry: the habitual liar is the easiest target in a lawsuit. In real life, she can run from one person to another, from one situation to the next, lying as she goes, and no one compares notes. There are no court reporters or transcripts of testimony; no one reveals what every witness has said to every other witness, and nobody pores over everything the liar has written on the subject to see whether it's all consistent. But in litigation, that is exactly what happens—and suddenly the habitual liar is exposed. It's very rewarding to see.

The Professional Liar

The professional liar is the hardest to identify. He doesn't lie indiscriminately, like the habitual liar. He lies for a purpose. For example, a mechanic who routinely cons motorists about their "faulty" transmissions will have his diagnosis carefully prepared. A real estate salesman who doesn't want to acknowledge a leaky roof will respond quickly to an inquiry about the stains on the ceiling with a rehearsed, very spontaneous sounding statement: "That was old damage from a water leak in the attic. All it needs is a little touch-up paint."

The professional liar has thought the lie through and knows exactly what he's going to say, how it will fly, and whether the customer can easily verify it. Such a well-practiced lie will not be revealed by the liar's voice, body language, or appearance. The lie will be consistent, both internally and logically. The only sure way to detect it is to check the liar's statements against entirely independent sources. Have the roof inspected. Get a second opinion from another mechanic. Take nothing for granted.

Before you make a definitive call about someone who is truly important to you, always ask yourself whether the information you have about him is reliable. Is he being truthful? If your goal is to accurately evaluate someone, you can't afford to skip this step.

The Delusional Thinker

Every once in a while I find myself staring at someone, a look of disbelief on my face and my mouth ajar, wondering, "How can anyone be so clueless?" We've all encountered people who have lost touch with reality, if only in one specific area. This is a blind spot, as in "She's just got a blind spot where her sister is concerned." Some people have one or two blind spots. Others have enough to weave a complete set of blinders.

If you think you're immune, consider this: after participating in the questioning of over ten thousand jurors, I could count on one hand (well, maybe two) the number who admitted to having any racial bias. I don't need to refer to any surveys to say without fear of contradiction that more than one in a thousand people harbor some racial bias. But it seems that only one in a thousand is willing to admit it in open court. Some are simply lying; they know they're racist but aren't about to say so in a courtroom. The majority, however, really do believe they are bias-free, and for many that amounts to delusional thinking. If I took the word of every prospective juror who declared, "I don't have a prejudiced bone in my body," a lot of bigots would have sat as jurors in the cases I've worked on over the years. But I don't accept that type of information at face value, because I can't. It is too important to my client.

For the same reason, when a particular issue is important to you in evaluating someone *even if you believe she is fundamentally honest,* don't assume you can take everything she says as gospel. Ask yourself: Is there any evidence that she may be fooling herself? Have I stumbled across a blind spot?

Delusional thinking can be the result of someone else's suggestions, or we can develop blind spots ourselves. In working on the McMartin Preschool case and other child-molestation cases, I saw how easily the children could be persuaded that they had been asked to participate in sexual acts—not only with their day-care providers but, in one prominent case, with large animals that couldn't even have fit into the room. The youngsters' reality was altered by suggestions—they were brainwashed. Similarly, some of the blind spots I've seen in adults were probably the result of odd ideas implanted by their parents from an early age.

More often than not, however, adults brainwash themselves. Some behave dishonestly, and, rather than admit it, create elaborate justifications for their misdeeds. Others take credit for someone else's ideas or accomplishments. As time passes, perhaps they tell the story of their achievement over and over. With each successive telling, they become more comfortable with it, until eventually they delude themselves into believing it.

This type of delusional thinking can be difficult to spot. But you can't afford to miss it. You may have correctly concluded that in most respects someone is exceedingly honest and reliable, and you may have dismissed the potential that she would mislead you intentionally, even though her story feels wrong or doesn't add up. In view of her past honesty, the possibility that she's lying doesn't make sense: How could this essentially truthful woman make up such a story? In cases like this, consider the possibility that you've run into her blind spot—she's having a bout of delusional thinking.

The Physically Disabled

Years ago, I had a client who suffered from a nervous twitch. The twitch worsened when he was under stress: he would grimace and his head would jerk sideways. His attorney decided to explain this during jury selection, so that the jurors wouldn't misinterpret his neurological problem as a dishonest man's psychological response to tough questions.

Anytime you're evaluating someone who is disabled, it's critical to identify the disability and how it affects him or her. People with physical disabilities may not display the pattern you would otherwise expect. Make no assumptions about what the impact of a disability might be. It differs tremendously from person to person, often depending on whether the disability is lifelong or developed in childhood or adulthood, and on how much support the disabled person has had in coping.

I see many disabled people in my line of work. They're involved in lawsuits concerning their disability, and they often act as jurors, witnesses, lawyers, and judges. I've seen how differently people handle the loss of a limb or bodily function. On one end of the spectrum was a woman who suffered a severe and debilitating injury to both her legs in an automobile accident. She came from a very wealthy family and was bright, attractive, outgoing, and well educated. But because of her injuries, she had become surprisingly bitter and angry. Apparently feeling that something vital to her had been unfairly taken away, she developed a sense of entitlement. Without recognizing the significance of this woman's physical disability in her life, it would have been very difficult to truly understand her and predict her behavior. Her disability proved to be the trait that in many ways trumped all others.

On the other end of the spectrum was a juror in a case on which I recently worked. He was born with a deformed right arm, which was no more than a foot long; his hand wasn't much bigger than a large walnut. This obvious physical disability must have made him the brunt of vicious teasing in childhood.

After learning the basics about this man—his educational background, job history, family background, and life experiences—I was fairly confident that he would be a good juror for the defense, on whose behalf I had been retained. However, I was a little worried that because of his disability he might harbor some bitterness and hostility, which generally would not be good for the defendant in a criminal case. Also, because of the severity of his handicap and the effort undoubtedly required to overcome it, I thought he might not be particularly sympathetic to the defendant's plea for understanding and leniency. Because of these concerns I paid very careful attention during questioning to his body language and voice, as well as to his answers.

Everything I saw and heard suggested to me that he was a very well-adjusted, compassionate, and open-minded man: a good juror for this case. We left him on. I felt even better about this decision when I saw him raise his small right arm and hand to be sworn in as a juror. That degree of comfort with his disability reaffirmed my faith in him. Clearly, he had long ago come to terms with his disability and it did not negatively color his worldview.

With careful attention, you can determine what impact someone's disability has probably had on his view of the world. How does he refer to his handicap? Does he talk about it freely and comfortably? Excessive joking about it may reveal a deep-seated discomfort, but the ability to poke fun at oneself occasionally is always a good sign. Look to see how easily he moves among others and copes with physical obstacles such as stairs and doors. The more someone has mastered his environment, the more probable it is that he's integrated his disability into his life rather than letting it dominate him. Watch also for signs that someone prizes independence and has worked to achieve as much of it as he can. If he seems comfortable with himself and is as independent as possible, chances are his disability hasn't negatively influenced his worldview.

Often, however, a person's disability colors many aspects of his behavior and beliefs. You can identify such a person by a number of clues. Often he'll withdraw even from activities he could perform. He may be bitter toward others and toward life in general. He may expect to receive special treatment beyond that which is appropriate to accommodate his handicap. And he may use his disability as a rationale for his failures or unhappiness. Remember, satisfaction with life is a key predictive trait. If someone believes he has not achieved what he should have because of his disability, its impact on him will be that much greater. In such cases, the disability may overshadow the person's other traits and may be the driving force behind his character.

Any significant physical disability—whether it's heart problems, paralysis, epilepsy, or a stutter—needs to be viewed with special care. It would be unwise to assume that a disability defines a person, but by the same token, it would be naive to ignore the unique influence a serious disability may have on someone's life experiences and attitudes.

"I'm Not Myself Today": The Effects of Illness, Fatigue, and Stress

If you had met me in the winter of 1979, the fall of 1981, or the fall of 1987, you would have found me morose, humorless, unimaginative, weak, needy, weepy, and altogether quite debilitated. My appearance, body language, voice, words, and conduct would have been completely consistent. I was a mess.

But if two months later I ran into a friend of yours to whom you had described my pitiful condition, she would have thought you were crazy. I would have seemed very independent, outgoing, and happy.

So what happened? Like many women, after the birth of each of my three children, I suffered severe postpartum depression. My entire personality was altered by the physiological changes taking place in my body. Without knowing what was going on, you would have completely misinterpreted who I was and how I was likely to react under "normal" circumstances.

People's personalities can be severely affected by postpartum depression, PMS, chronic stress, and similar conditions. Personality can also be affected by the flu, a nagging cough, a toothache, or an upset stomach. But because most people try not to complain too loudly about their ailments, it's easy to miss the signs that someone is ill or under stress. If you didn't know he was nauseated, you might perceive someone suffering from a touch of the flu being quiet, inattentive, perhaps even rude. Similarly, you might think someone who is exhausted is bored, grouchy, not very intelligent, or possibly under the influence of drugs or alcohol.

Some medical problems are more obvious and last longer than others and it's usually not hard to see their impact on someone's behavior. When someone breaks a leg or suffers a bout of pneumonia, you'll probably attribute many of their grouchy moments to their condition. But temporary or less obvious conditions, like stress and fatigue, are easier to miss. You need to be on the lookout for them, however, because almost everyone's good humor and social graces take a backseat under these circumstances.

My friend Robert recently came very close to making a disastrous decision because he didn't realize one of his partners was under significant stress. Robert is an attorney in a small law firm, whose handful of partners have all shared strong personal friendships as well as professional ties over the past several years. Not long ago, one partner, Gary, suddenly became cold and distant. He and Robert had had some disagreements about a few minor issues in the previous weeks, but such differences of opinion never jeopardized their friendship before, and Robert didn't understand why they should now.

After two weeks of progressively more tense exchanges, the awkwardness escalated to open hostility at a firm meeting. Afterward, as Robert sat in his office sulking, Gary knocked on the door. Gary began by apologizing for his behavior, and told Robert how much he cherished their friendship. Slumping in his chair, Gary then dropped a bombshell: he and his wife were getting divorced. Gary was devastated.

Robert had neglected to look for possible explanations for his partner's odd behavior, even though there were strong indications that one of the exceptions to the rules was involved. Gary's actions were so out of character—and after all those years of friendship, Robert knew Gary's character well—that Robert should have realized that whatever was bothering his friend had nothing to do with their normal interaction.

When you see a sudden change in someone's behavior, look for signs of illness, fatigue, or stress. If you think his behavior is influenced by any of these, try to find out what exactly is wrong. You'll be able to tell by paying close attention to his body language and voice—and, if you're close to him, by simply asking.

The Impact of Drugs and Alcohol

Much of what has just been said about illness, fatigue, and stress applies equally to drugs and alcohol. They can produce symptoms of depression, anxiety, or hyperactivity. In some people drug or alcohol abuse is an illness, and might be considered nonelective. Others are recreational users, in which case the situation is totally elective. When evaluating people who sometimes seem to be under the influence, try to determine two things: How often do they use? And how does it affect their behavior?

Drugs and alcohol always affect behavior, but unless you know what a person is like sober you'll have a tough time knowing exactly what that effect is. Therefore, it's pretty foolish to make a judgment call about someone you first meet over a heap of empty champagne bottles at a New Year's Eve party. You need more information.

The most important thing to learn is whether the person has a substance-abuse problem. If so, it's a critical mistake to ignore the impact it will have on her behavior. Sometimes it's difficult to accept that a normally hardworking, considerate, intelligent person cannot be relied upon because she abuses drugs or alcohol. But in many cases, even when everything else you know about someone points in one direction, if she is a drug or alcohol abuser, one of the exceptions to the rules is at work. If you want to know the significance of that exception, just talk to the families, friends, coworkers, and employers of drug and alcohol abusers.

If, on the other hand, someone is just a recreational drinker, the most important thing to bear in mind is that what you see when he's been drinking is not necessarily what you'll get under normal circumstances. Alcohol can make people jovial or belligerent, aggressive or passive. The outgoing, witty life of the party and the loudmouthed party pooper may have very similar personalities when they're sober. Unless you recognize that drugs or alcohol may substantially change behavior, you may completely misjudge the traits you see when somebody is under the influence.

Cultural Influences

Many people think only of race or ethnicity when they consider someone's "cultural background." In fact, cultural background is much more. It is the influence of any peer group. Certainly race, ethnicity, and national origin influence us, but so do our religious background, age, regional origin, economic background, and sexual orientation. There are even professional cultures—among athletes, doctors, truckers, actors, the military, academicians, and almost every other identifiable group.

Attributing certain traits to certain groups is stereotyping. It's true that many stereotypes have some basis in fact, and that *some* stereotypes may accurately reflect characteristics of *some* members of the group: some Frenchmen are romantic, some Englishmen are witty, and some Scots are frugal. But reading people based on stereotypes is extremely unreliable. I can assure you, when I'm working for the defense I don't lean toward Scottish jurors on the theory that they will award lower damages.

As chapter 3, "Discovering Patterns," pointed out, you need to look beyond stereotypes to how someone's cultural experiences may have influenced her. The weight you should give a person's cultural background depends on just how deeply engrossed in that culture the person has been. What role did her culture play in her youth? And how much contact has she had with it since then?

- Did she go to school with other members of the same culture (for example, Hebrew school, Catholic school, Greek Orthodox school)?
- Does she regularly attend religious services?
- Was she raised, and does she still live, in a community populated mostly by members of that culture?
- Were her family's friends predominantly of the same culture?
- Do her current friends have the same cultural background?
- Does she patronize doctors, lawyers, shopkeepers, and others who have the same cultural background?
- Does she use cultural colloquialisms?
- Does she watch television and movies in her native tongue?
- Does she speak her native tongue at home?
- Does she wear clothing and hairstyles that reflect her culture?

Much the same line of inquiry is helpful when evaluating the influences of *any* culture. Imagine how someone may be influenced by a lifetime of emphasis on sports. Did your new boyfriend grow up living and breathing sports? Do he and his friends spend a significant amount of time playing in adult sports leagues? Is he an avid fan? When he's watching or playing a sport, does the rest of the world (including you) disappear? If so, his immersion in the sports culture may be a driving force in his behavior. Even if other characteristics don't suggest it, he is probably competitive, tough, macho, and able to concentrate. I know law firm recruiters who give high marks to applicants—male or female—who are successful athletes: the traits prized in jock culture frequently translate into success in the courtroom.

If your new brother-in-law was in the military, does he keep his hair short even though he's left the service? Years after retirement, does he still say "Yes, sir," or "Yes, ma'am"? Does he still carry himself with a military bearing? If so, the military mind-set undoubtedly had a profound impact on the way he views the world. He's probably disciplined, authoritarian, and conservative.

Whenever I'm involved in selecting a jury, I am very attuned to how someone's cultural experience may affect his other characteristics. One good example of this involves a man who had been immersed in two powerful cultures. I was working on a case in which a former police officer was the defendant. Those of us on the defense team were looking for jurors who did not have a bias against police officers or other authority figures. The juror at issue was a former Marine about thirty years old. He earned a master's degree in computer science after he left the Marine Corps, and was now working for the Department of the Navy. He still wore his hair very short and held his weight-lifter's body as stiff and erect as if he were still in the Marines. "Yes, sir" and "No, sir" were typical responses to the questions put to him. Everything about this man pointed to a law-and-order, no-nonsense, support-your-local-police-department mentality. Except he was African-American. And the sad reality is that in southern California, if not the entire United States, most young African-American men have had an unpleasant experience with the police, or are close to someone else who has.

Our jury questionnaire asked about confrontations with the police. This juror had replied simply, "I was stopped by the police one time with some friends." When asked to explain the situation further during the oral questioning, he replied, "You mean the incident where I was detained." As he said "detained," his jaw tightened. He snarled the word through gritted teeth. Without knowing that he obviously believed the police had treated him unfairly, we might have left him on the jury. As it was, I believed that his personal negative experience with the police would override all the other traits that would have suggested a sympathetic mind-set.

Recognition of cultural influences was also a factor in my recommendation to dismiss the Hispanic woman juror in the Simi Valley trial of the four officers accused of beating Rodney King discussed in chapter 6. Although she herself appeared to be unbiased, she acknowledged that her husband felt very strongly that the officers were guilty and should be severely punished. While I would never presume that all Hispanic marriages are dominated by the man, I am certainly aware that many are (and that this is not unique to Hispanic cultures). After further questioning, I was satisfied that the juror's husband dominated their relationship. For this reason I believed that whatever other positive traits she might have from the defense perspective, she should not be retained as a juror because she would have a difficult time overcoming her culturally induced bias.

I did not act upon a cultural stereotype in either of these examples. I tested it. Only after I was able to verify that the black Marine really had had an alienating experience with the police, and that the Hispanic woman really did have a traditional patriarchal marriage, did I conclude that those cultural influences might drive their behavior.

In some cases, investigation reveals that such conclusions are unfounded. For example, I recently participated in a program for the Ontario Bar Association in which one of my copanelists was a middle-aged, highly respected woman judge. At first, she seemed all business—confident, direct, and no-nonsense. At the podium, she typified the rather harsh, humorless professional culture in which many businesswomen, particularly in the field of law, are immersed.

After the program, I had dinner with the judge, and found that while her appearance and demeanor on the panel had pointed toward a strong "professional-woman cultural influence," once she was off that podium, it just wasn't there. She was warm, friendly, self-effacing, and funny. She talked of her children, not of her professional successes. She was not at all self-important or uptight, even going so far as to casually take a puff off another judge's cigarette during the cocktail hour. This is definitely not something I would expect from an uptight, all-business career woman.

Examples of cultural influences abound in everyday life. Here are a few, inspired by events I've witnessed over the past several months. All of them demonstrate how important it is to consider culture when you're reading people.

If you saw two men embracing each other and kissing on the cheek, would you assume they were gay? If you knew they were heavily influenced by a European culture in which men typically show such affection for one another and were comfortable with it, you would realize that such a conclusion is probably unwarranted.

If you saw a young woman dressed in a short skirt, four-inch-high platform shoes, a spaghetti-strap blouse that revealed both her belly button and her bra straps, dark lipstick, and long, multicolored fingernails, would you conclude she was loose and sleazy at best, and more probably a "working girl"? Not if you were aware of contemporary fashion culture. If every girl who dressed like this were a hooker, that category would include half the girls in southern California between the ages of fifteen and twenty-one. Even "good girls" dress that way these days.

You see a young couple proudly displaying their assortment of tattoos and exotic body piercings. Are they freaks? Social outcasts? Rock musicians? No, they are members of the MTV generation. Ten years from now, likely as not, they'll be teaching your children calculus or ringing you up in the grocery store.

Cultural influences are extremely complex and often difficult to recognize. Still, there are a few simple rules that can help you correctly identify when they are most likely at work.

- Remember that race and national origin aren't the only cultural influences. Also consider religion, age, geographical origin, sexual orientation, economic background, and profession, as well as the person's other peer groups.
- Never make decisions based on cultural stereotypes. Always test them against the life experiences of the person you're evaluating.
- When someone appears to be subject to a particular cultural influence, learn about the nature and extent of that influence, and from that information try to gauge its importance in shaping the person's perspective.

Coincidences Do Happen

Sometimes seemingly significant events are entirely meaningless. While a healthy skepticism is essential for reading people effectively, it's just as important to keep an open mind to the possibility that something is just an innocent coincidence.

In an earlier chapter I relayed the story of the woman juror who wore black gloves to court every day during the federal prosecution of the four officers for the beating of Rodney King. Had the woman been white and had the trial involved something other than an allegedly racially motivated beating, I might have assumed either that the woman was cold or that she just liked to wear gloves. Everyone on the legal team certainly wouldn't have wondered whether she was making a racial statement. The fact is, the racial background of the people involved in the case was purely coincidental.

Just because you see someone at the opera does not mean he is cultured or sophisticated, or even that he likes the opera. Maybe a friend gave him the tickets and he felt obliged to attend. Likewise, while it may be natural to assume that someone you run into at a baseball game likes baseball, maybe he's on a company outing or is courting a customer who enjoys the game. In either case, meeting that person in that setting is just a coincidence.

If someone has an obvious stain on his tie, can you assume he's a slob? Maybe. On the other hand, perhaps a waiter spilled some soup on him twenty minutes earlier and he hasn't had a chance to change. He may be the most obsessively fastidious person you'll ever meet. The spot on his tie may be meaningless—or worse, misleading.

In the continuous process of gathering and weighing information, you will catch a few red herrings. Don't assume anything; look for patterns; and expect to come across coincidences now and then.

Asperger's Syndrome

One of the most compelling e-mails that I received after the original publication of this book came from Lynn, a woman who suffers from Asperger's syndrome. In her communication she told me stories regarding instances in which both she and other people with Asperger's had been misread. A person with Asperger's has a physiological/neurological barrier to normal social interaction cues that a person with Asperger's is not likely to pick up. She correctly pointed out that I didn't pay enough attention to autistics in the earlier version of the book. Many people with Asperger's have been called "creepy," "jerks," "serial killers," and "rapists." Her heartfelt story sparked my interest in learning more about this syndrome.

Asperger's syndrome is a disorder that, despite its discovery in 1944, had not reached a level of medical acceptance until the mid-1990s. This neurobiological or developmental disorder appears in individuals across all intelligence levels and appears more frequently in males. It can range from mild to severe and appears in both children and adults. People with Asperger's syndrome are specifically impaired in social interactions by their inability to read nonverbal cues. Often times, you will find that a person with this syndrome might be hypersensitive to sounds, light, and smells. Additionally, these individuals prefer to live within predictable patterns and routines, where nothing ever changes. Other common symptoms of this disorder can include inappropriate or one-sided social interaction, clumsy body language, pedantic or monotone speech patterns, discussions focusing on only one or two subjects, lack of eye contact, awkward movements, and strange posture.

Lynn gave some wonderful examples of how certain behaviors of a person with Asperger's could be misconstrued by the person reading them. She tells of a friend who wears sunglasses inside not to hide a black eye or drug use, but because he can't tolerate fluorescent lighting. Someone who has trouble with eye contact may not be a self-impressed jerk; he may have Asperger's. Another person might ramble on about one topic that bores you to tears but they can't pick up on the cues that would tell them that you're bored. Yet another woman doesn't thank the person bagging her groceries only because she is terrified of speaking with others.

All of these examples are important because there are many more people than any of us would think who have varying degrees of Asperger's. Many of us think these people are disrespectful or worse. In fact, one of their biggest fears is that we will dislike them and not want to become friends with them.

The moral of this story is that stereotyping is not people reading. We have to evaluate all of the possible reasons why a person may be manifesting a particular social-interaction behavior. It must be horribly painful to be unable to naturally read others, much less to be misread by others.

KEY POINTS

Always consider whether you're missing a key piece of the puzzle: Some single factor can drastically alter an otherwise clear picture.

Be particularly alert for:

- *The elastic person.* With time and exposure he'll revert to his natural state.
- *The rehearsed presentation.* Take her out of her comfort zone and see how she handles herself.
- *Liars.* Most people are uncomfortable when they lie. That discomfort usually leaks out somewhere. But the more frequently one lies, the less it bothers him and more difficult it is to spot the lies from voice and mannerisms. You'll need to focus more on what he says and does, or verify his statements independently.
- *The delusional thinker.* Sometimes we unwittingly fool ourselves, not just others. It's not a lie, but a blind spot.
- *The physically disabled.* Don't assume someone who is physically challenged will see and react to the world as the able-bodied do.
- *Illness, fatigue, and stress.* Don't judge too harshly, but realize that what you see is what you can expect to emerge under similar circumstances in the future.
- *Drugs and alcohol.* They can change behavior so dramatically from moment to moment that they should always be considered.
- *Cultural influences.* Before you jump to any conclusions, determine if someone's culture deeply impacts him. If it does, learn as much as you can about the culture before you draw any conclusions.

Never forget, coincidences do happen: Sometimes seemingly significant events are entirely meaningless. Don't assume too much.

TWELVE

Reading People in the Internet Age

In order to find out how reliant you have become on technology, take the following short quiz.

- Does most of your daily communication take place via e-mail, even with your spouse or other family members?
- Do you prefer to use e-mail as a way to intentionally avoid verbal conversations?
- Can you list the free wireless "hot spots" in your area off the top of your head?
- Has it been a year or more since you set foot in a bank or shopping mall?
- Do you rush home from outings frequently to check your MySpace page?
- Have you memorized more e-mail addresses than phone numbers?
- Do you spend more time online playing games than interacting with humans?

If you answered yes to most of the above questions, it's time to seriously reexamine your future as a people-reader. Most people are simply unable to resist being swept into the technological age, with its lure of increased efficiency and decreased need for in-person communication. Business can be conducted cheaply online from anywhere in the world via e-mail, and software like Skype even allows people to videoconference for free. There are even discussions taking place about whether or not the Americans with Disabilities Act applies to Web sites, especially with regards to the needs of the vision-impaired.

Although technology has increased our efficiency in the professional world, it has decreased our ability to monitor our children's personal lives. The ease of cyberspace communication causes parents a significant amount of anxiety, knowing that so many of their children use the Internet (which is increasingly available for free) to cultivate personal relationships.

In our adult discourses, Internet correspondence is supplemented with live contact that enables us to read someone in all Seven Colors. However, when that is not possible (or safe to do, as in some instances), this chapter will discuss the significant amount of information we can glean about someone online.

How Much Is Left to Read

In modern times we have many more contacts, but much less personal contact. Computers, cell phones, pagers, and BlackBerry devices have replaced the need for live contact. Some modern business cards contain four or five contact numbers in addition to e-mail and a Web site. (Ironically, however, even with all of this technology, we can never seem to get ahold of anyone!)

Let's face it, if all we have available to read someone is their e-mail correspondence or Web site postings, we are at a distinct disadvantage—but that disadvantage is not insurmountable.

This chapter will show you how you can most reliably form impressions on many different levels, even in cyberspace. So even when you don't have the chance to test the information gleaned from your virtual "reading" skills against other information you have from and about the person that was acquired through other means, there is a wealth of information you can read online.

E-mail "Relationships"

E-mail has replaced the telephone as the primary mode of communication for many of us. You may e-mail back and forth with someone assisting you in making travel arrangements so frequently either in a business or personal environment that you feel that you know her. You even have a mental picture of what you think she looks like. When you finally meet her in person you might be shocked to discover she is nothing like you imagined. In fact, with the popularity of unisex names, you may have even mistaken her sex. Talk about the reliability of first impressions!

E-mail "first impressions" can be wrong on multiple levels. Many people have great e-mail manners (sometimes as a result of time spent on social Web sites), only to be obnoxious in person, or vice versa. This is one of the reasons we still meet people in person for important things like job interviews and don't just hire based solely on someone's résumé.

You can gauge only so much from words on a page. You miss critical information that you could otherwise glean through body language, facial expressions, voice inflection, pauses, and so on. Worst-case scenario, someone else is answering her e-mail! We see this more and more often with busy professionals who give their assistants the freedom to correspond under their name.

Now surely, most of us recognize the drawbacks to relying solely on virtual communication. But because our society nonetheless continues to forge ahead into cyberspace, it is important to discuss methods of compensating for the absence of live clues, and suggest ways in which we can elicit more reliable information. But first, consider what types of contact you absolutely *must* continue to have in person.

"You're Hired" and "I Do"

Even in the age of technology, our most important meetings are still done in person. These include job interviews, taking oaths, and—unless the groom-to-be is fighting a war overseas—marriage proposals. There is a reason we have suicide hotlines, and even suicide support Web sites encourage visitors to *call* a hotline to talk with someone. With the essentials, technology should be a last resort.

Jury selection is another process that is so important that our judicial system requires it be done in person. Even if the jurors have been given questionnaires previously, that process is always followed up by in-person questioning. Similarly, when we summon our citizens for jury duty and send them to a courtroom to decide a case, they are not just given huge boxes of transcripts to read and dismissed. Why not? Because some things in life are just too important to leave to chance when it comes to reading people, we don't cut corners when we need to make important decisions; we gather all of the relevant information that we can.

This brings me to the second example of "I do," the taking of an oath to tell the truth. Consider the following scenario. A young female witness steps into the courtroom. Her inappropriately short skirt immediately prompts several audible *tssks* from the gallery. She tentatively wobbles through the audience in obviously uncomfortable shoes, with makeup running down her face from crying. As she raises her visibly shaking right hand to take the oath to tell the truth, she stares wide-eyed at the defendant, looking absolutely terrified. As she prepares to respond to the oath, her gaze immediately drops to the floor; her answer is given in a voice that is barely audible as she stares at the tips of her stiletto heels and tentatively replies: "I do."

Now imagine how that scenario would have appeared on paper:

BAILIFF: "Ma'am, please raise your right hand. Do you swear to tell the truth, the whole truth, and nothing but the truth, so help you God?"
WITNESS: "I do."

Can you imagine the magnitude of what the person reading the transcript would have missed? The way this witness took the oath will likely influence how the jurors view everything she said on the stand! One of our most important jury instructions explains to the jurors that they are allowed to consider, among other things, motive, bias, interest, and a witness's demeanor while testifying. Jurors are permitted and even encouraged to notice how witnesses' demeanor and body language complements or contradicts their testimony.

Some of Wendy's experiences as a prosecutor during police interrogations illustrate this need. There is a reason these are done in person, and often videotaped. The suspect's demeanor during a police interview is a key piece of evidence. If a man accused of killing his wife and who learned of her death just hours beforehand is seen in the videotape of his police interview jovial, smiling, and joking around, this will be powerful evidence for a jury. Can you imagine the difference if all the jurors had was a dry transcript of the interview? The police don't interview suspects over the phone either, for precisely the same reasons. And can you imagine if the police started interviewing suspects via e-mail? With no controls over how long they had to respond, who was actually responding, and no indication of mannerisms, appearance, voice quality, or expressions, how effective an investigation tool would that be?

Seven Colors Online

Before you turn on your computer monitor at the office in the morning, my best advice, if you have something important to convey, is to get up out of your chair and walk over to the person's office to talk to her in person—especially if your subsequent actions will depend on the other person's reaction to whatever information you have to convey. Consider the following illustration of the Colors you are, and are not, able to reliably read online:

Reading People in Cyberspace

	LIVE	PHONE	E-MAIL
Personal Appearance	X		
Body Language	X		
Voice	X	X	
Communication Style	X	X	X*
Content	X	X	X*
Actions	X		
Environment	X		

*Assuming the person you think you are communicating with is who you are, in fact, communicating with!

A recent *New York Times* article by Daniel Goleman, author of *Social Intelligence: The New Science of Human Relationships*, discussed "social neuroscience," defined as the study of brain function as a result of interaction.* The article stated that a computer screen does not provide the brain with the signals it needs to "calibrate emotions." In-person interaction, on the other hand, has been proved to help one person's

---

*"E-mail Is Easy to Write (And to Misread)," *New York Times*, October 7, 2007. *www.nytimes.com/2007/10/07/jobs/07pre.html?_r=1&oref=slogin*).

brain stay on the same emotional wavelength as that of the person with whom he is interacting.

If e-mail is the only medium through which you are attempting to read another person, the main Colors you have available to read are Communication Style and Content. You may therefore find yourself assigning more weight to these cues than would be necessary and appropriate if you had more information to use. In many cases, however, e-mails and the circumstances surrounding their transmission may provide you with considerable information.

Despite the obvious drawbacks, you can read quite a lot about people online on a number of levels if you pay close attention to detail. In addition to text, e-mail correspondence may include a variety of font and format styles, symbols, graphics, detailed taglines, links, photos, and many other cues, including when and from where the e-mail was sent. Similarly, text, link options, and graphics of Web sites provide even more information that will assist you in drawing conclusions. This chapter will explore how you can read others online, creatively perceiving more of the Seven Colors than you might think possible.

Virtual Appearance

Unless someone has a Web cam on his computer (and many people do!), if you want to know what someone with whom you are corresponding online looks like, you might have to rely on a photograph attached to the tagline of his e-mail in the same way a realtor puts his photo on his business card. This is the only way people online can show you what they really look like. Or *do* they? What kind of photo has he chosen to append to his e-mail tagline? Is it the photo from his driver's license or passport? Unlikely. The photos people include in their e-mail "signatures" are often some kind of glamour shot or professionally done headshot courtesy of their company photographer. And how do we know *when* the photograph was taken? As with any kind of business directory, there is a strong temptation to keep using a great photo, regardless of how outdated it is. I know a criminal defense lawyer in Los Angeles who uses a personal photo that is at least thirty years old. This might indicate that he is vain, or perhaps just lazy. You would need to find out if he has updated anything else to know for sure.

These issues certainly arise in the context of online dating, except that the cyberspace façade—with all its opportunities for misrepresentation—doesn't even give us the comfort of knowing whether the photo that was submitted matches the person with whom you are corresponding!

Cyberbody Language

Is there such a thing? Well, not really. It's impossible to visually read this Color online unless someone is using a live-stream service like YouTube—technology that is currently being utilized widely. The current extensive use of video blogging and MySpace pages have made it easier to read someone in more Colors online than merely reading *about* them through words on a page. If you are attempting to read body language through a photo on someone's Web site or tagline, you may still be able to glean some cues, such as folded hands, crossed arms or legs, and posture. Keep in mind, however, that some Internet photos people post of themselves may be posed or altered. Photoshop, a digital-imaging program, is used to airbrush and reconfigure photos so often that it has actually become a verb—"to photoshop"—and an adjective, to describe a "photoshopped" picture. Even the effectiveness of reading body language through videoconferencing is compromised by the artificial nature of the medium. Although the participants can see each other, a videoconference is no substitute for a natural environment.

So is there any way—besides relying on a photoshopped image or a grainy YouTube clip—to read the body-language Color online? Not very reliably, is the easy answer. Because of this, many expressions have cropped up for people to describe what kind of body language is accompanying their message—terms like "lol" (laughing out loud) "sigh," "yawn," "big hug," and "smile" are used, although most of these are commonly understood as obvious exaggerations. And these self-described gestures still lack verifiability, especially when you consider that the reason reading live body language is so valuable is because in contrast to the conscious descriptions of body language provided online, natural body language is largely unconscious and therefore much more predictive. Online body language expressed by the sender is more aptly analyzed for its content.

Also note that the sender's use of expressions such as "lol," while intended to convey something specific (in this case that they find something amusing), unintentionally conveys other things, such as their casual approach to e-mail correspondence; possibly their age, because many older adults are unfamiliar with what these contractions mean; and even their level of professionalism and judgment, depending on whom they are sending the message to. If these body-language expressions are used by an advertising executive when she e-mails her new boss, it might throw into question her judgment, and consequently her capability as well.

Online "Voice"

Through our computer keyboards we can select keystrokes that will mimic vocal intonations. For example:

- ALL CAPITALS: A word or phrase in all capitals transmits anger or excitement, depending on context and the use of punctuation.
- *Italics*, underlining, and **bolding** show the same kind of emphasis as would be expressed through vocal intonation and to express emotion.
- Punctuation such as exclamation points, question marks, and signals like asterisks and the famous "*@*&*#*!" phrase are also used to enhance meaning, and often indicate a lighter tone to the message.
- Parentheses signify what the sender does not consider to be quite as important as the rest of the message.
- In general, messages that include a moderate to high level of font changes and nonletter characters indicate a higher level of familiarity and a more casual demeanor than more formal messages.

At first blush, you might think that in this fashion you could decipher the same types of cues you would by listening to someone talk out loud. Unfortunately, that isn't really accurate, as *involuntary* vocal variations are more reliable than spoken words, just as body language is more reliable than appearance. Someone can only type the emphasis he *wants* to convey, not what would be subconsciously conveyed if he were talking live. For this reason even a phone conversation is preferable to an e-mail if the topic is important. And also remember that many people have neither the time nor the patience to bold or italicize their text. Some people don't even bother to capitalize.

E-mail Etiquette: Communication Style

As with verbal communication (see chapter 7), we read a lot into electronic communication style. If a Reflective communicator sends a long and flowery e-mail to a Noble who responds with a one-word answer, the Reflective will immediately feel put off and offended. The Noble, on the other hand, will be irritated that the Reflective just bombarded him with irrelevant information that wasted both the space on his computer screen and the time it took for him to read the message. Both of these people have just read the other negatively, all due to something as simple as a difference in communication styles.

Before jumping to a conclusion based on someone's communication style, consider the circumstances surrounding the e-mail's delivery. If someone is sending email from her BlackBerry, even a Reflective is tempered by the challenge of typing with her thumbs. The amount of text she may be able to comfortably type from her BlackBerry may make her look like a Noble! A curt e-mail reply might also mean that the other person is in the middle of something and can respond with only a couple of words. In this fashion, communication style must be analyzed in the context of the environment. We can discern environment from what someone tells us in his e-mail— if he explains that he is in the middle of a meeting, for example—or if we see in the e-mail that it was sent from his BlackBerry, in which case a shorter-than-usual message makes sense.

E-mail Content: Spelling Errors

Many people are incredibly articulate verbal communicators. Some of these same people, however, cannot express a thought on paper to save their lives. This is why speech writers make as much money as they do. And even worse, some otherwise very competent professionals would lose a spelling bee to a seven-year-old. These problems severely impact their ability to come across as intelligent and capable when they correspond through e-mail, and consequently affect the way they are mistakenly read by others.

Harry, a friend of mine and professor at a local university, is an incredibly proficient and highly skilled writer who has authored several scholarly books. But during the workday he often interrupts his coworkers and staff with questions yelled out of his office, such as "How do you spell 'personnel'?" and "Does 'dessert' have one 's' or two?" Dictaphones were invented for people like Harry to speak into at night, and an important part of his personal secretary's job is to type up the resulting documents each morning. Once these documents are typed, spell-checker is thankfully included in Harry's word-processing programs in case even his competent secretary misspelled a word. Harry does not, however, have a good spell-check in his e-mail account, and consequently, many people who correspond with him through that medium question whether they have the wrong e-mail address! Suffice it to say, the Harrys of the world are advised to stick with live communication because their e-mails, in stark contrast to their other forms of communication, do not exude professionalism.

On the other hand, the poor grammar in some people's e-mails truly does stem from lack of care; their e-mails merely reflect their usual negligence. If someone is sloppy in other areas, they will come across as sloppy online. In addition, depending on the content of the e-mail, poor grammar and spelling may severely impact the sender's credibility. If a woman on a singles site receives a response from a man claiming to be a Harvard graduate with a literary degree who misspells not only "Cambridge" but also "Massachusetts," she will justifiably second-guess his authenticity.

If you are attempting to read someone solely via e-mail correspondence, you should keep such limitations in mind. Resist the temptation to discount someone immediately based on e-mail syntax and spelling errors; opt instead to gather more information before passing judgment. This doesn't mean you should immediately set up an in-person meeting with someone you met online. Search engines like Google can provide a wealth of information about someone against which you can test your observations.

Cyberspace Actions

I recently saw a flyer from the Anti-Defamation League advertising a class that included a segment on "Understanding and Addressing Cyberbullying." This topic would include a discussion about online hate activities and fostering a culture of "e-safety." Isn't this a sign of the times! Once confined to the school playground, bullying is now possible online! In today's world many people perform actions in cyberspace that you can read like real-life actions. Reported instances of online harassment have included threatening or vulgar e-mails, posting embarrassing or defamatory information about someone on public Web sites, and spreading rumors via electronic chain letters.

One common online action that occurs every day in the world of business and marketing could be dubbed "cybernetworking." When some people send you an e-mail, they also deliver their résumé or bio—information appended to the end of their e-mails in the form of an extended signature or tagline. This supplemental information ranges from simple facts like the person's full name and contact information to a curriculum vitae complete with graphics, photos, and a link to her Web site. Due to the promotional nature of many taglines, you can often learn far more background information about a person if he e-mails you than you ever would if you met him in person. Some e-mail taglines include career highlights like "Winner of the Golden Spoon Award" or "Bestselling author of *The Stock Market in the New Millennium.*" Such feats would be awkward to mention if these people just met you at a party, but delivering the information via an automatic e-mail tag does not convey the same sense of egotism and is becoming increasingly appropriate.

Someone's intentional selection of an e-mail tagline will tell you something about his personality, especially if he is using a personal e-mail address. Some professional e-mail taglines contain boilerplate occupational information and a link to the company Web site. While law firms, hospitals, and federal organizations list details about some of their executives, a majority of companies (like book publishers) keep their employees' information private.

Personal e-mail taglines, on the other hand, contain what the person has *chosen* to include. You can read something about her priorities, depending on whether she included a link to a promotional video of her last singing gig or a link to footage of her son making a touchdown at his junior high school football game. Again, this is valuable information that is unlikely to come up during an initial meeting with the person.

Other cyberspace "actions" are really just regular actions performed online, like the gracious friend who searches the Web for articles on buying a new home and sends them to her girlfriend who is in the market for a house, or the coworker who sends links to political Web sites to her colleague who has just landed a job reporting on national politics. Unfortunately, as discussed in chapter 9, the most revealing actions are those that people engage in when they think no one important is watching. So unless you have hacked into someone else's computer (in which case getting an accurate read on them is the least of your problems), the Internet is not the most reliable forum for reading the Actions Color.

E-environment: Reading the Surrounding Circumstances

Imagine you are at your desk one morning, soon after having started a new job. You have just finished reading an e-mail from your new boss containing specific instructions on how to complete an important new assignment you have been given. You have read the information in her e-mail carefully, and paid close attention to her instructions, wanting very much to perform well in your new position. Just as you are about to delete her e-mail, you notice one very important piece of information: it was sent at three A.M.

Congratulations, you may have just learned one of the most important things about your new boss and her priorities. This observation may actually turn out to be more valuable to you in the long run than the content of the e-mail. Your new boss may be either a hopeless insomniac or a workaholic, but more likely the latter. This is because although many people have trouble sleeping at night, only a portion of insomniacs turn to their jobs for comfort in the middle of the night. Many people will attempt some sort of soothing activity such as soft music, television, or a glass of warm milk.

Someone who is up in the middle of the night working takes her job very seriously, and likely expects that her employees will, too. Also notice the volume of text she is sending. Has she sent only one e-mail to you, or is she sending out block e-mails to your entire division on various topics? If you determine your new boss is routinely up working for a significant amount of time overnight and she is still at her desk every morning at eight A.M., you can bet this is not a woman who will understand or approve of your coming in late, taking a long lunch hour, knocking off early, or asking for extensions on your work.

Now let's suppose this e-mail is not from your boss, but from an employee that works *for* you. Before you get carried away with praising the obvious dedication this employee has for his job, are there other explanations for the three A.M. time stamp? Sure, and you will need to explore the other possibilities (which could also apply to an e-mail sent from your boss) before jumping to conclusions. As a starting point, you want to know if these hours are part of the other person's usual business practice. Apart from the insomnia explanation, some people may be so enamored with their job or such workaholics that they can't stop working at night. Other people will explain that the only time they can get any work done at home is after their kids and spouses go to bed. One of the less likely explanations—but certainly not out of the realm of possibilities—is that the person is up all night using some kind of stimulant. Obviously, as with the other possibilities, before reaching this type of conclusion you will want to examine the surrounding circumstances. If the employee weighs eighty pounds, has a terrible complexion, is consistently missing work, and is always falling asleep at her desk, you might want to consider involving your Human Relations department. But if she is in impeccable physical health and demonstrates no other erratic or questionable behaviors, it may not raise any alarms.

And in the cyberspace age also remember that you may not really know *when* the e-mail was actually sent. If a company server goes down, the computer systems in some large offices just collect everything in the outbox and then send out all of the e-mails whenever the server is back online, which is usually when all of the e-mails will end up being time-stamped. If you relied on a time stamp as an indication of productivity, late-night server failures would result in everyone appearing to be incredibly efficient workers, having composed and sent fifty e-mails all at eight in the morning! In addition, because there is often no reliable way to tell from *where* e-mails have been sent, you may be unknowingly corresponding with someone who sent an e-mail at noon in their time zone, when it was three A.M. in yours!

Reading People *Through* Their Use of Technology

You can learn a lot about people by paying attention to the extent of their use and reliance on technology, as well as from the type of technology they use. Some people pride themselves on knowing how to use all of the latest gadgets from The Sharper Image, while others wouldn't dream of apologizing for the eight-track tape player in their office, next to the manual pencil sharpener. Note that in this fashion you are also reading their respective attitudes, security, and comfort level about aging. The sixty-year-old accountant with a phone attached to his ear and an iPod attached to his arm may be making a desperate attempt to appear youthful and "with it," or he may be like my husband and genuinely love gadgets and want to keep abreast of the times. You won't know which explanation fits unless you read his other Colors. If this man also has a head full of blond hair plugs, wears trendy clothing, and always has a surfboard fastened to the top of his car, you may have identified more indications of insecurity with aging. The sixty-five-year-old accountant in the office next door with natural gray hair, a bookshelf of reference material, and a pencil and a pad of paper *in plain view* by his telephone who appears comfortable with his age may be viewed as more confident and capable by comparison. His comfort level even changes the way his personal appearance is perceived; his gray hair does not scream old, but wise. On the other hand, he may be out of touch.

Love It or Leave It

This phrase embodies many people's attitudes toward the swell of technology that is engulfing our society. Some people are very vocal about their negative feelings toward heavy reliance on technology. I have friends who will use their company e-mail at work for work-related business, but refuse to buy a personal laptop, or carry a PDA or a BlackBerry. Some people even refuse to carry cell phones or pagers because they do not want their interpersonal relationships to be interrupted. I know people who refuse even to get call-waiting for this same reason. These people value personal relationships and cherish quality of interactions over quantity or speed. If you work for someone like this, it is in your best interest to sacrifice the time it would take to walk to her office if you need to tell her something instead of sending an e-mail.

Some people prefer to communicate electronically, and so depend solely on their computers or BlackBerry devices. Someone like this would prefer that you e-mail him rather than attempt to track him down any other way. You need to learn more information about someone in order to determine whether his refusal to carry personal communication devices is due to concerns of courtesy or of accountability.

Paying attention to how someone uses technology can also reveal information about her sense of social correctness. Some technophiles are perfectly comfortable taking a phone call in the middle of a business meeting. They may even carry on a short phone conversation at the meeting without getting up to walk outside. Believe it or not, I have watched attorneys take phone calls in court, when the judge is on the bench—hard to believe, but true. This behavior also speaks volumes about others who believe it to be somewhat inappropriate. Old-school professionals would *never* condone this practice. Text messaging is less obvious and less disruptive than a phone call, but if you're texting in the middle of a meeting or on a date, it similarly reveals that your priorities are elsewhere, and it also signals poor judgment. Texting may be a hallmark of the younger, technology-inundated generation, who are new to the workforce and who honestly believe that this conduct is acceptable (in which case hopefully they will be assigned an older mentor). It could also represent someone who is just self-absorbed and couldn't care less about being disruptive.

The Allure of Anonymity or the Ease of Efficiency

The reason why people choose to operate as much as they do behind the cyberspace curtain can tell you a lot about them. An engaging Web site can be a valuable promotional tool, but it can also provide a façade that is easy to hide behind. Someone's Web site can provide a glimpse into her personality through her choice of message, graphics, and selected links. This will give you the opportunity to observe both what she wants you to see and what she unintentionally reveals about herself. For example, is the most prominent feature a "Contact Me" button or a series of grandiose testimonials? The former may indicate a desire for personal communication while the latter may indicate insecurity or poor judgment if the claims are too over-the-top. However, all of the testimonials may be 100 percent true, which is why you will need to navigate someone's Web site in its entirety in order to get an accurate read of her. Also note what other Web sites it links to: legitimate world news organizations, gossip sites, or sites that are all "currently under construction" or state "page not available." There are also those Web sites that are geared specifically toward human error in typing popular Web site pages, such as "wikepedia.com" instead of "wikipedia.com."

In addition, many people simply communicate better in cyberspace. When a shy or insecure person is sitting in front of a computer screen, he likely has time to formulate thoughts and responses in a low-stress virtual atmosphere. Many of us know people who behave like fish out of water at parties and other social events, but are incredibly articulate and witty on e-mail. Consequently, online dating has become one of the preferred ways to meet people. It's easy: you can proceed at your own pace, and you don't have to try on every outfit in your closet before you send an e-mail (you have already posted your best photograph online!). Many social Web sites and chat rooms even allow you to attend online "parties" without leaving the security of your home.

When you come across someone who would much rather communicate from behind the veil of cyberspace than be out there in person, in order to get an accurate read on him, you are going to have to analyze more than meets the (visual) eye. The file clerk who appears shy and unapproachable in the office may be the life of the party on sites like MySpace, Friendster, and Facebook. How will you be able to determine this? You have to see someone's behavior in a variety of circumstances in order to acquire enough information to read him correctly. That same seemingly shy file clerk obviously has a strong social side. So in order to get a more reliable read on her, you would want to not only observe her demeanor and behavior at the office, but also at the company picnic, at happy hour, and at the company holiday party.

Façade: Pretentious or Predator?

I recently heard a new country-western song by Brad Paisley, "Online," which goes, "I'm so much cooler online." The song is a great example of how someone can basically blog anything he wants with regard to his background, demographics, attitudes, and opinions. The lyrics of the song refer to the man as being something other than what he is (taller, physically fit). The importance of his song is the public acknowledgment that many people hide their real selves behind their monitors, typing or blogging information that may not be true. The dangerous implications here are far-reaching, as in the case of sexual predators. Internet journalists can post materials that are largely unchecked for accuracy, and yet because of the material's widespread availability, they can still influence the opinions of scores of readers.

There are several reasons that people disguise themselves online. Some reasons are innocuous, such as wanting to describe themselves as more physically attractive than they really are. For example, one of my client's teenage daughters is currently plagued with a severe case of acne. Her Facebook page, however, showcases a series of gorgeous photos of her in a bikini on the beach from a distance, with her complexion completely out of view. The new media adaptation of fudging height and weight on a driver's license is to provide misleading self-descriptions or post outdated photos of oneself online. Other people will lie about their age, what kind of job they have, or misrepresent their financial status in an effort to appear successful.

Wendy recently handled a spousal abuse case where the defendant maintained a quite impressive Match.com page that was highly inconsistent with his statement to the police. His claim of acting in self-defense was belied by his enhanced online physical description and his boasting on Match.com that he was a body builder who worked out five days a week. Similarly, his claim of being a wine connoisseur on his Match.com profile contradicted his assertion in the criminal case that he never drank alcohol of any kind, which was provided to corroborate his statement about not drinking at the time of the offense.

But on the other end of the spectrum, some people disguise themselves online in order to prey upon unsuspecting victims. Sexual predators often pretend to be the same age as the twelve-year-old victims upon whom they prey, or sometimes even pretend to be other young girls in order to gain the friendship and trust of the unsuspecting victims. Without having the benefit of all Seven Colors to read, how do you tell the difference? While I wish we could provide an easy answer to this dilemma, let me just point out that the Internet has not only created this problem; it has also given us tools to help solve it. Google and similar sites allow us to research anyone, anywhere, in no time. Young Internet users (and their parents) should seek from their online friends enough information to then independently verify they are who they represent themselves to be. Like the buyer not trusting his realtor and Googling a seller, the Internet has given us an extensive database in order for us to "trust but verify" the true identities of those with whom we correspond.

The importance of verifying online identity is highlighted by a heartbreaking story that was in the news recently about a young girl who killed herself over a boy named "Josh" who never existed. A story that proves that even when parents are monitoring their children's online activity, the opportunity for fraud inherent in such correspondence can lead to tragic results. National news carried the story of thirteen-year-old Megan, who began an online MySpace correspondence with Josh, whom she and her mother, who consented to the contact, thought to be a sixteen-year-old boy. Megan became very enamored of Josh, and was devastated when he turned on her one day and began to say horrible things about her, leading Megan to commit suicide by hanging herself in her closet. It turned out that "Josh" was actually a fictional boy made up by some neighbors down the street who had a daughter with whom Megan had had a falling-out. Their mean-spirited practical joke cost Megan her life.

In addition to using online research tools, make sure you corroborate the online information with information that was gathered in the real world. Consider a young woman who is preparing to interview for a legal secretary position. Having grown up in the technological age, she knows that the fastest way to research her potential new boss is online. The first thing she does is Google the lawyer she wants to work for, carefully reading her corporate bio and her firm's description. She then prints out some articles about the firm's history to read before the interview.

Unfortunately for this ambitious young woman, her competition for the job is an older woman who grew up in a time where the best way to learn about someone was to spend time observing her. So the older woman looks at the court calendar to find out what department her potential new boss is in, and then goes and watches her in trial. She notices her suits, what kind of pen she uses, the condition of her briefcase, her demeanor and communication style, who comes to court with her, and how she speaks. As a result, when she comes in for her job interview she has not only gathered a large amount of useful information with which to tailor her own style, but she is able to deliver, Dale Carnegie style, some music to the litigator's ears: well-thought-out compliments on what she did well in her last jury trial!

How Much of a Technophile Have *You* Become?

Let's face it, most of us can relate all too well to many of the problems described in this chapter. We have all, to some extent, been initiated into the virtual age. While new technology has certainly allowed us to become more efficient and productive in many ways, don't let your reliance on technology cause you to lose focus on reading people in the real world.

The Dangers of Multitasking

Technological advancements allow us to multitask at higher levels than ever before. Many people defend their reliance on technology by pointing out the necessity of using the latest gadgets to keep up with everything they need to do. As if being able to send e-mails while talking on the phone wasn't convenient enough, now we can correspond with others, do online banking, or surf the Internet even during the most important of business meetings, right from our handheld devices. "So what if we miss some of the minor points covered at the meeting?" many people rationalize to themselves, defending their divided attention as the price of efficiency. But what is the real cost?

Our old-fashioned coworkers who are actually focused on the meeting at hand will be at a huge advantage, because in paying attention to the speaker, they are able to use their people-reading skills to figure out what their boss really conveyed during the meeting. While Sharon was busy bidding on a dining room set in an eBay auction, her old-school coworkers Ellen and Wendell were not only bonding with the boss by maintaining steady eye contact with her and squared body language during the meeting; they were reading her like a book. Regarding *personal appearance,* they saw the sweat on her forehead as she described the financial crisis facing the company, and noticed that her usually manicured fingernails had been chewed down to nubs. In examining her *body language,* they watched this usually calm woman pacing back and forth as she spoke. Although her *communication style* was direct and to the point, they heard the cracking in her *voice* as she asked for the swift cooperation from the entire team, offering extra benefits to those who volunteered for additional assignments. They noticed her out-of-character gracious *actions* as she made a point of holding the door open for everyone before the meeting as they filed in to their seats and offered everyone water before the meeting began. With respect to her *environment,* they observed that she brought two company higher-ups to the meeting who sat quietly taking notes as she spoke.

In short, instead of taking advantage of modern technology, Ellen and Wendell read the boss through all Seven Colors, and as a result of their observations, sprang into action to quickly rectify the company's dire situation. Sharon, on the other hand, might have left the meeting with a new dining-room table, but with little knowledge of what went on beyond what was printed on the agenda. As a result, Sharon's smart people-reading coworkers who perceived the urgency of the situation and acted accordingly will be able to buy their next dining room set off the showroom floor with the money they are making as a result of their promotions.

The same example reflects the continued importance of attending company and industry seminars and networking events. Sure, you may be tempted to forgo actually traveling to and attending a conference when you could just attend an online "Webinar." But think about what you would miss in terms of reading your peers and others in the industry (not to mention the chance to be favorably read yourself). Gain the advantage by capitalizing on valuable people-reading opportunities and equipping yourself with the maximum amount of useful information on which to reach reliable conclusions.

Don't Rely Solely on Internet Research to Read People

None of this is to say you should throw away your computer or PDA. Certainly, there is a wealth of information you can, and should, glean from online resources, or by picking up the phone and calling around. The older woman no doubt would be well-advised to *also* read the firm description and the attorney's bio. But there is no substitute for live observation and real-life interaction. Don't let the ease of and convenience of the Internet become a disabling crutch that prevents you from acquiring additional valuable information and making the most of each interaction.

KEY POINTS

Recognize the drawbacks: When you are reading someone in cyberspace you will miss an enormous amount of information. Be prepared to supplement what you learn online with live contact if you can.

Take advantage of online solutions to online problems: In cases where arranging personal meetings with online contacts might be dangerous, acquire as much information as you can and then corroborate it with search engines like Google.

Never conduct important personal business online if you can help it: Don't conduct online business that involves posting your personal information. Most banks warn customers against posting their PIN numbers online.

Cyberspace Seven Colors: Although online reading is better than nothing at all, keep in mind that you need to pay attention to every detail surrounding someone's online persona in order to acquire useful information.

Question what someone's reliance on technology says about him: Is he hiding behind a false identity for illicit purposes or is he just insecure? Corroborate his information online yourself in order to validate his claims.

Don't let your own use of technology decrease your people-reading skills: Resist the urge to rely solely on the ease of Internet research to acquire information. Go the extra mile to read people face-to-face and you will gain the advantage over the competition, who are likely relying on the Internet as much as or more than you are!

THIRTEEN

Reading People in the "Age of Terror"

Detecting Criminal Activity

In a world forever altered by the tragic events of September 11, 2001, the value of developing a skill set for reading people exceeds job interviews, hiring nannies, or finding prospective mates. Fine-tuning our understandings of the Colors could save lives.

Recently, I read an article about specially trained Transportation Safety Administration (TSA) behavior detection officers who are stationed in the nation's airports, evaluating passengers based on their "micro expressions." Micro expressions are facial traits such as lack of eye contact, lack of a smile, darting eyes, clenching lips, licking lips, sweating, and "making clandestine signs."* A passenger in a security-screening line demonstrating any of these characteristics is especially susceptible to being isolated for additional evaluation by TSA officers. This is because these expressions, as discussed in chapter 5, are often indicators of concealment or discomfort.

My husband Randy is six-foot-two with blond hair and blue eyes, and had the opportunity to "meet" a TSA behavior detection officer. He was rushing to the security gate at Phoenix Sky Harbor Airport and forgot he was toting a large duffel bag that weighed about sixty pounds. At the security area, a pleasant TSA employee reminded him that he wouldn't be able to bring the bag onboard the plane, as it was a great deal larger than the allotted carry-on bag. Randy—in such a

*"BDOs SPOT More Than Just Opportunities at TSA," *www.tsa.gov/press/happenings/boston_bdo_spot.shtm*).

rush and now a bit embarrassed at having forgotten to check in his bag earlier—returned to the ticket counter (a good hundred yards away) and checked the bag as requested, then rushed back to the security gate as his flight was boarding.

Unfortunately, Randy has the misfortune of sweating profusely in any temperature above seventy degrees, whether he is inside or outside a building. When he got back to the security gate dripping with perspiration, another female TSA officer asked for his boarding pass and identification. While she was looking at his boarding pass, yet another TSA officer approached him and asked if he was having a bad day and why he wasn't smiling. Randy looked him directly in the eyes and said, "Wouldn't you be having a bad day, too, if you had to walk two football fields to return your bag to the ticket counter in one hundred and twelve-degree Arizona heat as you're rushing to catch a flight?" Keep in mind that Randy looked like a character in a *Saturday Night Live* skit that had a running faucet attached to the top of his head. The officer continued to engage him, likely to evaluate Randy's Colors, and asked where he was headed. Randy replied, "Burbank."

Randy's facial expressions and sweating were micro expressions that professionals are trained to recognize, but the temperature that day in Phoenix was 112 degrees, and the airport's air-conditioning wasn't working properly. Many people are not smiling when they are rushing, especially to catch a flight. Additionally, if he had been aware of the time and had looked closely at Randy's boarding pass, the officer would have known that Randy's flight was currently boarding.

If you were the TSA officer, how would you have applied the Seven Color approach to reading my husband's situation? Here is one possibility:

1. *Appearance.* Randy was blond-haired, blue-eyed, six-foot-two, dressed in khaki cargo pants and a Lacoste T-shirt. He was wearing Prada shoes, a nice watch, and a gold wedding band.
2. *Body language.* He was perspiring, frowning, and rushing.
3. *Voice.* His voice was deep but somewhat out of breath due to the "hike" to and from the ticket counter.
4. *Communication type.* His communication technique consisted of responding to a question with a question.

5. *Communication content.* The content of that communication was very factual and explanatory.

6. *Actions.* Randy's actions were directly in response to the TSA officer's actions. He stopped immediately when asked, put his bag on the ground, faced him directly, and proceeded to answer all of his questions.

7. *Environment.* The environment in which this interaction occurred should have been the most telling in terms of this person's evaluation of my husband.

And to supplement the information obtained by observing the micro expressions, you could reason that traveling through Phoenix in August means expectedly high average temperatures (without even factoring in the problems with the airport's air-conditioning!), and what may have been warning signs in one case were actually circumstantial conditions here, in response to the temperature and Randy's rushing to make a flight that was already boarding.

Recent articles on the Transportation Security Administration Web site detail the findings of behavior detection officers (BDOs) and the implementation of SPOT (Screening Passengers by Observation Techniques) training, which includes classroom instruction on observing and analyzing behavior and on-the-job training. One article recounted that SPOT had recently arrested a man for impersonating a U.S. soldier because they recognized that not only was his long hair inconsistent with military regulations, but they noticed that his uniform had conflicting rank insignias. Another article mentioned one of the more interesting SPOT detections: the observation of several people at an airport who were sitting separately but communicating with one another through clandestine gestures; the group later admitted they had been paid $5,000 to travel through airports and observe security!

Seven Colors of Red

What I call the "Seven Colors of Red" describe how careful assessment of strangers can aid you in detecting caution signs in each Color, and help you and those around you stay alert and safe in our unfortunately high-security age.

Consider the following example. Imagine you are standing in line to buy coffee in an airport terminal and you notice a well-dressed dark-haired man sitting near one of the gates. He is wearing a conservative suit with a short haircut. As you look closer, in contrast to his professional suit, instead of the expensive wristwatch you might expect, you notice that he is wearing a large diving watch with a timer. He is holding a newspaper, but it becomes clear to you that he is not reading it. Although you often see him look down, you never see his eyes move across the page. Instead, each time he looks up his eyes are trained primarily on the security checkpoint station at the entrance to the terminal. On rare occasions, he averts his gaze from the security checkpoint in order to scan the rest of the terminal completely, from left to right. Now suppose in scanning the area yourself you see two more men sitting in different positions in the next gate over who appear to be similarly dressed, and are engaged in the same behavior. Are you just being paranoid, or are you watching these men prepare for the next big act of terrorism?

Would you have been just as suspicious if the men described were blond or redheaded instead? What if they were speaking Korean? What if they were women instead of men? How can you tell if you're stereotyping, and where do you draw that line? Couldn't the first man have had his gaze transfixed on the security line of passengers because he was waiting for his wife who was dropped off late at the airport, and he was concerned that they might miss their flight? This would also explain why he was obviously unable to concentrate on reading his newspaper, and he might have glanced around the rest of the terminal periodically just to make sure his wife hadn't come through security when his eyes were downcast and he missed her. The other men you observed might all have been in similar predicaments, or it may have just been a coincidence that all three were dressed and acting similarly. After all, it is not unusual at all for people to be wearing suits in the airport as they travel to and from business trips. So how do you discern between the sinister and the innocuous? When are your observations cause for concern?

Paying attention to clues across all Seven Colors will help. Unlike reading people you know and with whom you're familiar, reading strangers requires you to take more time to observe, interpret, and attempt to identify their patterns. Anything you can do to eliminate interference and distractions on your end to increase your concentration will also help you to detect more information and reach more reliable conclusions.

What Does a Terrorist Look Like?

The answer is: just like the rest of us. Studying behaviors should never be an excuse for profiling. Not all terrorists look alike, just as not all attorneys look alike. Having said that, however, regardless of what kind of criminal activity you suspect, there are some aspects of personal appearance that may alert you to something being off-kilter.

- Pay attention to unusually loose clothing.
- Be aware of awkward bulges in clothing.
- Take note of someone who seems to be intentionally dressed so as *not* to draw attention (nondescript slacks, neutral tones).
- Notice clothing that doesn't fit quite right with the surrounding circumstances.

But make sure to temper your observations with the latest fashion trends. Teenagers wearing baggy shorts with their back pockets level with the backs of their knees and young women in oversized men's button-down shirts are more likely to be dressed that way because they want to look cool rather than because they're about to commit a crime. But older people dressed like this might warrant closer scrutiny. I have been involved in cases where older criminals commit crimes, often in conspiracy with younger cohorts, taking advantage of the decreased suspicion they arouse as a result of their age. When you do observe suspicious attire, immediately consider whether your observations in the other Colors confirm or deny your suspicions.

Hair Style and Color

A common complaint many parents find themselves frequently making to their teenagers is to "cut that hair!" It is unlikely anyone would need to impart this advice to a terrorist or other savvy criminal. While young people often complain that they are hassled by the police because of their "wild" hairstyles (and clothing to match), sophisticated criminals do not have this problem. Although there are, of course, exceptions to every rule, criminals hoping to escape notice are unlikely to have dreadlocks, Mohawks, or long hair of any sort. Besides drawing attention, long hair, especially if it is in a ponytail, can be grabbed, which is something a criminal who may need to make a quick escape can't afford to risk. As a general rule, look for hair that is short, neatly cut, and nondescript. Similar common-sense rules apply to facial hair. Someone about to commit a crime and therefore trying to blend in is unlikely to have long sideburns or a goatee. The caveat here is that long hair or facial hair is something that can be quickly shaven after a crime is committed, giving the criminal an entirely different look so as to escape detection. Depending on the crime, however, there is a balance between wanting to be able to commit the crime without being noticed, and the value of needing to change his or her appearance afterward.

Regarding hair color, common sense dictates that if the goal is to fly under the radar, less is more. Criminals are trying to blend in, not look like the latest billboard for popular hair products. Their hair color, like their cut, will be professional, muted, and unmemorable.

Body Language: Revealing or Rehearsed?

Once while waiting in Los Angeles's Union Station, I couldn't help but notice a young woman on her cell phone, constantly walking back and forth in front of the listings of scheduled train arrivals and departures. Finding her pacing a bit curious—and remembering the recent "cell phone bandit" videotape (showing a bank being robbed by a woman pretending to be on her cell phone)—I paid closer attention to the phone that the pacing woman was using. The cell phone was up to her ear, but I could still see the design on the faceplate, which told me that although she was talking up a storm, she was not really connected to another person. I moved closer in order to overhear her "conversation," and found it rambling, virtually one-sided, and in a fast-paced and nervous tone of voice. Certain that I had stumbled into a crime in the making, I suddenly heard the woman exclaim "Hello? Hello?" in a terribly irritated voice, as she realized she had lost her connection. I then watched her clearly redial a number and resume speaking.

In this example, my suspicion arose from the woman's nervous body language. True, she was also young, dressed in a mismatched outfit, and carried a backpack instead of a purse: all of which pointed to the (erroneous, in this instance) conclusion that she was up to no good. You will not have the luxury of such cues with smart criminals. Their body language, like their choice of nondescript clothing, accessories, and hairstyle, will be designed to escape notice and detection. But the difference here is that, because of the unconscious nature of body language, if you are watching closely, you'll realize that people may try their best not to display any revealing body language, but will be unlikely to be able to completely pull it off.

James Bond's nemeses generally display a chilling serenity, but you can bet their lack of body language and expression resulted from multiple takes in the studio. Few of us can successfully achieve this result, even with practice. In fact, criminals who *attempt* to display a total lack of body language may actually become more conspicuous instead. Because true body language is largely subconsciously executed, someone attempting to cease all movement will look terribly uncomfortable. Along these lines, consider the following indicators.

"The Eyes Have It"

Ask any parent who has observed an obviously guilty young child deny having gone into the cookie jar without permission: the truth is in their eyes. Whether it is looking away when speaking or avoiding eye contact completely, human discomfort with lying or engaging in dishonest behavior is often revealed through our eyes, the "windows to the soul." In addition, if people are nervous (as can be the case when committing a crime), their eyes often give them away. Blinking often or looking around a lot may be a sign of something sinister to come. Most people don't do this. If you are with your family or friends, your attention is on them. I can say when I am watching my kids or conversing with my husband or siblings, my eye contact is with my family. If you are waiting alone in the airport, most of your glances will be relatively random, within the comfortable two- to three-second window of personal space, or directed toward your boarding gate. Unless you're nervous, chances are your gaze won't be darting from exits to other gates to the security checkpoint.

Noticing lack of eye contact is good advice whether you are a TSA officer or a department store loss prevention manager. Most crimes are less likely to be successfully pulled off by engaging in more eye contact. Even under the influence of drugs and alcohol, people will avoid your gaze in order to disguise their glassy red eyes or dilated pupils. Criminals will also avoid eye contact with you for the same reason that they do not want to wear anything memorable. The less you notice them, the less likely you will be able to identify them again.

- Also watch for people who make consistent eye contact with certain people and almost total lack of eye contact with anyone else.
- Be on the lookout for indications that two or more people standing or sitting apart seem to know each other or are a part of the same group. (This is highly significant if they are not sitting together. You may have to watch someone for a period of time to see if he makes contact with certain people when he gets up and walks around, but is not sitting with them in the waiting area.)
- Pay attention to people who are sitting together but not exchanging much eye contact. (If a group of people are sitting together and they are all focused on some other location, they could either be up to no good or could be waiting for the late arrival of a companion.)
- Watch for other indicators of companionship and whether their conversation seems lighthearted or forced.
- Also consider the possibility that a group of total strangers have just had their attention diverted and noticed something interesting at the same time.
- Minimize *your* distractions in order to make reliable observations. You will have to watch people for a period of time in order to confirm your suspicions.
- Choose your vantage point carefully to ensure that your method of observing others does not cause you to become suspicious yourself. Most public places afford plenty of places to sit and people-watch where you can blend into the mix.

Log this information away in order to compare it to your observations in the other Six Colors.

Criminal Demeanor

In my experience, I've learned that it is the rare criminal who actually enjoys committing crimes. For most, crime is simply a means to an end. Whether it's a terrorist plot or a shoplifting scheme, people involved in a conspiracy or otherwise about to commit a crime will generally not look happy. Sure, many of the rest of us don't always look happy, either, especially when we are waiting around in places like airports and train stations. But terrorism is an incredibly serious crime, and consequently, we can reasonably expect these criminals to look serious and very *focused*. Common sense dictates that it takes a high degree of concentration to pull off complicated criminal schemes. The more complex the plan, the higher degree of focus you are likely to observe.

- Look for people who appear to exhibit a high level of concentration, which will often manifest itself physically. (This can manifest itself on one's face with clenched teeth, intense staring, and a furrowed brow.)
- Make note of general muscle tenseness, which again is largely unconscious. You can detect muscle tenseness by watching how a person moves and walks. If you have the opportunity to observe her performing simple tasks such as buying something in a store or handling her bags, you may notice her movements are jerky but deliberate.

While some people absolutely hate traveling and display unusual tenseness, the vast majority of people do not exhibit these characteristics. Most of us are usually exhausted with all of the walking and waiting. When a particularly long day of travel is taking its toll, we may begin to exhibit irritability and discomfort. But even in this state, we will not be staring intensely, clenching our teeth, or flexing our muscles. On the contrary, we are more likely to be sprawled out on a bench or slumped in a chair, resigned to our fate as we wait for our delayed flight, train, or bus. But keep in mind that many people do get irritable when traveling, and this should not be mistaken for suspicious behavior.

Pulling off a serious and immediate crime generates an incredible level of anxiety. While some people exhibit a certain amount of anxiety or irritability when flying, the majority of us have attained a certain comfort level that minimizes the overt manifestation of anxious emotions.

- Be alert for people who seem unusually short-tempered and anxious at the airport.
- Look for people with extraordinarily irritable demeanors.
- Carefully consider someone who may find it impossible to engage in even innocuous interaction, such as responding to a simple request for directions.

Remember we are not just talking about catching terrorists here; you may notice people displaying unusual irritability in any venue, from the library to a public park. But always keep in mind that because anyone can have a bad day, these observations must continually be measured against the other Six Colors.

Criminal Nervousness

We all get nervous and show it at times. But there is a difference between displaying strong signs of nervousness right before taking the stage to perform a solo with the symphony and displaying the same strong signs of nervousness while standing in line at Starbucks. Someone can be wearing a suit as professional as the most conservative politician, but if he is incessantly tapping his toes, loosening his tie, or sweating profusely, he may be worth a second look. Unlike the example of my husband Randy—whose actions and environment provided an explanation for his sweating—someone about to commit a crime may be sweating while sitting still in air-conditioning on the most comfortable of days.

- Closed body movements or repetitive movements may also be a sign of nervousness or discomfort.
- Look for constant toe tapping, fiddling with objects, and general fidgety behavior.

This type of nervous behavior is typical of anyone about to commit any kind of crime. It can also indicate drug use or too much caffeine.

Detecting the Criminal Voice

Like body language, many vocal cues are also involuntary. Listen to whose voice cracks with nervousness when discussing mundane topics. And listen for inappropriate vocal intonations, because nervousness will often produce unusual vocal characteristics. Notice who speaks in a whisper instead of a normal voice, and pay attention to whether someone sounds angry, nervous, or uptight.

Wendy has prosecuted numerous conspiracy cases, where the players were noticeably suspicious by virtue of their concerted *lack* of contact with anyone, much less each other. Watch for people who are intentionally avoiding contact with anyone, which is even more unusual if they arrived at the location with other people or appear to know other people in the area. In order to analyze vocal cues, you may therefore have to confine your listening skills to how people sound when they respond to someone else talking to them. While I am not suggesting you approach suspicious-looking people in order to ask them a question, they too must go through security, where they may be asked something by airport personnel. This may be your only opportunity to listen to how they sound in response to questions from security staff. Lest you think that security staff can always make a correct assessment, keep in mind the limited window of time they have to observe these people as they come through security, and consequently the limited amount of Colors they can perceive, much less having the chance to observe any patterns of behavior. If you are able to overhear conversation *between* suspicious-looking individuals, pay attention to voice intonation and note which topics or statements seem to carry emotional value. However, some hardened criminals will not have any emotion in their voice. Whether or not they are clinical sociopaths, they will sound cold, calculated, and nonemotional, probably intentionally. The characteristics of criminal conversation are *unlikely* to include things such as:

- Joking around
- Loud discussions about any topic
- Displays of anger, sadness, or elation
- Obvious arguments

These people don't want you to notice them or remember what they were discussing, lest anything they say should arouse suspicion, or should you ever be questioned afterward.

Communication Style: Companionship or Conspiracy?

When I observe a man and a woman having a conversation, I can tell you what their relationship is to each other with a high degree of certainty just by watching their interaction. There are distinct differences in the way they will interact visually, physically, and spatially depending on whether they are family members, colleagues, or romantically involved. Like the couple I observed in the restaurant in chapter 2, I can also tell you the stage of their relationship by observing the way they communicate with each other and react to each other.

So how do people about to commit a crime together interact? Do they appear distracted? Irritable? Relaxed? Obviously, they are unlikely to be cracking jokes and slapping each other on the back. They are far more likely to be tense and short with each other than jovial and easygoing. This will probably be their communication style with other people as well. They are certainly not going to come across as Reflective communicators. They will likely display the characteristics of a Noble, using communication solely for the purpose of transmitting or receiving data as quickly and unobtrusively as possible. When forced to interact with others, they will keep their communication to a minimum. They are not going to joke around with other people or start conversations with strangers unless their part in the criminal conspiracy is to create some kind of diversion. If seeking to fly under the radar, someone about to commit a crime will turn away, speak in a low voice, and answer questions with the shortest amount of words possible.

Criminal Content

Assuming you understand the language being spoken and that you have the opportunity to listen in on a conversation, paying attention to content can teach you a lot about the people you are listening to. If you are listening to a conversation between criminals, you will likely not hear a discussion about who is going to pick up Fluffy from the vet. But at the same time, be aware of the use of code words in communication, and pay attention to whether what they are saying makes sense in context. Sometimes you may hear a discussion that becomes suspicious by virtue of the inane topics being discussed. An extended discussion of a subject that appears to be ridiculously trite may in fact be a discussion about something else. Pay particular attention to the mention of specific times and locations.

And pay particular attention to vocabulary. Is their vocabulary simple or scholarly? The terminology criminals use can give away their background, their socioeconomic level, even their religious beliefs. Are they using profanity or other harsh language? This, of course, may signify a lack of morality, but smart criminals know better than to speak like this, lest their words draw attention. Some criminals are quite articulate and highly educated. This is where astute observations about body language and communication style can make a big difference. Knowing all of the things to look and listen for will place you in the best position to arrive at reliable conclusions.

Criminal Actions

What kinds of things do criminals do and what should you be looking out for? You are unlikely to witness a man in a suit and dark glasses bring a briefcase into the airport terminal, set it down, and walk away. So what, then, will you see that should raise a red flag? The answer to this question depends in part on the location of your observations. A man walking through the airport would be expected to be dragging a piece of luggage; the same man walking through a power plant or City Hall would not. As a general rule, you should take note of actions that are unusual under the circumstances or do not fit with the surroundings. A woman taking photographs of animals at the zoo is not suspicious, but if she is taking photographs of hallways inside the county administration building, it might be cause for concern.

Also note that conspiracy trumps chivalry. Most men are gracious in public. They hold doors open for other people and make sure everyone gets off the elevator before they do. I have noticed that in many of the cases with which I have been involved, that as a general rule, a man who is about to commit a crime, in his quest to remain undetected, will not prolong any social interaction, even at the expense of common courtesy. And after the crime is committed, what I have observed most often is conduct designed to facilitate a quick getaway, many times involving rude behavior such as cutting in line and pushing others out of the way in order to flee the scene.

Lack of Normal Activities

Think about your last trip through an airport. What did you do as you waited for your flight, or during your layover? Most of us do the same kinds of things. Above all, we eat. We snack our way through the airport both out of boredom and because most flights have done away with complimentary meals. Throughout our wait, we can be found in and out of the food court. As a general rule, terrorists or other criminals who are about to pull off a major crime will not have much of an appetite, as you might imagine with the expected heightened levels of anxiety. You are unlikely to find these people in line at the food court: not only because they are not hungry, but also because they are not going to be hanging around heavily populated areas.

We also tend to browse in the various gift shops. While many airport or train station passengers hang around the newsstand long enough to read an entire current edition of *People* magazine without buying it, you are unlikely to find criminals standing *anywhere* for this amount of time where they are likely to be noticed or spoken to. While they may be sitting among other people who are holding a newspaper, they will not be engaging in this activity in a place where they might stand out or be asked if they "are finding everything all right" by a store employee who is trying to make a sale.

So what do criminals do to pass the time? Usually, the answer is *nothing.* This may be due to their level of anxiety as well as their focus on whatever it is they are about to do. Therefore, pay attention to people who do not appear to be able to concentrate on anything. Most people pass the time in airports or waiting rooms by reading, doing crosswords, talking, eating, or some other intentional behavior. Look twice at the person who has been on the same page of a book since you noticed her. Someone about to pull off a crime will be so distracted with her criminal plan that she will be unable to engage in any other intentional activities.

The Criminal's Environment

In public places, especially if we are in a waiting area, our immediate environment is often a reflection of the activities in which we engage to pass the time. As indicated earlier, because most of us eat and drink in the airport, while waiting for a flight we are likely to be surrounded by a variety of carry-on bags, food wrappers, and soda cans. Criminals, on the other hand, are unlikely to be seated in the middle of this kind of mess. First of all, unless they are planning a suicide mission—in which case they won't care who saw them beforehand—they will be sitting in areas where they are less likely to be seen because their goal is to prevent other passengers from getting a good look at them. And they will probably choose fairly neat areas, lest other passengers wander over searching for some strewn-about newspaper sections to borrow as reading material to pass the time. And regarding social environment, notice who is sitting with whom. If someone is not sitting alone, observe whether or not she is sitting with others of the same nationality, similar attire, and similar demeanor.

Transportation

You are walking past City Hall when a shiny black stretch limo pulls up to the curb. Heads are turning, jaws are dropping. Wow, who could possibly be inside? The governor? Paris Hilton? One thing is for sure: it is not a terrorist. Criminals will never make any kind of a scene heralding their arrival, unless they're creating a diversion to draw attention from the nondescript character gaining access to the rear of the building!

Criminals are unlikely to drive their own vehicles to a location and leave them there, where they can be easily traced down via license plates, registration, or fingerprints or other DNA samples left in the car. They are much more likely to be dropped off. So then what does a criminal drop-off look like? Probably like the rest of the conspiracy: *nondescript and forgettable.*

So if they do not get dropped off at the curb by a driver in a Bentley or *any* kind of a memorable car, for that matter, how do they arrive? Do they take a taxi or the bus? Do they walk? Given the quest for anonymity, many criminals will not opt for public transportation to avoid giving curious bystanders the opportunity to look at them for any significant period of time. Plus, DNA samples can be left in buses and taxis, and wearing gloves to avoid leaving fingerprints will itself arouse suspicion.

That leaves private drop-offs, which provide profilers with a wealth of information. Is a man dropped off by what appears to be his wife and three loud kids, with whom he exchanges very public displays of affection, or is he dropped off quietly by three other men who look exactly like he does? What words, if any, are exchanged during the drop-off? And if nothing is said as he gets out of the car, why not? When was the last time you got out of someone else's car and said *nothing*? No "Thanks for the ride," "See you later," or "I'll call you"?

And what kind of vehicle is it? We have long warned our kids that if they see a van with no windows parked on the street, they should cross and walk on the opposite side of the street. As a general rule, smart criminals don't drive vehicles with large window areas. And you won't see a terrorist dropped off somewhere by anyone in a convertible. Obviously, there are exceptions to this rule, but again, you have to factor all of this information into the mix in order to make an accurate assessment of the situation.

KEY POINTS

Criminals blend: Use all of your senses to read nondescript people in light of all of the surrounding circumstances to pick up clues. You may miss noticing these people unless you are carefully reading in all Seven Colors.

Be on the lookout for discomfort: Someone about to commit a crime is likely to be uncomfortable and unhappy. You can detect this through everything about the way the person looks and moves around his environment.

Body language may be the most reliable indicator of criminal activity: Even criminals can "look the part." Therefore, pay particular attention to body language that is inconsistent with appearance. Take note of nervous behavior, especially if there is no obvious reason for it—for example, when someone is just sitting in the airport or train station.

Be alert for a lack of social grace: Criminals are unlikely to display common social courtesy because they seek to avoid any social contact at all. Notice people who go out of their way to avoid having to open a door or pull out a chair for another person.

Look for accomplices: Many crimes are committed by committee. Coconspirators may be in the same area as one another, and may even look and behave similarly. Look for shared elements of appearance and body language.

FOURTEEN

Listening to Your Inner Voice

The Power of Intuition

The African-American defendant weighed more than 275 pounds and acted as if he had a serious "attitude." Even in a suit and tie, he looked menacing. The prospective juror, on the other hand, was a young, petite, well-educated white woman from a wealthy family. It was a murder case, so the attorneys took their time interviewing the woman. We questioned her for hours, and she said nothing in all that time to indicate that she would be particularly charitable toward our client. In fact, the more we learned about her background, the more she seemed to fit the profile of a person who would probably vote to put our client in prison for life—or worse.

At the end of the day, the lead attorney on our team turned to me and shrugged. "Well," he said, "she's history, right?"

"I'm not sure," I replied. "We may want to keep her. Something still tells me that she may have an open mind." I knew from the look of skepticism on the attorney's face that he was going to need a much more specific reason than that to put the woman on the jury. No way would he bet his client's life on a mere hunch.

That night, I lay in bed and tried to figure out why my intuitive feeling about the woman seemed so much stronger than the objective facts I had learned about her in the courtroom. Where did my hunch come from? Why did I have such a powerful feeling that it was right?

Of course, the evaluations of jurors that I make for my clients are much too important to depend on guesswork. *I never guess* about who should sit on a jury. But intuition is not guesswork, and it has always played a major part in my work. Over the years, I have learned to pay close attention to my deeper feelings about people and situations. Often, sudden flashes of intuition have led me to conclusions about people that appeared, at first, to be totally at odds with the rational workings of my mind. And on most occasions, these intuitive conclusions have turned out to be right.

As a result, I have become totally convinced that intuition is both *very* real and *very* powerful, and I know that it can be very useful in reading people. At the same time, I have become convinced that there is really nothing very mysterious about how intuition works. Contrary to what many people will tell you, I believe that intuition is a normal part of our mental equipment that most of us simply don't understand very well. If we understood it better, we could use it more often and more effectively.

In the eyes of many, intuition is some kind of special mystical gift that is given to only a few chosen people. But I believe that we *all* have natural intuitive abilities—and that we can all improve our intuition enormously by working at it.

I was flattered some years ago when *The American Lawyer* called me "the Seer" because of my ability to understand jurors and predict how they will act. And I sometimes wish that I did, in fact, have second sight. It would make my job, not to mention the other parts of my life, a lot easier.

But I am definitely not clairvoyant. My ability to predict human behavior is based not on some mysterious sixth sense that only I possess, but on *the use I make of the ordinary five senses that every human being possesses.* It is not "second sight" but curiosity, focus, observation, and deduction that have made me successful in court.

What Is Intuition?

The very word "intuition" carries a strong charge of mysticism, suggesting some mental voodoo that defies analysis or description. Professional psychics are said to use it to perform astounding feats, from predicting who somebody will marry to forecasting the fate of the world. I admit that some of the things that psychics do look impressive at first glance.

But what is it, exactly, that psychics *do?* When you strip away all the show business, *what is the process* that lends them to seemingly astounding conclusions? When you look closely, you can see that psychics are simply people who are very good at reading people. They have trained themselves to be especially sensitive to the signals that people send out about themselves. Over time, they amass a great deal of information about human nature, and they become very adept at pairing certain types of human signals with certain types of human behavior.

The information they gather is stored in their brains in two different ways. Part of it remains *conscious* knowledge, which they draw on and use with complete awareness of what they are doing. But most knowledge slips down into the *subconscious* mind, and psychics call upon it without being fully aware of the process that permits them to use it.

This is why some psychics are undoubtedly sincere in their belief that "voices" are speaking to them when they make intuitive predictions. They are simply not fully aware that the information that allows them to make accurate decisions about people was originally gathered by their own conscious minds and stored away in their subconscious. Their "gift" is their natural ability to gather and store information, and to retrieve it from the subconscious.

The average person doesn't pay such close attention to his or her perceptions and experiences. We don't even notice most of them. Consequently, most of our experiences about life and people are deposited behind the opaque curtain of our subconscious within a few days, or even moments, after we are exposed to them.

But even though we may not be consciously aware of these experiences, they become part of our stored knowledge. If certain events led to a bad or good experience once, when similar events occur again something inside us may hoist the flag we call intuition. This flag may come in different guises: déjà vu, free-floating anxiety, getting a sick feeling in the pit of our stomach when something feels wrong, or becoming excited when something feels right.

Thus, *what we call intuition is nearly always the surfacing of a submerged memory, a barely noticed event, or some combination of the two.* The "feeling" doesn't come to us over the cosmic ether, but drifts up from our own subconscious. This means that all we have to do to greatly improve our intuitive abilities is find new ways to gather information, store it, and retrieve it from the subconscious.

Searching Your Mind

Our subconscious holds thousands of experiences and observations, much as a computer stores information in its hard drive. However, when we use a computer, we can click on the "Find" button and instantly retrieve any information we want. Access to our subconscious is much more haphazard, particularly if we weren't paying much attention when the information was loaded.

I've always been very attentive and observant, and I've also been fascinated by how particular aspects of a person's appearance, actions, voice, or behavior forecast his thoughts and actions. As a result, I've amassed a very large subconscious database of various human characteristics and what they are likely to mean in various people under different circumstances. This vast database is the foundation of my intuitive responses to people and situations.

By the time jurors enter the courtroom, are called to the jury box, and ready themselves for the first question, I've usually formed an initial impression of each of them. As I watch them more closely and listen to their responses to the lawyers' questions, this impression is almost always borne out. There is nothing psychic about that. It's simply that the way each of these jurors looks, talks, and acts fits the pattern of one or more segments of the thousands of other jurors I've seen walk through the doorways of hundreds of other courtrooms. Sometimes I'm hard-pressed to say what it is about someone that leaves me with a particular impression. But in most cases, by the time the decision is made to accept or reject the juror, I've discovered the source of my intuition and can logically explain myself to counsel.

Let's return for a moment to the juror we mentioned at the beginning of this chapter. The lead attorney agreed to have her return for a second day of questioning, though he let me know he was going to be a hard sell. My hunch that this young white woman would be good for our client remained unshakable—though still mystifying—until the afternoon recess of the second day, when I realized what I must have subconsciously noticed about her.

The courtroom was arranged in a fashion common in courtrooms across the country. The jury box was on one side of the room. The counsel table, where the defendant sat with me and his lawyers, was near the middle of the room, just a few feet in front of the low swinging doors to the aisle that runs down the middle of the spectators' seats and ultimately out to the hallway. Every time a juror comes or goes, he or she must pass by the counsel table. Most jurors, not surprisingly, cut a wide path around the defendant, particularly if he's a large, gruff-looking man charged with murder. This jury was generally no exception. Some of them looked as if they were tempted to jump over the railing next to the jury box rather than come anywhere near the accused.

But the young woman who had been the subject of my attention and frustration for the past two days didn't veer away from our client. She seemed to go out of her way to walk close to him—close enough that he could have reached out and grabbed her. Furthermore, unlike most jurors, she didn't take her eyes off him but seemed intent on scrutinizing him "up close and personal." This was truly extraordinary behavior under the circumstances.

As I've watched thousands of jurors walk by—or, more accurately, around—defendants charged with violent crimes, my subconscious storehouse was full of such images. While I had not consciously registered that this woman's behavior was dramatically unusual, my subconscious had raised a flag. Her behavior made it apparent that she was not afraid of the man, as most jurors would be if they had already judged him guilty of murder. Also, she was plainly inquisitive and had not formed a rigid opinion about him. Her attentive looks as she passed him revealed that she wanted to know if he'd really committed the crime, and would want to gather as much information as possible about him if she were asked to decide that question. What more could we ask of a juror?

Building Your Database

Since your intuition depends on the quality and quantity of your information, your first step is clear: *improve the database*. A valuable database is filled with useful information, not random impressions.

Chapters 1 and 3, "Reading Readiness" and "Discovering Patterns," showed you how to gather information and tell the important traits from the inconsequential ones. Other chapters have illustrated how to interpret various characteristics. If you consistently practice these techniques, you'll automatically fill your database with useful information.   •

You'll accumulate data a lot faster if you pay attention to everyone you meet, not just the people who are most important to you. If you're naturally curious about even strangers or casual acquaintances, you'll be way ahead of the game. Don't be shy about tactfully asking about someone's clothing, jewelry, or hairdo. If you don't feel like commenting, simply notice. Your inquisitiveness can be put to good use.

The more closely you observe everyone with whom you come into contact, the quicker you'll build up your database. I can illustrate the point with a fashion statement that's proliferated around the country the last ten years: the eyebrow ring. I first saw one on the street in downtown Los Angeles, worn by a young man who looked like the lead guitarist in a grunge-rock band. My first thought was "How weird." My second was "Boy that must have hurt." My curiosity was aroused, and I began noticing other people who wore eyebrow rings. Whether the person was a clerk at the market, a teller at the bank, or one of a group of young men and women hanging out at a coffeehouse, I paid attention. I was curious to know why each particular person might have chosen to pierce an eyebrow. I noted whether each seemed conservative, arty, a little on the wild side, intelligent, well-educated, flaky, respectful, dirty, whatever.

Since then, I've seen hundreds of eyebrow rings. They're often worn not by scruffy teenage men but by young girls who otherwise look like daughters of the middle class. Unlike tattoos, eyebrow rings can easily be removed, so they indicate a less fundamentally rebellious nature. Most of the young people with pierced eyebrows seem to be arty, individualistic, expressive types, who are making a fashion statement rather than a political or cultural one.

In recent years, I've accumulated a substantial store of knowledge about eyebrow-ring wearers. I don't expect to retrieve it very often. In fact, much of this knowledge may remain in my subconscious forever. But if a young woman with an eyebrow ring came into my office tomorrow to apply for a position as a file clerk, my intuition would probably tell me to keep an open mind—it might look odd, but if everything else seems in order it's no cause for alarm.

If you have always simply recoiled from people who wear eyebrow rings, assuming they're all unemployed, unwashed druggies, don't expect much help from your intuition if you find yourself needing to accurately evaluate a person who wears one. You simply won't have accumulated a sufficient database to warn you to look beyond the stereotype.

The next time you get a haircut, wait on a customer, or walk down the street, stop, look, and listen. Be attentive. Engage people, or at least look at them. Note any unique characteristics. If you're going to develop your intuition, you need to keep looking and listening until you get a sense of the whole person, until a pattern develops. Every time you do this, you'll be filling your database with valuable information.

Tune In and Turn Up Your Intuition

No matter how unobservant you may have been in the past, your database is still stocked with thousands of experiences. Improving the quality and quantity of the information in your subconscious storehouse will help you use your intuition more frequently, but you can also make better use of the data you already have. You can begin to tune in and turn up your inner voice right away by following four steps:

1. Recognize and respect your intuition.
2. Identify what your intuition is telling you.
3. Review the evidence.
4. Prove or disprove your theory.

Recognize and Respect Your Intuition

Before you can hear your inner voice, you have to turn on your receiver. You have to believe your subconscious may be reaching out to tell you that you are either on the right track or headed toward a cliff. When you find yourself thinking "This rings a bell," or "Something isn't right," or "I have a good feeling about her," stop and listen. Usually, you'll have time to step back from the situation and reflect on it before making any decisions.

If you have a hunch, *do not* just go with your gut instinct. As much as I value intuition, it is not some pure, unimpeachable knowledge from beyond. Intuition can be influenced by your own often faulty memory. You should know why you're reacting to a person as you are before you let a hunch dictate your actions. Something about the current situation might be stirring up a recollection, but who knows what? You may have an adverse reaction to a man named Ralph for no better reason than that your next-door neighbor when you were six was a bully named Ralph—and you haven't known a Ralph you liked since. That's hardly a good reason not to go to work with someone named Ralph or hire a mechanic named Ralph.

The first step in the process of learning from our intuition, then, is simply to recognize and respect it. *Don't ignore or dismiss it, but don't follow it blindly either.* Think of yourself as a dog who hears a noise in the distance. You stop, become alert, and turn your ears in the direction of the noise. By doing that, you'll be turning on your intuition receptors.

Identify What Your Intuition Is Telling You

Simply recognizing that you have a funny feeling isn't very helpful if your objective is to make intelligent decisions. With a little self-examination you should be able to identify not just that you have a hunch, but what that hunch is.

If, for example, a woman has an uncomfortable feeling when she leaves an interview for a job as a cashier for a man who runs an auto-parts business, she should try to identify her concern. Is she afraid he is going to sexually harass her? Is she worried about the amount of overtime he expects? Is she afraid the business isn't doing well, and she may be looking for another job no sooner than she takes this one? If a man has just met a woman and decides to ask her out because he has a good feeling about her, what exactly is that feeling? Is it that she is going to be fun? Is his intuition telling him that he has met the future mother of his children? If a woman has an aversion to the new bookkeeper after passing him in the hallway for the first time, what might account for her reaction? Did he seem arrogant? Unfriendly? Sleazy?

Identifying your hunch is usually a matter of replaying the chain of events that led up to it. At this point, you're not trying to find the factual evidence that supports your feeling, you're just trying to identify what the feeling is. If you can, try to pinpoint the first time it occurred to you that something was wrong, or right. Free-associate. Ask yourself who the person or place reminds you of, and then reflect on the first image that pops into your head, no matter how absurd it may seem. At some point you'll feel the click of recognition:

"I think the store owner is attracted to me."

"I'll bet that woman has a great sense of humor."

"That new bookkeeper struck me as a real jerk."

It's important to focus on exactly what your intuition is saying, rational or not, because without focus you can't move to the next steps in the process and test the validity of your hunch.

Review the Evidence

Once you've identified what your hunch is, the next step in using your intuition is examining the evidence—that is, all the information already at your disposal. Mentally rewind the encounter and play it back in slow motion, carefully evaluating physical appearance, body language, environment, voice, words, and actions. As you review what happened while your intuitive response was forming, you will be tuning in to its source.

In the case of the fellow who got a good feeling about the woman he just met, he may recall seeing a calendar on her desk featuring his favorite cartoonist. Can he rely on that alone to conclude that he and the woman would have a great time together? No. But at least he has identified the evidence that led him to that initial gut feeling.

As for the woman who took an instant and seemingly inexplicable dislike to the bookkeeper, she may recall he wore the same aftershave favored by the creep her mother used to date. As soon as the woman realizes that her aversion to the new bookkeeper is simply an association between his aftershave and her mother's ex-boyfriend, she can dismiss her intuitive warning bell as a false alarm. She may or may not end up liking him for other, more rational reasons, but at least she won't get off to a bad start just because of a misleading gut instinct.

If the woman who interviewed with the owner of the auto-parts store has identified her hunch as a concern the boss might harass her, she now must look at the available evidence to see if it supports her suspicion. As she replays the interview, she might recall that the man approached her with a swagger and a smug smile when she first entered the room, maintaining only brief eye contact before looking her up and down. As he escorted her to her chair, he touched her first on the arm and then in the small of her back. Once the interview began, he lowered his voice like a late-night disc jockey on a local jazz station. This pattern, coupled with a few suggestive remarks such as "I'm really, really, looking forward to working closely with you," created a fairly solid body of evidence that harassment was a possibility.

As you become more familiar with the clues to reading people, you will be able to better evaluate the evidence available to you. Knowing, for example, that an attempt to come within someone's personal space (touching the arm and back) often signifies sexual interest adds weight to your intuition. Without that knowledge, you might doubt your instincts and chide yourself for being too uptight about physical contact. As you evaluate the events that produced your intuitive response, remember that self-censorship is an obstacle when you're trying to tune in to your intuition. Don't be sabotaged by insecurity or political correctness. At this point in the process, let your intuitive response to a person's looks, environment, voice, and demeanor be your guide.

Prove or Disprove Your Theory

Once you've recognized that your subconscious is reaching out to you, identified what it's trying to tell you, and reviewed all the available evidence, you will probably have formed a theory about the origin of your intuitive response. Sometimes you don't need to take the process any further, as in the example of the woman and the bookkeeper with the unfortunate choice of aftershave. But when you haven't reached a comfortable conclusion, the final step is to test your theory.

Maybe you didn't have enough clues to make a call. Or there may have been plenty of clues, but you didn't notice them as carefully as you wish you had now that you know their importance. When we first meet somebody we are bombarded with new data, and it's easy to overlook details. There's also the possibility you encountered someone on a bad day, or think you may have, and want to see if your concerns are borne out. Now, having carefully reflected on your first impression, you can approach him again with your attention fully focused on the specific additional information you need to test your intuition.

The man who wants to know if his new acquaintance really does share his sense of humor might begin his investigation with a casual chat. He could start by asking her about the calendar. A ten-minute conversation should let him know whether there's a rational basis for believing they're on the same wavelength.

The woman considering the job at the parts store might conclude that she doesn't need any more information to know that the owner may come on to her if she takes the job—there's plenty of evidence pointing in that direction. But if she really needs the job and doesn't want to turn it down unnecessarily, she could ask for a second interview. This time she can consciously tune in to aspects of the man's appearance and behavior that might indicate a lecherous nature. She should be able to gather enough information to make the call now that she's focused on the possible problem. She can scrutinize the environment for such items as wall calendars, posters, and cartoons that might offer clues to the owner's tastes. She could look for family photos or other items that might shed some light on his personal life. She might also speak with female employees and, as tactfully as possible, ask how the boss treats them. This time she'll watch his gaze even more carefully; if he touches her, she'll be alert to whether he does so in a sexually suggestive way.

When you're out to test your theory, plan in advance. Prepare a few pertinent questions and ask yourself what character traits might reveal the most about the issue you're concerned with. Be very alert this time around, in case a second chance is all you get before you have to make a decision.

The Four-Step Process in Action

I vividly recall an experience in O. J. Simpson's criminal trial in which I followed each of the four steps in this process. A young Hispanic woman had been selected to sit on the jury. Our pretrial research, questionnaires, and the oral questioning led us to believe the woman would be receptive to the defense theory of the case and not particularly swayed by the prosecution's theories, especially its emphasis on spousal abuse.

The morning after the jury was selected, the young woman caught my eye. I had a strong feeling something was very wrong. I knew better than to ignore my intuition, even though no one relished the idea of further evaluating the jury that had been selected after months of effort.

After a little thought, I realized I was concerned that she had been abused herself. Once I had identified what my intuition was trying to tell me, I was able to focus on what had raised this red flag. Very quickly, I saw the basis for my concerns.

Previously, this juror had been very attentive in court. She frequently looked at the attorneys, the judge, and Mr. Simpson. She was absorbing everything in the courtroom. She was involved. But that morning she sat with her face turned away from us, staring off into space. When I looked at her more closely, I saw a small bruise on the side of her face, which she was either consciously or unconsciously trying not to reveal to us. When I brought this to the defense team's attention, everyone's red flags rose to full mast.

Someone can get a bruise on her face in a number of ways that have nothing to do with an abusive husband or boyfriend. But my intuition, calling upon my years of experience and stored knowledge, was telling me that if any of those other circumstances applied, the woman would not have been so preoccupied. What's more, if she had merely suffered an innocent bump, she wouldn't have averted her face: she was embarrassed, or trying to hide evidence of a home life she probably realized would cause her to be excused from the jury, or both.

The last thing any of us wanted to do was shame or alienate the juror by asking the judge to allow further questioning, especially of such a personal nature. But eventually the defense team agreed we had to take that risk. During the questioning that followed in Judge Ito's chambers, the juror acknowledged that her boyfriend had hit her the night before. Judge Ito excused her.

This time, my intuition was consistent with the most obvious interpretation of the facts. But that isn't always the case. Many times intuition flies in the face of other, more obvious evidence. When that happens, it's crucial that you know how to think through your hunch to the facts underlying it. I've experienced this many times during my career, and I'm often the lone voice trying to convince a reluctant legal team to keep or dismiss a juror. One of the most memorable occasions was the trial of an English cabdriver accused of killing four people, whose bodies were never found.

The defense team in that case included the defendant, who was very actively involved in the jury selection process. We were all wary when one of the jurors revealed that he had accompanied police on several "ride-alongs" in their squad cars. Wouldn't he be partial to the police if he had requested to ride around with them? The knee-jerk reaction was to dismiss him. The lawyers and the defendant assumed that anyone who wanted to see the police in action was a staunch supporter of the force. But something told me the man would be a favorable juror.

One of the cabdriver's principal defenses was that the police had not followed appropriate procedure in the investigation and that as a result, their conclusions were unreliable. A second defense contention was that both the police and the prosecutors had made up their minds that the man was guilty without objectively evaluating the evidence themselves.

When I asked myself what my intuition was telling me, I decided it was saying that this juror would be critical of the police *if* the defense was able to prove the investigation was not handled properly. If the sloppy police work was due to the detectives prejudging the defendant before the investigation was concluded, I thought, this juror was even more likely to be critical.

Knowing what my intuition was telling me, I carefully evaluated the information I had about this prospective juror. First, it was clear that he was at least vaguely familiar with normal police procedures and the importance of following them. This meant he would understand why a deviation from proper procedures could taint the investigation and, consequently, the prosecution's case. Also, even though he had ridden along in a patrol car on a few occasions, he was not an auxiliary or volunteer police officer, and had no aspirations to become one. He was simply curious about the process and wanted to experience it himself. This suggested he had an inquiring nature and would be open-minded as we presented our case, even if we were critical of the police investigation.

Finally, and perhaps most significantly, the man was openly gay. I believed that an openly gay man who had undoubtedly been judged on the basis of his sexual orientation alone would be critical of the police if we could prove they prejudged the defendant. I hadn't focused on this issue at first, but on reflection, it became vital to my final analysis.

In this trial we hoped the jury would see that the prosecution had likewise made an unfounded judgment, which they were not willing to reevaluate despite any evidence that might contradict it. This stubborn refusal to objectively evaluate the evidence applied not just to the detectives but also to the district attorney's office: this was actually the third time the defendant had been tried for this alleged crime. The first trial resulted in a hung jury, the second in a mistrial. Nonetheless, the prosecution doggedly pursued the defendant a third time.

As I tuned in to this information, I became more satisfied that the juror would evaluate the investigation with an open and analytical mind. I believed he would also be receptive to the argument that the defendant was the victim of prejudgment, if we could prove it.

We decided to "turn up" the volume on my intuition by asking more about the man's experience as a gay person and his views about the state's possible prejudgment of the defendant. The more we questioned the man, the more certain I was that he'd be good for our side. The defense team, including the defendant, was extremely reluctant to leave him on the jury, but eventually deferred to my judgment. The man became an active participant in the jury deliberations that resulted in our client's acquittal.

Heeding Your Second Thoughts

It's not unusual to get a strong feeling about someone from the moment you first meet him. But sometimes a gut feeling will emerge only after weeks or months, as a result of more information you've acquired over time. The "Discovering Patterns" chapter cautioned you to constantly test your first impression against new information. An intuitive response to a person should always be viewed as new information and never ignored, no matter when it finally emerges. Heeding your second thoughts can make the difference between a missed opportunity and an inspired decision.

An example of this occurred during the McMartin Preschool trial. All the prospective jurors had filled out extensive questionnaires weeks before in-court jury selection began. One juror, an African-American woman, made a number of comments in her written questionnaire that strongly suggested she would be very pro-prosecution. She acknowledged having read or heard much of the extensive media coverage that preceded the trial. She admitted that, on the basis of everything she had read and heard about the case, she believed the defendants were guilty. Everyone on the defense team, including me, had crossed her off the list of potential jurors.

The oral questioning took place about two weeks after the written questionnaires had been turned in. When she sat before us answering the lawyers' questions, this woman recanted much of what she had written two weeks earlier. She claimed to have reflected further on the case and on the defendants' right to a fair trial. She apologized for being so judgmental and assured us she would be open-minded. Normally, I would not even have considered selecting her. These words and actions suggested that she wanted to sit as a juror in a high-profile case and was trying to sell us on her ability to be fair. But for some reason I believed her. Something was telling me she really would be open-minded.

After coming to this realization, I began the process of reexamining everything she had said as well as how she looked and acted. I noticed that when she spoke to us, she made very direct eye contact. She leaned forward slightly in her chair. Frequently, she sighed as she acknowledged the comments she made in her questionnaire. She expressed her regret at being so judgmental. She seemed to be struggling with the realization that she had passed judgment on others, just as so many had judged her as a black woman. She spoke slowly, sincerely, with an even cadence. It was as if she were searching her heart and soul for the absolute truth about how she felt.

By this point in my career, I had seen many people misrepresent themselves just to get on a jury in a high-profile case. I knew how they looked and acted when they were trying to sell themselves to the judge and attorneys. Their body language, tone of voice, and speech patterns were stored in my subconscious database. The gut feeling I had about this woman was based on the fact that she didn't fit that pattern. We left her on the jury, which found my client not guilty.

Are Women More Intuitive Than Men?

We end this chapter with a question, the answer to which we believe validates our view of intuition.

Many of us know someone who truly seems to have a gift for understanding people or even predicting the future, and that person is usually a woman. When I tell people my definition of "intuition"— that it's basically a subconscious message percolating up from the storehouse of information gathered by our five senses—I'm often challenged to explain the psychic powers of somebody's grandma, aunt, or mother: "She knew when one of her friends was going to catch a cold two days before it happened," or "She predicted the car crash that killed little Jimmy Smith," or "She could always tell when I was lying to her."

Maybe there are some people, somewhere, who actually *do* sense vibrations, can describe the character of someone they know nothing about, and see into the future. I have never met one. As we explained earlier in the chapter, I chalk up these powers to observation and deductive reasoning. I have noticed, however, that true to conventional wisdom, women do tend to be more intuitive than men. There's a straightforward reason for this, and it's as obvious as the reason Mom always knew when you were lying.

More so in previous generations, but even today, most moms spend more time than most dads closely watching their children's behavior and mannerisms. Almost everyone looks different when he or she lies, even if it's a subtle difference that a stranger might not notice. When you were a child, the smallest change in your expression was instantly apparent to your mother. She wasn't psychic. She just had an enormous database on the topic of *you*. The moment you made a move that differed from your standard "honest" pattern, her subconscious picked up on it. Maybe it was something as minor as the angle at which you were standing. Maybe even she would not have been able to tell you exactly how she knew you were fibbing. But the fact is, your pattern was different. As you grew up and spent less time with Mom, her intuitive powers probably started to decline—at least when it came to you.

Today, this dramatic disparity between the roles of men and women has diminished, and in many families has disappeared altogether. But women still more frequently assume the role of caregiver, communicator, observer, and peacemaker in the family. And women typically are raised to be more sensitive to their own and other people's feelings. They're also socialized more to notice clothing, haircuts, shoes, jewelry, and other aspects of personal appearance. They read fashion magazines far more than men do, and they key in on who's had plastic surgery, who's wearing a wedding ring, and who's gained five pounds. They watch. They notice. If you have any doubt, ask how much the men and women you work with remember about what the boss's wife (or the boss) wore to last year's holiday party. If the women don't win hands down, I'll be amazed. Larger database, better intuition.

Is this a generalization? Absolutely. We all know men who are more attentive, observant, and sensitive than most women. And I'll bet they're more intuitive as well. As women's roles in society have moved toward parity with men's, the intuition gap has also closed. Mr. Mom, not his wife who works outside the home, is now the one who knows intuitively when little Johnny isn't feeling well or the dog needs to go outside. And that is as it should be, given the nature of intuition. Personal and social experience, not chromosomes, give rise to intuition.

And what about the woman who knew when her friends were ill, or the one who predicted a car crash? If I had the time, I'd relish investigating those stories. I'll bet those sickly friends looked different, or smelled different, or asked for a cup of hot tea instead of the usual coffee. I'd also wager that the corner where little Jimmy Smith died had been a death trap for years. One bet I'd certainly make is that most of those psychic aunts and grandmas have sterling memories, great eyesight, and a keen interest in other people's business.

KEY POINTS

Intuition isn't a mysterious sixth sense: It's the whisper of your subconscious memory of forgotten or barely noticed events. To maximize it, build your subconscious database by paying closer attention to everyone.

Tune in and tune up your intuition: Follow this simple approach when you hear that whisper of intuition:

- *Recognize and respect your intuition.* But neither follow it blindly, nor reject it outright.
- *Identify what your intuition is telling you.* If you have a "hunch," ask yourself what it is. Are you afraid? Nervous? Excited?
- *Review the evidence.* Play back the events that immediately preceded your gut feeling, and try to consciously spot what you noticed only subconsciously the first time around.
- *Prove or disprove your theory.* Once you've identified a plausible basis for your intuition, gather additional information from which to consciously test your theory.

Don't just listen to your intuition as you form first impressions: Keep alert to intuitive messages that might emerge months or years after you've come to know someone. "Second thoughts" are often intuitive voices, too.

FIFTEEN

The Need for S.P.E.E.D.

Making Snap Judgments That Make Sense

I was driving with my family along the central California coast. It was getting dark and we were running low on gas. I saw a small convenience store and gas station off the freeway, so I took the exit and slowed to pull in to the lot. One car was parked in front of the store. There weren't any cars getting gas. I took in the rest of the scene: a young man in a baggy jacket was just entering the store, while two others wearing similar clothing stood at opposite ends of the building. They were not speaking to one another but were glancing nervously up and down the street.

Call it intuition or simply the result of years of involvement in criminal cases, but I had a very uncomfortable feeling. Something wasn't right. Should I pull in? Should I stop and watch to see if something was amiss? Or should I pull back on the highway and drive a few miles to the next town to get gas? I had just a few seconds to make up my mind. At the time, I felt I was probably overreacting, but I decided to drive on anyway. The next morning I read in the newspaper that the convenience store had been robbed at gunpoint by three young men.

In a perfect world, we would have all the time we need to size up a situation, read the people involved, and make our decisions. And we usually do. But in real life, situations sometimes unfold in a matter of seconds and snap decisions must be made. In the courtroom, I've become accustomed to making these rapid-fire judgments. Every case doesn't involve days, weeks, or months of jury selection, as most of the high-profile ones do. Sometimes I have only a few minutes to watch and listen to a juror before making a decision that may mean the life or death of a client. After years of practice, I have developed a method that substantially increases the odds of reading people accurately on the fly. I use it whenever I need to read with S.P.E.E.D.

Reading with S.P.E.E.D. isn't foolproof, but if you memorize the technique and practice it carefully, you'll greatly improve the quality of your decisions—no matter how quickly they're made. There are five steps to the process of reading with S.P.E.E.D.: **S**can, **P**are, **E**nlarge, **E**valuate, and **D**ecide.

The approach I use when I need to read with S.P.E.E.D. is essentially an abbreviated version of the people-reading techniques discussed in the previous chapters. But don't use it unless time is of the essence. Reading with S.P.E.E.D. is not as reliable as a thoughtful, patient analysis that allows time for patterns to develop more fully. Always remember: *The less time you have to evaluate someone, the more likely it is that your evaluation will be faulty.* Don't rush to judgment unless you absolutely have to.

While understanding people and predicting their behavior is not a process that lends itself to shortcuts, you do need some method of making snap judgments or you'll be unprepared for real-life emergencies. Reading with S.P.E.E.D. works for the taxi driver who must decide each night which fares are safe to pick up, the foreman who must decide whether a heavy-equipment operator returning from a long lunch has been drinking, and the father who must decide whether to leave his child at a pool party, trusting people he hardly knows to be vigilant enough to avoid a tragedy. It's equally effective whether you're buying an item at a flea market or stopping at an ATM while someone is loitering nearby.

Even when you've been forced to read a situation with S.P.E.E.D., stay alert for additional clues that may warrant a reevaluation of your snap judgment. If you quickly accept a ride home from someone and three blocks later you realize that he's drunk, don't hesitate to reverse that decision. Remember, few decisions are irreversible. Keep testing your impression against any additional information that is revealed over time.

Scan

Literally hundreds of pieces of information were available to me as I began turning in to the gas station in central California, among them: the time of day; the weather; the location of the convenience store on the lot with respect to the gas pumps; the position of the three men; whether they were talking; how they were acting; how they were dressed; and how their behavior compared with what I would expect from three young men who'd stopped for a snack or something to drink while they were out together for the evening. I couldn't possibly evaluate all that information in the few seconds in which I had to decide whether or not to stop. In order to quickly decide what information was critical and what was irrelevant, I needed to view it in the broadest possible way.

When faced with such circumstances, first *scan* the entire picture, then work your way from general impressions to more specific ones. Begin by taking in the backdrop: the environment, location, weather, and other physical aspects of the scene. It's as if you're looking at a stage and noticing the set and props. Then move on to the actors on the stage. How many people are there? What are they doing? How are they relating to one another?

After you get a general sense of the backdrop and the entire cast of players, focus on the individuals. Consider their physical appearance and body language, such as their eyes, movements, and speech. If you're speaking with them, watch their facial expressions and try to gauge how they're relating to you. As you do all this, *be alert to anything peculiar or unique*—anything that might define the person or the moment. Gather as much information as you can as quickly as you can, from the general to the specific. Make a first pass through all the information available to you.

Pare

Once you have scanned the stage and the actors, noting their appearance and behavior, *pare* the information so you can get a handle on it. To do this, *identify the items or traits that stand out.* When you're in a hurry, you will usually need to limit yourself to no more than five or six traits. If you focus on more than that, you probably won't have time to complete your evaluation before you need to react.

If you don't have a clear idea of what you need to decide about someone, you won't be able to quickly select the handful of critical traits. So before you decide on your short list of important traits, consider for a moment what question you need to answer. For example, assume a woman goes to a party with friends who are available to drive her home, but toward the end of the evening a man she met there offers her a ride home. Before she accepts, she should focus on her concerns and identify the information she needs to evaluate him.

If she wonders whether the man is sober enough to drive her home safely, she should focus on signs of intoxication. Is his speech slurred? Has he been acting in an exaggerated or inappropriate fashion? Is his conversation coherent? How much did he drink? Does he show any signs of poor balance or impaired motor control?

If her concern is whether his intentions are honorable, she should focus on an entirely different set of facts. Has he been a gentleman toward her thus far? Has she noticed how he's treated other women at the party? Is he a friend of someone she knows, who can reassure her that he's not the next Ted Bundy? Was there anything suggestive in his body language, voice, or words when he offered to give her a ride home?

When you must make a decision quickly, you need to identify what your primary concerns are and then focus on the traits that pertain *directly* to those concerns. You won't have time under these circumstances to look carefully at everything.

Enlarge

Once you've pared down the hundreds of bits of information available to you, the next step in the process when reading with S.P.E.E.D. is to *enlarge* those few traits that are most important and bring them into clearer focus. Think of it as if you were looking through a telescopic lens. As you scanned the environment, you saw a handful of features that you want to view more closely. You now focus on those, and zoom in.

You'll need to concentrate if you expect to be able to enlarge the key traits quickly and clearly. Eliminate any distractions. If you know you'll have only a short period of time to read someone in a meeting, then before it begins, turn off the phones, radio, or TV. Clear your mind of what you'll be having for dinner or whether you need to stop off at the cleaner's on the way home. Close the door so no one will enter the room and tear your attention away from where it needs to be. When the meeting starts, maintain that same focus.

This is exactly the process I used when I made that critical decision not to pull in to the gas station. I had only a few seconds to increase my awareness of the key events unfolding before me. Once I scanned the entire environment and identified my concerns sufficiently to be able to pare down hundreds of pieces of information to just a few, I focused on the most important ones. I focused on the two young men standing outside the convenience store. I watched them carefully and saw they were not looking at or speaking to each other. Instead, they were looking nervously up and down the street—and at my car as I drove in. I noticed their body language, which reeked of anxiety. And I tuned out my children, the noise of the car radio, and every other distraction. It was as if the rest of the stage, the props, and even the other members of the audience disappeared, leaving only the actors, who became the exclusive focus of my attention. In the process, the minute details of their behavior emerged even more clearly.

Evaluate

Now that you've focused on and enlarged the most important pieces of information, you need to *evaluate* them. To do this, use the tools we've discussed throughout this book—but consider this the lightning round. You must continue to concentrate. The more focused you are, the more accurate your evaluation will be.

Look for deviations from normal behavior. Does it make sense that three young men out for the evening would visit a convenience store and not go in together, but instead have one enter the store while the other two position themselves like sentries? Does it make sense that the two young men who stayed outside would not be speaking to each other? Wouldn't you expect them to talk, laugh, and joke, rather than stand quietly, looking nervously up and down the street?

Look for extremes. How far apart are the men? Do they talk a little, or not at all? Do they seem particularly nervous or vigilant? Is there any other logical explanation for their behavior?

Always ask yourself whether a pattern has developed that points in a particular direction. There was nothing unusual about three men pulling into a convenience store–gas station and not getting gas. It happens all the time. Likewise, it may not mean much that only one of the three men went inside. Maybe the other two just needed some air. It might not even be that unusual that the two men outside were not speaking to each other—perhaps they weren't getting along. Even the fact that they were looking up and down the street didn't necessarily mean they were up to no good. Conceivably, they could have been watching for friends who were supposed to meet them there. But put all these clues together, and a pattern became clear. This particular pattern told me that there was a reasonable chance something was wrong, and I should be careful.

Decide

You have scanned, pared, enlarged, and evaluated; *now you need to make a decision. If you don't decide, and decide quickly, you run the risk that the decision will be made for you.* Had I delayed too long at that gas station, one of the armed men might have gotten jumpy and demanded that I get out of my car, or worse.

When you're reading with S.P.E.E.D., there's always the chance that you'll make the wrong decision. That's true in any situation, but in cases where snap judgments are required, the margin for error is a lot greater. That's why I always follow one rule: *If you must err, err on the safe side.*

One of the reasons I've had such a good success rate as a jury consultant is that when in doubt, I take the path least likely to have adverse consequences. I'm sure that among the people excused on my say-so because I was uncertain of them were a number who would have been wonderful jurors. If I make a mistake and excuse someone who would have been a good juror, it doesn't matter, as long as I am confident in the one I pick as his replacement. On the other hand, if I have concerns about someone and we leave him on the jury anyway, rather than search for someone about whom I feel better, the consequences could be catastrophic. Better safe than sorry.

Engineers use the term "fail-safe design," which means that products are designed so that if they fail, they do so in a way that ensures no one will get hurt. A machine that malfunctions automatically shuts off. A bolt that breaks will drop into a location where it won't do any serious harm. The concept of fail-safe design should be applied to the decision-making process—especially when you're reading with S.P.E.E.D.

At the gas station, I quickly considered my options and their consequences. If my concerns proved well founded and a robbery was under way, I would expose myself and my family to potentially serious harm if I pulled in to the station. But if I chose to drive to the next town and it turned out the men were not robbing the station, at worst I'd waste a few minutes. My decision was easy. I knew the next town was just a few miles down the road and I had plenty of gas to get there. If I had been driving on fumes, and passing up that gas station meant we might be stranded on the roadside at night, the decision would have been more difficult.

Weighing the consequences of a decision is crucial. The dad who takes his child to a pool party may wonder whether there will be adequate adult supervision, especially if his child can't swim. As he evaluates the scene, he might look to see how many other parents are around, and if the adults seem attentive. He could ask whether the kids will be playing unattended near the pool, and whether the adults will be drinking alcohol. After he's gathered and weighed all the information, the final decision should hinge on the consequences of his decision. If he is concerned that the environment presents a risk that his child may drown, he may choose to stay at the party himself, especially if there's no compelling reason for him to be elsewhere.

The more important the decision, and the more devastating the consequences could be if you are wrong, the wiser you are to err on the side of caution. If you don't have enough time to eliminate the risk, take the safe course.

Practice Makes Perfect

Reading with S.P.E.E.D. gets easier with practice. As you become more attentive, focused, and perceptive, you'll be able to identify and understand important traits more quickly. And you'll become more confident of your ability to make sensible snap judgments as your decisions improve and you begin to trust your people-reading skills.

Don't be surprised if you feel a bit overwhelmed at first by all the information you'll have to scan, pare, enlarge, evaluate, and decide. The process may seem unwieldy at first, but after a while it will become second nature—like driving a car. I remember how completely overwhelmed I felt by all the things I had to keep in mind when I first got behind the wheel. It was all I could do to handle the clutch, accelerator, and gear shift—how could anyone expect me to use my turn signals, check my rearview mirror, and watch for oncoming traffic, too? Yet within a few months, I no longer even thought about shifting; it just happened.

As you practice reading with S.P.E.E.D., you'll become as proficient at it as you are at driving. Whatever you do, *don't give up*. While reading people in everyday circumstances when you have plenty of time will greatly enhance your relationships, it's perhaps even more important to be able to make the right decisions when time is short. Both skills require the same tools, and both will help you gain control over your life. Whenever I think of that gas station, I thank the fates that I was able not only to read those young men, but to read them with S.P.E.E.D.

KEY POINTS

Take your time if you can: But if you must decide about someone quickly, remember to use the acronym S.P.E.E.D.

- Scan. Start with the big picture—the entire stage upon which the events unfold—and work your way down to the subtle clues projected by the individual actors.

- **Pare.**   Keep in mind the issue you need to resolve as you identify the five or six elements of the whole picture that stand out most.
- **Enlarge.**   Zoom in on those five or six key elements as if you were a telephoto lens, until your concentration is focused on them alone.
- **Evaluate.**   Look for a pattern within those key traits and for deviations or extremes within the patterns.
- **Decide.**   When you're in the lightning round, if you don't decide, and decide quickly, your decision will be made for you by others or by the haphazard manner in which events unfold.

When in doubt, take the safest course: Err on the side of caution. You may miss a few golden opportunities, but you may also avoid disaster.

Most important, practice, practice, practice: It may seem difficult at first, but with practice, reading people accurately will be as automatic as driving your car.

Physical Traits and What They Reveal

To sharpen your observational skills, the next time you meet someone new imagine you're taking a snapshot of her. Freeze her for a moment, then mentally step back and look her up and down. You'll be scanning her for physical characteristics and noting consistent traits, as well as the one or two that may stand out. What follows is a list of the types of things you should notice. It may seem long, but in reality you can take in most of this information very quickly. And it gets easier with practice.

PHYSICAL CHARACTERISTICS

BODY
height
weight
proportion/shape
overall size
physical condition (muscular, wiry, soft)
posture (slouched, potbellied, erect, stiff)
body hair

FACE
eyes (open, squinty, red, dilated, watery, droopy)

lips (open or tight; smile, frown, grimace)
teeth (crooked, white, clean, false, missing; braces)
nose (red, bulbous; broken capillaries)
ears
head hair (bald; thin; color, style, cut, condition, cleanliness)
facial hair (beard, mustache, eyebrows, nose and ear hair)
complexion (pale, red, blushing, sweaty, dry)

wrinkles (smile lines, crow's-feet, furrowed brow, bags under the eyes)

EXTREMITIES

hands (callused, clean, wrinkled, tanned)

fingers

fingernails and cuticles (length, condition, color; manicured)

feet

toes

toenails

SKIN

pigmentation

birthmarks

moles

warts

scars

acne

pallor

wrinkles

rashes

hives

sweatiness

PHYSICAL IRREGULARITIES/
DISABILITIES

physical deformities

prostheses

body braces (back, leg, neck, ankle, knee)

scars

unusually thick glasses

hearing aids

bandages

casts

ORNAMENTATION/JEWELRY

earrings

necklaces/chains

bracelets (wrist, ankle)

rings (toe, finger, nose, eyebrow, pinkie; college, high school, sport, fraternal organizations)

cuff links

tie tacks

watches

watch fobs or chains

ornamental pins

lapel pins

fingernail jewelry

MAKEUP

foundation

lipstick

lip liner

eye shadow

eyeliner

eyebrow liner

blush

mascara

powder

fingernail polish

toenail polish

fake eyelashes

body makeup

ACCESSORIES

hats

belts

purses

scarves

gloves

socks

stockings/nylons

garters

ties (bow, regular, bolo)

suspenders

pocket scarves

hair adornments (bows, barrettes, pins)

glasses (type, style)

headbands

CLOTHING

shirt/blouse

pants/slacks

dress

shoes

jacket

coat

cape

sweater

vest

shorts

bathing suit

"BODIFICATIONS" (ELECTIVE ALTERATIONS OF THE BODY)

body piercing—whether or not any jewelry is currently in the holes

(ears, nose, eyebrow, tongue, navel, nipple, cheek; holes)

plastic surgery, if noticeable (eyes, face, ears, breasts/pectorals, other implants, tummy tucks, fanny lifts, liposuction, face peels, nose jobs, tattoos [both decorative and eyebrows], collagen injections)

manicures

dyed hair

lash/brow tinting

eyebrow plucking

HYGIENE

hair

face

ears

nose

hands

fingers

nails

feet

teeth

breath

body odor

clothing

Once you have armed yourself with information by noticing the various traits on this list, you can begin to interpret them. The following are eleven common characteristics and what they may mean. The only way to accurately interpret the meaning of these physical traits is to view them in context with other physical characteristics as well as mannerisms, environment, voice, and actions.

Complexion

Complexion may reveal much about someone's behavior and values, particularly if he or she tries to change it.

TAN A tanned face may reveal that the person's job or hobbies put him outdoors for considerable periods. A tan may also indicate that someone is vain and appearance conscious, or only that he just returned from a vacation in a sunny location. To figure out which, you'll need to look at other clues. For example, if a man is very tanned, deeply wrinkled, and has calluses on his hands, he has probably spent a lot of time working outdoors since few outdoor hobbies would leave heavy calluses. On the other hand, if you saw a man who had manicured nails and an immaculate suit along with bronzed skin, the odds are he thinks he looks better that way and has the time to pursue a dark tan, either outdoors or at a tanning salon. This much attention to skin tone indicates vanity and image consciousness.

PALE SKIN People whose skin is very pale generally have few outdoor hobbies and don't work outdoors. There are, as always, exceptions: someone may protect her skin out of health consciousness, or she may be ill, or she may be from the Pacific Northwest, or somewhere else where there are extended periods of overcast weather. In years past, I found that light-complected people with softer, paler skins tended to be less physically active and health conscious than those who showed at least some exposure to the sun. But as people have become more aware of the harmful effects of the sun, this conclusion is sometimes off-base.

IRREGULARITIES Facial irregularities such as moles or warts, particularly if they're conspicuous, are significant because today most people can afford to have such blemishes removed. Sometimes these irregularities point to a socioeconomic background in which physical appearance was, by necessity, a very low priority. But often someone's reasons for retaining a facial blemish are more complicated. If someone doesn't bother to remove a large, dark mole from the tip of her nose it may mean she is very comfortable with herself, moles and all.

Or it may show she doesn't want to cater to our image-conscious society, in which case it may also reveal rebellious leanings. But remember, there have been famous actresses and models known for their "beauty marks."

Hygiene

Hygiene is one of the most significant and noticeable traits. Poor hygiene reveals a wealth of information about a person, but it's essential to make the distinction between people who are unkempt and those who are dirty. People who are messy but clean fall into an entirely different category. The rumpled look is covered in the "Dowdiness" section later in this appendix.

Hygiene can speak of a person's education, social class, perception of himself and others, intelligence, organization, laziness, carelessness, security, self-image, rebelliousness, cultural background, consideration for others, desire to please, and desire for social acceptance.

The signs of poor hygiene include:

- unkempt, greasy hair or scalp
- dirty hands, face, and/or body
- dirty fingernails
- dirty, stained, or missing teeth
- bad breath
- body odor
- dirty, smelly clothing

People with poor hygiene may be

- oblivious to the effect they have on others. This indicates a high level of self-centeredness; a lack of common sense; and inability to read the reactions of those around them. They are out of touch.
- insensitive. They might know but not care about the effect they're having on other people. This may indicate a lack of education or uncaring attitude toward others as well as, again, self-centeredness.

- mentally ill or drug or alcohol abusers. People who are depressed often neglect their personal hygiene. Those with other chronic mental illnesses, including drug and alcohol abuse, also frequently ignore personal hygiene.
- unable to care for themselves because of a chronic medical problem.
- from a very poor socioeconomic background. Few people can't afford to be clean. But some people raised in poverty were never taught the basics of personal hygiene, and occasionally they never pick up the habit of bathing. They never got into the habit of bathing regularly or putting on fresh underwear each morning.
- lazy. Some people just don't want to make the effort to keep clean.

Personal hygiene, like all traits, must be viewed in light of other traits. My first case, fifteen years ago, involved a man charged with the kidnap, rape, and murder of a ten-year-old. The Los Angeles media called him "the Ice Cream Man" because he enticed the young girl into his truck while selling ice cream. He had a long, scraggly, unkempt, filthy beard and mustache and long, dirty fingernails. His fingers were stained yellow because he smoked and didn't wash. His eyes were frequently encrusted. This complete inattention to hygiene signaled the worst type of socioeconomic background. Indeed, he had been abused as a child and was uneducated; he had no goals in life, and even less self-esteem. He wanted to die, and the jury gladly accommodated him. He remains on death row today.

On the other hand, an isolated lapse in the hygiene department doesn't warrant too much consideration, especially if you can identify a reason for it. I know a fabulous trial lawyer who speaks several languages and is a model of professionalism. He also has a passion for rebuilding old cars. As a result, scrub as he may, he frequently has grease under his fingernails. His dirty fingernails are inconsistent with the rest of his pattern and don't indicate poor hygiene. Instead, they provide insight into his hobbies and, perhaps more important, his practical and unpretentious nature.

Fastidiousness

Fastidiousness can be reflected in a perfectly trimmed beard, freshly pressed clothing, a precisely positioned pocket scarf, and any similar trait. Like all traits, it varies in degree. I've known people who press their T-shirts and even their sheets. Others constantly straighten and restraighten their clothing or their desks. This degree of fastidiousness is unusual. When it reaches an extreme, it may mean the person is suffering from obsessive-compulsive disorder.

Except for the few people who suffer from this clinical disorder, I've generally found that the more fastidious a person is, the more he'll tend to be egotistical, structured, inflexible, unimaginative, vain, and concerned about the opinions of others. Almost invariably, fastidious people have acquired the trait from their parents, so fastidiousness usually reflects a strong parental influence.

Those on the opposite end of the spectrum may wear shoes that are heavily scuffed and worn-out, shirts with holes, torn seams, or missing buttons, or pants with an unraveling hem. My first consideration is whether this lack of personal maintenance is anything more than an indication that money is tight. If someone's clean and any items that can be maintained inexpensively have been, I can usually conclude little more from this feature alone. But if money doesn't seem to be the issue, I look for characteristics of the dowdy person, described later.

Writing, Logos, and Pictures on Apparel

Words or images displayed on clothing are virtual advertisements for someone's lifestyles and values. They may reflect the person's employment, hobbies, religious preference, cultural background, politics, and more. They may also provide clues to his or her personality. The sleeping cat worn by the elderly grandmother is a symbol of nature, serenity, compassion, warmth, and contentment. It is hard to imagine a young, macho Marine picking out that shirt at the department store. He'd probably favor a picture of a bulldog or a pit bull—which would gladly eat the cat—symbols of power, aggression, virility, and confidence. Sexually suggestive statements should be noted, as should humorous and intellectual ones. Most people do not randomly put on clothing with particular words, logos, or pictures. Rather, they choose what embodies their personality, depicts their interests, or reflects an image they want to present. For example:

- Prominently featured designer logos can indicate someone who is image conscious and perhaps lacks confidence. She may be trying to buy credibility with a designer label.
- Souvenir T-shirts from other cities and states, national parks, and so forth may tell you the person is a traveler or outdoorsman.
- T-shirts or polo shirts with sports insignias can indicate someone who is either a fan or a player. His haircut and degree of athleticism will often tell you which. Interestingly, some team logos have even been adopted by certain gangs as a type of uniform.

Many of these inferences are fairly obvious, but remember that seeing a pattern is the key. Everyone owns a few T-shirts with insignificant pictures or logos, but someone who consistently wears a certain label or logo is consciously trying to broadcast a personal priority.

Tastefulness

Taste is a slippery concept. Every culture has its own definition of good and bad taste—don't misjudge a person by mistaking cultural preferences for poor taste.

For example, I've occasionally heard people comment that skimpy bikini-style swimsuits on men are tacky and inappropriate. But these swimsuits are standard fare in Europe. American men may feel uncomfortable in, or around, such revealing garb, but Europeans do not, and it doesn't reflect at all on their tastefulness.

You can learn a lot from someone's taste in clothing and other physical trappings if you're familiar with his background and culture.

Good taste can reveal

- good judgment and awareness of societal norms.
- a sensitivity to image and the opinions of others.

- sophistication. Those who have learned to dress tastefully also tend to act and think with equal social sophistication.
- prosperity. Tastefulness, like trendiness, can be expensive.
- parental influence. Taste is typically learned from one's parents, along with manners. You usually won't see one without the other.

Poor taste tends to reveal just the opposite of these traits. But taste is such a tricky category that any guidelines I give you come with a warning: be careful to look at all the other traits before passing judgment.

Regional Style

Southwestern jewelry, African clothing, a European-style bathing suit, cowboy boots, a fisherman's hat—any distinctive clothing, jewelry, or accessories—is often a tip-off to where someone was raised. If not, it probably signals that the person either lived in the area and enjoyed that period of her life, or identifies with the location for some reason. Keep your eye out for items with a distinctive regional style; they almost always have special meaning.

Not long ago, I pulled in to a gas station in Beverly Hills behind a brand-new, bright red Jaguar convertible. A fiftyish woman stepped out, holding a small, white, immaculately groomed poodle with red bows carefully placed in its fur. The bows matched the color of the car perfectly. The woman's makeup was flawless. She had platinum-blond hair and was wearing high heels and a royal blue formfitting velour pantsuit. If ever I saw a woman who had cultivated the wealthy Beverly Hills image, here she was. Apparently, it was important to her to project an image of youthful sexiness, wealth, and success. In Beverly Hills, her appearance may have caused others to see her as she intended. But what would they think in Little Rock or New York City?

Cultivated Images

A distinctive image that someone intentionally tries to cultivate can reflect his true nature or simply his attempt to look a part. Some of the more common images people adopt are Country, Hollywood, Punk, Hippie, Grunge, Jock, and GQ. In general, it is more likely that a younger person has chosen a particular style to reflect a role, rather than his true nature. But old or young, it usually takes time and additional information to know whether someone is playing a part or is the real thing.

I recently conducted a focus group in which one of the mock jurors was a fifty-five-ish white man. He had a neat, long, gray ponytail, and his tanned, wrinkled skin showed the effects of years in the sun. His socked feet were clad in Birkenstock sandals, and he wore a T-shirt emblazoned with a hand-painted butterfly. This man exuded the image of a diehard hippie.

I wondered at first whether he truly held the liberal, creative, artistic, nonconformist views epitomized by the hippie movement, or whether he was just a middle-aged man who wanted to look hip. It turned out that he was a sociology professor at a local university, lived in a rural area outside of town, and drove a ten-year-old pickup truck. Since his lifestyle matched his hippie persona, I believe the nonconformist appearance was probably an accurate reflection of the inner man.

On the other hand, country bars all over America are packed with urban cowboys decked out in Stetson hats and snakeskin boots. To tell how much of their appearance is a conscious effort to adopt the Marlboro Man image—strong, macho, independent—requires more information. So watch out. Though you're looking for a rough, tough he-man with down-home manners and small-town values to match, you may find nothing more than a big-city boy in costume.

Flamboyance versus Conservativeness

Flamboyance is characterized by bright colors, shocking or distinctive styles, eye-catching jewelry, and the like. Conservatism is reflected by classic styles, subdued colors, and careful, meticulous grooming. Almost all of the many traits listed earlier in this chapter can range between the extreme ends of this spectrum. It's in where someone's traits lie in the spectrum—gaudy earrings, a toe ring, a flashy belt—that you'll find clues about whether she is more flamboyant or conservative at heart. But remember: to be flamboyant at heart, you don't need to dress like Liberace or Elton John.

The most clear-cut difference between these two types is their desire for attention. Those who are flamboyant generally want to stick out; those who are conservative usually want to blend in. I've found that extremely flamboyant people are sometimes insecure, lonely, needy, and bored and dissatisfied with their life. But flamboyance is one of those traits that can reflect polar opposites. Flamboyant people can also be confident and self-assured.

Whether they are lonely or confident, flamboyant people generally share a few characteristics. They

- are creative, artistic, and imaginative.
- usually have at least some money since flamboyant clothing and jewelry are generally fairly expensive and not very practical.
- themselves are not very practical.
- are nonconformists. They don't care what other people think of them, as long as they've got an audience.
- are independent, and maybe even a bit flaky.

Conservative people, on the other hand,

- are likely to care about the opinions of others and want to fit in and be accepted.
- are conformists who feel most comfortable when they meet social norms and expectations.
- are often practical, authoritarian, and analytical.
- are less creative or imaginative than flamboyant people. They tend to be more conventional thinkers.

Someone may dress very conservatively out of insecurity, in an effort to be accepted or to fit in, or they may be very secure and confident. To uncover their motive, you'll have to examine other clues. It usually takes some careful observation and questioning before you can tell if your conservative friend is confident or afraid to stand out. The same goes for flamboyant people—it requires more than a snapshot to determine whether they are lonely and needy, or gloriously liberated. But in either case, careful attention to someone's appearance will be an excellent place to start to develop the pattern that ultimately will reveal the answer.

Practicality versus Extravagance

Many people are simply middle-of-the road in their fashion statements, neither flamboyant nor conservative. But most fall into one of two distinct camps with respect to practicality and extravagance.

Anything that emphasizes comfort, cost, or utility over style will point toward the practical person. It usually takes me very little time to determine whether someone is more interested in comfort and practicality than style and image. Many different features of most people's appearance help place them in one category or the other.

Does a woman

- wear matching accessories with her outfits, or prefer basic blacks and browns that are easy to coordinate?
- have long, carefully painted, manicured nails, or are they short and functional?
- wear flats or high heels?
- have a high-maintenance haircut?
- wear large jewelry that can easily snag her nylons, or get in the way generally?
- wear a lot of makeup, which is expensive and time-consuming to apply?

Does a man

- wear color-coordinated ties, pocket scarves, socks, or other clothing?
- wear a lightweight running watch or a heavy Rolex?
- wear walking shoes or Italian loafers on his morning stroll to work?
- have his nails manicured?
- get frequent haircuts, or allow his hair to grow a bit long before having it trimmed?

The nature of someone's toys also says something about whether he is practical or extravagant. Someone who golfs only rarely but owns an expensive set of clubs, or who plays tennis infrequently but has several tennis rackets, is probably extravagant, not practical. The same can be said of someone who chooses an expensive, high-maintenance car.

I can make some generalizations about someone once I have determined how practical or extravagant he is. People who are interested in comfort and practicality are usually

- at ease with themselves and their position in life.
- not self-centered.
- willing to be nonconformists, if that's what it takes to be comfortable.
- frugal.

Extravagant people often

- are image conscious.
- suffer from poor self-esteem.
- desire acceptance and approval and need the respect and admiration of others.
- genuinely enjoy "the gift of giving." Giving people presents brings them pleasure.

Before you assume that someone will have traits typical of the extravagant person, take a good look at where he spends his money. If he spends it where it will be very much in the public eye—on clothing, jewelry, cars, big parties, and so forth—then he probably fits the extravagant profile. But someone can spend a lot of money without having the typical extravagant personality traits. The normal rules won't apply if he usually spends money where few people will see it— for instance, on vacations, a summer house only his family will visit, or quiet contributions to his favorite charities.

Sexual Suggestiveness

Some people wear clothes and accessories that are exceptionally sexy, even in the context of our very sexualized culture. The man or woman who wears sexually suggestive clothing may be tremendously confident or very insecure. What is consistently true, however, is that he or she is trying to get attention. Such an individual is often outgoing, self-centered, and vain. Revealing garb worn at inappropriate times also indicates a lack of good judgment. It's also likely, although not a given, that the wearer is sexually liberated, though he or she may also just be a confident tease.

Dowdiness

Dowdiness is yet another of those categories that can signify polar opposites. Men and women who seem dowdy (men like this are usually called rumpled or unkempt) tend to be out of the social mainstream and insensitive to most issues of appearance.

Common signs of dowdiness include:

- Wrinkled but fairly clean clothing
- Shapeless, outdated, or bland clothing and accessories
- Messy, uncombed hair
- An unflattering or out-of-date hairstyle
- Well-worn shoes

Dowdiness can signify

- *lower socioeconomic background.* Good grooming is often a reflection of financial status. Obviously, there are exceptions; many people who grew up without much money are stylish dressers. But if a person consistently wears rumpled clothing, there is a good chance she was never taught otherwise. This occurs in lower-class or lower-middle-class homes more often than in families that are well off, but it can exist at any socioeconomic level.
- *the artistic, intellectual, or "absent-minded professor" syndrome.* Some dowdy dressers simply don't pay attention to the way they look. These are typically people whose intellectual or creative life eclipses all other concerns. Engineers, scientists, inventors, and artists often fall into this category.
- *preoccupation elsewhere.* Some people have decided their true pas-

sion in life is travel, or dog breeding, or record collecting, or surfing the Internet. They just don't put much time or energy into their appearance, and they don't care what the outside world thinks. They often associate with others with similar interests who look and dress just as they do anyway.

• *sloppiness.* There are those who aren't obsessed with their computer or lost in an effort to find a cure for cancer or put a man on Mars. They're just slobs—pure and simple. Their house is a mess. Their car is a mess. Their locker at work is a mess. And yes— they're a mess. Appearance just isn't high on their list of priorities.

APPENDIX B

Body Language and What It Reveals

There are as many body movements to pick clues from as there are people and moments in the day. Like the list of physical characteristics in Appendix A, the list that follows, long though it is, does not include all the potentially revealing aspects of someone's body motions. But it does contain those you will see most often. Review it with a mind toward broadening your vision. No one notices all these possible clues all the time. But you'll start picking up more and more if you at least think about them from time to time.

WHOLE BODY MOVEMENTS

WALK
slow/fast
bouncing
tentative
striding
pacing

POSITIONING
in groups
in couples
alone
closeness to people
erect
chest out

slouching
sitting on edge of chair, or lying
 back

MOTION
shaking
trembling
rocking
shifting
twitching
wiggling
strutting
skipping
running

swaying
still
dragging
rapid jerky motions
stepping away
stepping forward
leaning forward or back
turning away

HEAD
nodding
shaking
hanging down
tossing
circling
looking down or up
looking around
looking in mirrors
nose in the air

FACE
EYES
open or shut
staring
moving back and forth
moving up and down
blinking
winking
closing frequently
wincing

squinting
smiling
rolling
looking over eyeglasses

MOUTH/JAW
lips open
lips tight
smiling (toothy grin, smug, relaxed)
lips pursed
frowning
yawning
turned-up corners
licking lips
biting lips
teeth clenched
mouth twitch
grimacing
set jaw
grinding jaw
dry
running tongue over teeth

EYEBROWS
moving up or down
furrowed

MISCELLANEOUS
wrinkling of nose
facial tics

EXTREMITIES

TOUCHING
handshakes (fishy, firm, two-
   handed, held)
poking
petting

backslapping
leaning

ARMS, HANDS, LEGS, AND FEET
tapping fingers or feet

touching fingers together

twiddling thumbs

obscene gestures with
   hands/fingers

hands over mouth

hands on chin

hands to temple

hands on hips

hands in pockets

hands on lap

wringing hands

clenching fists

scratching face or ears

twisting hair

flipping hair

stretching

scratching head

crossing and uncrossing

flailing

FIDDLING

biting nails

picking at nails

twirling hair

rubbing beard or mustache

touching or picking at clothes

twirling glasses

playing with watch

clicking pens

VOCALIZATIONS

breathing (deep, shallow, short,
   rapid, slow, rapid exhaling
   "whew")

burping/belching

sighs

swallowing

gulping

coughs (nervous, deep, dry,
   clearing throat)

humming

whistling

becoming quiet

becoming loud

Each of the traits or emotions discussed in the next sections is revealed most clearly through a combination of many different body motions, as well as environment, voice, and actions. Don't be overwhelmed by the fact that the same body motions can mean many different things. If you look at the whole pattern, you will almost always arrive at the right conclusion.

Arrogance/Humility

A would-be king holds himself above the masses. A true prince walks among them.

The essence of arrogance is an attempt to exalt oneself above others. The core of humility is the recognition that no matter what one's status may be, one person is no better or worse than another.

Not surprisingly, arrogant people try to separate themselves from the masses, whereas people who are humble opt for unpretentious contact and communication with others regardless of their "rank." Those who are arrogant are not necessarily secure, whereas humility usually reflects a certain deep-seated security. As a result, humble people are much less likely to be overcompetitive, particularly with friends or family. They are more forgiving, understanding, and compassionate.

In placing someone on the arrogance/humility scale, appearance may be telling. The arrogant person's attire, grooming, and behavior often reflect his effort to set himself apart and above; he may wear expensive, pretentious, or impractical clothing, or dress more or less formally than others. And he'll often act aloof, bored, or pretentious. Humble people tend to dress and act in a more down-to-earth style.

Arrogant people frequently

- preen
- glance at their reflection in mirrors and windows
- attempt to be the center of the discussion
- make grand, flamboyant gestures
- keep greater than average physical distance from others (although some arrogant people feel entitled to invade others' personal space and do so inappropriately)
- bore easily and quit listening (arrogant people don't really care what others have to say)
- make sexually suggestive movements and postures
- boast
- adopt affectations and put on airs

Signs of humility are

- focusing on others rather than oneself
- good listening skills
- self-deprecating humor

- a quiet demeanor
- courtesies such as giving up a chair or opening a door for someone

It's important to make certain there is a pattern of arrogance. A loud, boisterous woman may also be considerate, and a quiet man might not be listening to a conversation simply because he's tired. Look for more than one symptom.

Confidence/Leadership

A politician sits quietly, back straight, eyes forward, hands still in his lap, a slight smile on his face, as he waits for the debate to begin.

Not surprisingly, leaders tend to be confident, and followers tend to be insecure. Consequently, identifying leaders requires sensitivity to the traits shown by anyone who's confident, and vice versa. And spotting followers is the same as identifying those who are passive and insecure.

Leadership and confidence do not have to entail an outgoing, domineering, aggressive personality. There are quiet and confident leaders, and there are loud and aggressive ones.

Leaders and others who are confident may

- typically lead (and often control) conversations
- usually have a number of people around them as a result of their personality
- position themselves at an appropriate distance from people when talking (although a "control freak" will usually invade someone's personal space)
- volunteer for unpleasant tasks
- be good listeners
- have a self-assured smile, not overstated or toothy, but sometimes almost smug
- walk with confidence, almost striding, frequently with their arms moving rather significantly
- have a firm handshake
- be better-dressed
- have good hygiene
- dress conservatively and appropriately for the occasion

- dress in more expensive and more tasteful clothing
- seldom follow any faddish trends
- be willing to engage in conversation
- be physical and athletic
- make good eye contact
- have a conservative haircut or hairstyle
- have erect posture
- square their body to the person they're speaking to
- carry the trappings sometimes associated with responsibility, such as a briefcase, calculator, cellular phone, pager, calendar, or day-planner

People often expect leaders to be outgoing or aggressive, and overlook quiet, confident ones. Not all leaders and confident people strut like bantam roosters. Quiet, reserved leaders will still usually have a firm handshake and engage in direct eye contact. In conversation, they will be attentive and good listeners.

Leaders usually settle into a position of power in any room. If there is a table, they will tend to gravitate toward the end of it. If there are people scattered throughout the room, the leader will usually be more centrally located. Leaders usually don't show signs of nervousness and frequently take good care of their health and bodies.

Confusion

Visualize the windup toy, scurrying in one direction until it hits the wall, rebounding and heading off in another direction. The movement is random, not orderly.

You'll seldom see confusion in complete isolation from other basic emotions. Frequently, someone who is confused will also be frustrated or indecisive and will show signs of those emotions. But even when coupled with other emotional states, confusion can usually be spotted. When someone is confused, she has lost her bearings and is trying to find them.

Symptoms of confusion include:

- Verbal repetition
- Repetitive motion

- Picking items up and putting them down
- Conflicting or inconsistent behavior
- Shifting or shuffling
- Signs of indecision
- Signs of frustration

Defensiveness

Picture a cat cornered by a dog. It's backed against a wall, hair standing on end. It's looking for a chance to run away, but ready to attack if necessary.

Most defensive gestures are instinctive ways of protecting ourselves. Feeling defensive is extremely unpleasant; it's a product of feeling attacked. At the very least, someone who's feeling defensive will also be feeling awkward and vulnerable. As a result, his behavior usually reflects a desire to avoid the situation, either by physically or verbally moving or by deflecting the attack.

Most people detest confrontation, and when we feel defensive it's usually because someone has confronted us. Sometimes we also feel defensive if we fear a confrontation is about to erupt, or if we mistake a neutral comment for a challenge. Not surprisingly, many symptoms of defensiveness resemble the symptoms of anger, but you may also see signs like those of nervousness or secretiveness.

Symptoms of defensiveness may include:

- Crossing arms, legs, and/or ankles
- Clenching teeth, jaws, or lips
- Averting the eyes
- Body squared, not turned away (confrontational)
- Hands on hips
- Quick exhaling
- Closing the mouth tightly and refusing to talk
- Leaving the awkward situation

Drug and Alcohol Use

Denial is the biggest problem. Don't ignore the obvious symptoms.

Drug and alcohol abuse extends across all socioeconomic boundaries, cultures, income levels, occupations, and ages. The signs are fairly obvious and well publicized. What's more difficult than seeing them is admitting to yourself that you're seeing them, especially in a loved one. Once you're aware of the symptoms of substance abuse, don't refuse to acknowledge them.

Look for signs of intoxication not only in chronic abusers but also in people who indulge only occasionally. You don't want to get in the car with a drunk driver even if he gets drunk only once a year. No matter how responsible and reliable someone is when sober, drug and alcohol use can turn Dr. Jekyll into Mr. Hyde, altering behavior in both obvious and subtle ways.

Symptoms of drug and alcohol use include:

- Slurred speech
- Extremely rapid speech
- Inappropriate behavior, especially if exaggerated (too close or intimate, too loud, too quiet)
- Red eyes
- Partially closed eyes
- Bags under the eyes
- Mood swings (animated/depressed behavior)
- Loss of inhibitions
- Shaking
- Bulbous, red nose
- Odor
- Inconsistency, particularly dramatic inconsistency, of appearance and behavior between one occasion and another
- Poor hygiene
- Withdrawal from normal social activity
- A large torso and thin legs, or a potbelly on a thin person (both body types are typical of alcoholics)

Embarrassment

Think of a young boy strutting into the cafeteria. He trips and falls in front of everyone. His face turns red; he brushes himself off, awkwardly trying not to show his embarrassment, and slinks off to a table in the corner.

Embarrassment is often missed since people who are embarrassed invariably try hard to conceal it. Many people react to embarrassing situations by going away quietly and hoping the awkward moment will be forgotten. Others will try to laugh it off. It's important to be able to recognize the signs of embarrassment, because unless you're attuned to them you can easily mistake embarrassment for anger, defensiveness, or even nervousness. Or you might miss the signs altogether and assume someone is insensitive or antisocial, when in fact he might be deeply ashamed of his embarrassing actions and just not know how to apologize for them.

Symptoms of embarrassment include:

- Nervous laughter
- Avoiding eye contact
- Shaking of the head
- Turning away
- Flushing
- Avoiding people; leaving the room

Fear

Visualize a deer, frozen in its tracks in the middle of the road, eyes wide, body stiff.

The deer in the headlights is a perfect metaphor for how people frequently look in the initial stage of fear. Surprise is the main emotion at that point, but if the fright continues, defensiveness and nervousness also kick in. Fear is, of course, one of our most basic emotions. Only rarely do most of us experience fright—as distinguished from anxiety—but it's worthwhile to know the symptoms.

Symptoms of fear include the signs of surprise:

- Wide-open eyes
- Screaming
- Hands over the face
- Being frozen or paralyzed
- Flushing
- Gulping and swallowing
- Looking around (looking over one's shoulder)
- Clutching hands together or gripping another object tightly (white knuckles)

- Placing hands in front of the body
- Leaning or shifting backward
- Turning away (especially the upper body)
- Quick, jerky flailing or stretching out of the extremities
- Grabbing other people
- Shaking
- Heavy breathing
- Quick, shallow breathing
- Holding the breath
- Walking quickly
- Rigidity or stiffness
- Licking lips
- Taking small, tentative steps (as in searching a dark room)

Different people respond differently to fear. When I visited France two years ago with my friend Denise, we found this out firsthand. While we were at a stoplight, a man jumped into the back of our car and stole some of our luggage. Denise began screaming uncontrollably, while I became paralyzed. Social scientists have found one of two reactions kicks in when most people are confronted with such an aggressive and hostile act: "fight or flight." Denise and I are living proof that the menu of possible responses is much broader: we did neither. Generally, whatever symptoms a particular person exhibits, a little attention should reveal whether he or she is afraid.

Resentment

Picture a high school girl who wasn't picked to be a cheerleader, watching as the squad practices. Her arms are folded, her eyes are slightly closed, her body stiff.

Resentment is usually a by-product of anger or jealousy. Whatever its origin, resentment usually shows itself in a cluster of mannerisms designed to put distance between a person and the one she resents.

Symptoms of resentment include:

- Crossing the arms
- Stiffening of the body

- Grimacing
- Pouting
- Avoidance
- Looking away
- Signs of anger

Lawyers can be an egotistical bunch. That's what gives them the drive to succeed, but it can also lead to a competitiveness that can turn to resentment overnight. I've been involved in many trials where two or more lawyers represented a single defendant. Each lawyer usually brings different talents to the table, but almost invariably one will emerge as the lead counsel. Who that is may even vary from day to day or week to week. As this ebb and flow of courtroom supremacy takes place, I often see classic signs of resentment develop. The lawyers' chairs will slide slightly farther apart. Their arms will be folded. One lawyer's gaze will be fixed in the opposite direction as the other speaks. I'm sure if you were to ask the players in a scene like this whether they were aware of their body language, they would say no. But like so many mannerisms, those of resentment can creep in unnoticed, especially by the one displaying them.

Secretiveness/Openness

Think of a poker player, expressionless, peering over his cards, which he is holding tightly and close to his face.

People who are open expose themselves to you in their manner and speech. Secretive people reveal very little of themselves and carefully guard personal information. Often they prefer to keep the various areas of their life compartmentalized, and are open about one or more of their worlds—work, play, school, the dating scene—but secretive about others. Secretive people may literally keep their distance, as if afraid that if they get too close you will be able to size them up more effectively.

Symptoms of secretiveness include:

- Whispering
- A "guarding" posture, with shoulders hunched
- Covering mouth with hand

- Body turned partially away from the other person
- Tightly closed lips
- Set jaw
- Seldom invading the personal space of others since they don't want others in their space
- Avoiding social interaction or other circumstances in which they might be expected to reveal something of themselves
- Revealing little emotion
- Brief, almost mechanical handshake
- Frequently glancing down during a conversation
- Looking around the room when being addressed, rather than returning a gaze
- Instinctively and routinely covering or removing any personal material from view

Signs of openness include:

- Body fully facing the person to whom one is speaking
- Standing fairly close to the other person (although not within personal space)
- Frequent and prolonged eye contact
- Warm, relaxed smile
- Kissing or embracing when greeting
- Firm, sometimes prolonged handshake
- Enjoying social interaction

When gauging whether someone is secretive, consider whether specific behavior is an isolated trait or part of a slew of secretive habits. The truly secretive person will generally exhibit many secretive traits, not just one or two. If someone who is normally outgoing won't say much about why she was on the phone all day, don't jump to conclusions—who knows, maybe she's planning your surprise birthday party. And the person who habitually locks his desk drawers before he goes to lunch each day but is otherwise outgoing and open may be hiding something, or he may have been the victim of a lunchtime burglary. You won't know without more information.

Sexual or Romantic Interest

A seductress from a 1940s detective movie rubs her palms slowly down her sides to straighten her jacket. She walks slowly into the room, looking the gruff detective up and down, then sits slowly on his desk and crosses her legs.

Sexual attraction usually spurs people to make contact. Any action that reveals, emphasizes, or draws attention to someone's sexuality can be seen as a sign of sexual interest. There are scores of behaviors that are well-known tip-offs to sexual interest, and many books have been written on the subject. What follows is just a brief list of the most obvious traits.

Sign of sexual interest include:

- Making eye contact
- Exaggerated smile
- Laughter
- Staring
- Winking
- Blinking
- Wetting lips
- Crossing and uncrossing legs
- Thrusting out the chest or hips
- Walking with a swagger or wiggle
- Primping
- Lounging back
- Coy smile
- Flipping of the head or hair
- Entering someone's personal space
- Any revealing clothing (particularly if not appropriate for the occasion)
- Touching oneself (smoothing nylons or playing with shirt buttons)
- Touching the object of one's affection
- Excessive makeup, perfume, or cologne
- Overdressing for the occasion
- Whispering or other attempts at intimacy
- Intent listening
- Intently looking the other person up and down
- Trying to isolate the target of one's affection by getting him or her alone

Surprise

The lights go on and everyone yells, "Happy birthday!"

Surprise may be the result of fear, excitement, or pleasure. The response is usually the same regardless of the reason for the surprise: quick body movement and a temporary loss of control over the smaller muscles. Usually, someone will quickly resume his "presurprise" posture.

Symptoms of surprise include:

- Stepping backward (if standing) or leaning backward (if seated)
- Mouth dropping open
- Eyes widening
- Extending the arms and legs
- Jumping upward
- Gasping or screaming

The symptoms of surprise usually don't vary much, whether the news is good or bad. The last day of the O. J. Simpson criminal trial proved this point in many people's minds. The media frequently replayed the physical reaction of Mr. Simpson's friend and attorney Robert Kardashian to the not-guilty verdict. Pointing out that Mr. Kardashian's mouth dropped open as the verdict was read, commentators suggested that he was surprised. The writer Dominick Dunne was also seated in the gallery. Mr. Dunne firmly believed that Mr. Simpson was guilty. For Mr. Kardashian, the acquittal was good news; for Mr. Dunne it was terrible news. Yet Mr. Dunne's facial expression, while slightly more extreme, resembled Mr. Kardashian's very closely.

Suspicion/Disbelief

Visualize an elderly English judge, peering down from his bench, fingers sliding his glasses down his nose just enough so you can see his eyes over the top of them, as he slowly shakes his head back and forth.

The difference between suspicion and disbelief is a matter of degree. To suspect is to have doubt but not yet to have formed a firm opinion. The suspicious person is still thinking about what to believe, and consequently the characteristics of suspicion include those of pensiveness. Suspicion most often arises when someone doubts the truthfulness of a statement. When he makes up his mind that the statement is in fact false, the characteristics of pensiveness give way to those of disbelief.

Symptoms of suspicion include:

- Furrowed brow
- A squint in the eyes
- Turning the head slightly down and looking slightly upward (the peering-over-the-glasses look) or tilting the head slightly
- Tightening of the lips
- The signs of pensiveness

Once disbelief has set in, the symptoms may be:

- eye-rolling
- head-shaking
- grimacing
- turning up the corners of the mouth
- exhaling quickly "through the teeth"
- those of frustration

Worry

Think of a nervous father pacing back and forth as he awaits news from the delivery room.

When someone is worried, he is also normally anxious, nervous, or afraid. Consequently, whenever I see signs of anxiety, nervousness, or fear, I associate them with worry.

Symptoms of worry include:

- Repetitive action, such as pacing
- Biting nails
- Wringing hands
- Shaking
- Fidgeting
- Rubbing the face
- Running hands through hair
- Lack of focus

The hand-wringing, pacing, fidgeting brand of worry or anxiety isn't hard to spot. But the same can't always be said of the dull, constant anxiety we feel at times. Someone watching the last few minutes of her daughter's basketball game with the score tied 50–50 will probably show many of the classic signs of worry or anxiety, but how about the woman who has been fretting constantly for days that she may fall victim to the cutbacks at work? She may look anxious, but just as likely she will show signs of attentiveness and pensiveness, as she concentrates on her problem and how she can handle it. Or she may have lapsed into depression over the thought of being laid off and what that might mean to her family, in which case symptoms of depression would dominate her emotional picture. The important point to keep in mind is that worry, like almost every emotion, can take many forms. Keep your eyes open for all of them.

ABOUT THE AUTHORS

Jo-Ellan Dimitrius, Ph.D. has consulted in more than six hundred jury trials, including the Rodney King, Reginald Denny, Robert Blake, John du Pont, O. J. Simpson, and Enron cases. She has appeared on *The Oprah Winfrey Show*, *The View*, *Dancing with the Stars*, *Good Morning America*, *Today*, *Larry King Live*, *Face the Nation*, and *60 Minutes*, as well as on the BBC and TV Asahi. She has consulted with many Fortune 100 companies and political candidates.

Dubbed "The Seer" by *The American Lawyer* magazine, she is listed in *Who's Who in America* and is the 2007 recipient of the Brennan Award, named in honor of Justice William J. Brennan, Jr., from the National Trial Advocacy College. She was the first non-lawyer recipient of the award.

Jo-Ellan is a national and international speaker with the American Program Bureau.

Mark Mazzarella has been a practicing trial lawyer in San Diego for more than thirty years. He is a past chairman of the twelve-thousand-member litigation section of The State Bar of California, has been selected as one of San Diego's top attorneys in the corporate litigation category by the San Diego *Daily Transcript*, has been featured in *Super Lawyers* magazine, and is listed in *The Best Lawyers in America*. He writes and lectures extensively.

Wendy Patrick Mazzarella is a trial lawyer with the San Diego County District Attorney's Office, and was recently named one of the top ten criminal attorneys in San Diego by the San Diego *Daily Transcript*. She began her career as a defense attorney and have extensive experience selecting juries from both sides of the criminal justice system. She writes and lectures nationally and internationally on a variety of subjects ranging from "reading people" and "impression management" to legal and business ethics.